ICDL/ECDL: Syllabus 4 Office 2000 (Volume 2)

Student Manual

4000987/
ICDLUS

Australia • Canada • Mexico • Singapore
Spain • United Kingdom • United States

Approved
Courseware
Syllabus
Version 4.0

ICDL/ECDL: Syllabus 4, Office 2000 (Volume 2)

VP and GM of Courseware:	Michael Springer
Series Product Managers:	Caryl Bahner-Guhin and Adam A. Wilcox
Developmental Editors:	Jennifer Schmidt and Adam A. Wilcox
Keytesters:	Clifford Coryea
Series Designer:	Adam A. Wilcox
Cover Designer:	Steve Deschene

For more information contact:

Course Technology
25 Thomson Place
Boston, MA 02210

Or find us on the Web at: www.course.com

For permission to use material from this text or product, submit a request online at: www.thomsonrights.com

Any additional questions about permissions can be submitted by e-mail to: thomsonrights@thomson.com

Trademarks

Disclaimer

ISBN 0-619-24239-6

Printed in the United States of America

1 2 3 4 5 PM 06 05 04 03

Unit 15

Access basics

Unit time: 45 minutes

Complete this unit, and you'll know how to:

A Define database and database-related terminology, and plan a database.

B Start Access and open, create, view and close a database.

C Create, save, close, and delete tables.

D Get help.

Topic A: Database basics

Explanation

A *database* is a collection of data or information. For example, a phonebook is a database that contains the names, phone numbers, and addresses of individuals and businesses.

Databases that organize data into tables are referred to as *relational databases*. Each relational database can have multiple tables that contain data regarding entities, such as products, sales, or customers. An *entity* is any object that has a distinct set of properties. If you need details from two different entities in a single report, such as product details and sales details, you can access the corresponding tables to get the information.

A program that enables you to store data in and retrieve it from relational databases is called a *relational database management system*, or *RDMS*. Microsoft Access is an example of a RDMS.

Database terminology

To become familiar with relational databases, you need to understand basic database terminology. The following table defines several database-related terms.

Term	Description
Data value	An item of data. For example, in Exhibit 15-1, 500 in the Min_order column is a data value.
Record	A single set of related data values. For example, in Exhibit 15-1, each row is a record because it contains data for a single product.
Field	A particular type of information or data value, which is represented by a column or cell in a table. For example, in Exhibit 15-1, each column represents a field. Field 1 contains the product ID and Field 2 contains the product description.
Table	A collection of records. The records and fields in a table form rows and columns. For example, Exhibit 15-1, shows a table named Product. It contains six fields and ten records.

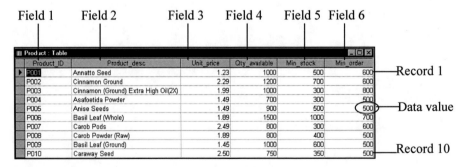

Exhibit 15-1: The Product table

Do it!

A-1:   Discussing database terminology

Questions and answers

1 What is a database?

A collection of data or information

2 What is a relational database?

data Bases that organize data into tables

3 Microsoft Access is a RDMS. (True) or false?

4 What is a field?

A particular type of infor data represented by a column or cell in a table

Database planning

Explanation

Thorough planning ensures that no data is missing or redundant and saves time on future modifications to the database. It is important to plan the type of data you need to store. For example, assume you want to keep track of the following items:

- Products
- Sales
- Retailers

You must design a database that can store data related to these three different entities, each in its own table.

Below are some items to consider when planning the design of a database:

- The purpose of the database
- The number of tables and type of information to store in each table
- The fields to be stored in each table
- The type of information you want to retrieve from the database
- How data will be entered in the database
- The types of reports you want to generate

Do it!

A-2:   Planning a database

Questions and answers

1 Lets say you are working in the sales and marketing department of Outlander Spices and you also keep track of the retailers. You have to create a database containing all information related to the operations in your department. What is the purpose of the database?

2 What type of information do you need to store in the tables?

3 What fields do you need in the tables?

4 What kind of information do you want to extract from these tables?

Topic B: Getting started

Explanation

Microsoft Access is a relational database management system (RDMS) that you can use to store, organize, and retrieve information in an effective manner. Within a RDMS, you can create, edit, view, and retrieve relational database data.

Starting Access

To start Access, click Start, then choose Programs, Microsoft Access. When you start Access, the Microsoft Access dialog box appears inside the Access window.

Do it!

B-1: Starting Access

Here's how	Here's why
1 Click **Start**, then choose **Programs, Microsoft Access**	To start the Microsoft Access program.
2 Observe the Office Assistant	(If it appears.) The Office Assistant is an animated character that you can use to locate help information.
3 Observe the title bar	**🖉 Microsoft Access**
	It shows the name of the program.

Opening databases

Explanation

To open a database:

1 From the Microsoft Access dialog box, select Open an existing file and click OK.

2 Navigate to the folder you want, and then select the name of the database you want to open.

3 Click Open.

Do it!

B-2: Opening a database

Here's how	Here's why
1 Observe the Microsoft Access dialog box	When you start Access, this dialog box gives you the option of creating a new database, or opening an existing one. By default, Open an existing file is selected.
Click **OK**	To open an existing database. The Open dialog box appears.
2 From the Look in list, select the current unit folder	To see the files in the current unit folder.
Select **Concepts**	
Click **Open**	To open Concepts. The title of the window is Concepts : Database.

Creating and saving databases

Explanation

To create and save a database you would:

1   Choose File, New to open the New dialog box. In the General tab, Database is selected by default.
2   Click OK and the File New Database dialog box opens.
3   Use the Save in list to specify the folder in which you want to store the new database.
4   In the File name box, type a name for the database.
5   Click Create and a new database is created in the specified location.

Only one database can be open at a time in Access. If you already have a database open, and you then open or create a new database, the first database will close.

Do it!

B-3:   Creating and saving a database

Here's how	Here's why
1 Choose **File, New...**	The New dialog box appears. By default, the General tab is active.
Verify that Database is selected	
Click **OK**	The File New Database dialog box appears.
2 In the Save in list, navigate to the current unit folder	If necessary.
In the File name box, type **My database**	
Click **Create**	The Concepts database closes and the new database opens, only one database can be opened at a time.

Database templates

Explanation   The Database Wizard helps automate the process of creating a database and its objects. When you create a database you can specify a template, and the Database Wizard will create the database objects based on that template.

To create a database by using the Database Wizard:

1 Choose File, New or click the New button on the Database toolbar. The New dialog box appears.
2 Click the Databases tab. From the list of database templates, select the template you want.
3 Click OK to open the File New Database dialog box.
4 Specify a location and a name for the database.
5 Click Create to open the Database Wizard.
6 Follow the steps of the wizard and click Finish.

Do it!   ## B-4:   Creating a database using a template

Here's how	Here's why
1 Choose **File, New...**	To open the New dialog box.
Click the **Databases** tab	To see the different database templates available.
Select **Order Entry**	To create a database for maintaining details about the company, products, orders, and other transactions.
Click **OK**	To open the File New Database dialog box.
2 In the Save in list, navigate to the current unit folder	(If necessary.) To save the database in this folder.
In the File name box, type **Outlander Spices**	To specify the name of the new database.
Click **Create**	The Database Wizard dialog box appears. This screen displays the details to store in this database.
3 Click **Next**	(To move to the next step of the Database Wizard.) To see the lists of tables and fields in the tables.
4 Click **Next**	To see the list of various styles for screen displays. By default, Standard is selected.
5 Click **Next**	To see the list of various styles for printing reports. By default, Corporate is selected.
6 Click **Next**	Here, you give a title to the database.

7	Type **Outlander Spices**	(In the What is the title of the database to be box.) To specify the title for the database.
	Click **Next**	
8	Verify that Yes, start the database is checked	To open the database after you exit the wizard.
	Click **Finish**	A dialog box with a progress bar first appears, indicating the rate at which the database objects are being created. Then, a message box appears prompting you to enter details about the company.
9	Click **OK**	To open the My Company Information form.
	Enter the details as shown	

Company	Outlander Spices
Address	61 Rock Creek Dr
City	Portland
State/Province	Oregon
Postal Code	97201-
Country	US

	Close the window	The Main Switchboard form appears with database options.
10	Click as shown	

Outlander S...   Form View   Restore Up

		(The Outlander Spices Database window is at the lower-left corner of the Access window.) To restore the window, and view the forms created by using the Database Wizard.
	Observe the Outlander Spices Database window	It shows the forms automatically created by the Database Wizard.
11	On the Objects bar, click **Tables**	To view the ten tables automatically created by the Database Wizard.
12	On the Objects bar, click **Reports**	To view the reports automatically created by the Database Wizard. There are six reports created by the Database Wizard.
13	Click ☒	(On the Database window.) To close the database.

Database views

Explanation

You can click the View button on far left of the toolbar to change the view of the database, or you can click the arrow next to the button to display the list of available views. The list of available views depends on the object that is open.

A complete list of views are:

- Print Preview
- Datasheet View
- Design View
- Form View
- SQL View

The Design and Datasheet view are the two most used views.

Datasheet view

Datasheet view shows data in a tabular format of rows and columns. Use the navigation buttons and the scroll bars to navigate within a table. You can scroll to the left or to the right by using the horizontal scroll bar. Also you can scroll down through the records by using the vertical scroll bar, as shown in Exhibit 15-2.

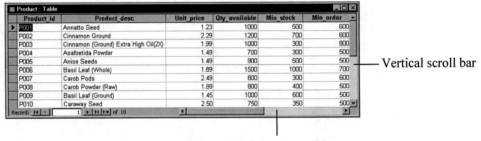

Vertical scroll bar

Horizontal scroll bar

Exhibit 15-2: The Product table in a Datasheet view

Design view

In *Design view*, the window is split into two horizontal panes, as shown in Exhibit 15-3. In the upper pane, there are columns for field name, data type, and a description for each field. The lower pane is the Field Properties pane, which lists additional properties for the filed selected in the upper pane, such as Field Size and Format.

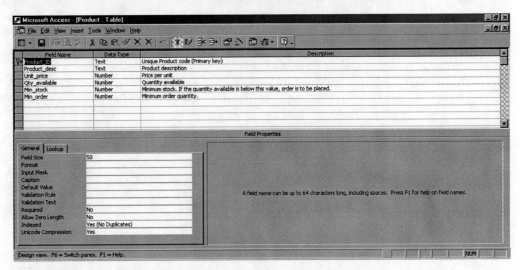

Exhibit 15-3: The Product table in Design view

Do it!

B-5: Examining views

Here's how	Here's why
1 Open Create_query	(From the current unit folder.) To open the Create_query : Database window.
2 On the Objects bar, click **Tables**	(If necessary.) To view the list of tables. There are three: Product, Retailer, and Transaction.
Select **Product**	
Click **Open**	The Product: Table window appears. This is the Datasheet view of the table.
3 Observe the fields in the table	Each column in the table is a field. The fields are Product_ID, Product_desc, Unit_price, Qty_available, Min_stock, and Min_order.
Observe the records in the table	Each row in the table is a record.
Observe the bottom-left area of the window	In this area the text 1 of 10 appears. This indicates that the first record is now active and there are a total of 10 records.
4 Choose **View**, **Design View**	To switch to Design view.
5 Observe the window	The Product: Table window appears in Design view, as shown in Exhibit 15-3.
Observe the Field Name column	The Field Name column lists the fields Product_ID, Product_desc, Unit_price, Qty_available, Min_stock, and Min_order.
Observe the Data Type column	To see that Product_ID and Product_desc are of Text data type, and Unit_price, Qty_available, Min_stock, and Min_order are of Number data type.
Observe the Description column	Each field has a description.
Observe the Field Properties pane	The field properties specific to data types are shown.

Toolbars

Explanation

There are several toolbars, such as the Formatting toolbar and the Web toolbar, that you can use to accomplish tasks quickly. To add a toolbar, choose View, Toolbars, and then, select the toolbar you want.

Customizing toolbars

You can also add and remove toolbar buttons by using the Customize dialog box. To open the Customize dialog box, choose View, Toolbars, Customize.

Do it!

B-6:   Working with toolbars

Here's how	Here's why
1 Choose **View**, **Toolbars**, **Web**	To add the Web toolbar.
Choose **View**, **Toolbars**, **Web**	To hide the Web toolbar.
2 Choose **View**, **Toolbars**, **Customize...**	To display the Customize dialog box.
Click the **Commands** tab	This tab shows categories of menus and associated commands.
3 From the Categories list, select **Edit**	To display the command buttons under the Edit menu.
From the Commands list, select **Delete**	You might need to scroll down in the Commands list to see the Delete command.
Drag Delete from the Commands list to the Database toolbar, as shown	
Observe the toolbar	The Delete button appears after the Format Painter button.
4 Click **Close**	To close the Customize dialog box.
Observe the Database toolbar	The Delete command has been added to the toolbar.

Closing a database and Access

Explanation

Updates are not permanently written to the database until it is closed. This means that any changes you make to a record or any other data will update to the database automatically when it is closed.

There are different ways to close a database:

- Choose File, Close.
- Click the Close box on the far right of the menu bar, as shown in Exhibit 15-4.
- Double-click the Database Control menu icon, as shown in Exhibit 15-4.
- Click the Database Control menu icon and choose Close.

Database Control menu icon   Close box

Exhibit 15-4: The Database Control menu icon and the Close box

There are also different ways to close Access:

- Choose File, Exit.
- Double-click the Access Control menu icon (the icon on the far left of the title bar.)
- Click the Access Control menu icon to display the Control menu, and then choose Close.
- Press Alt+F4.

Do it!

B-7:   Closing a database and Access

Here's how	Here's why
1 Choose **File**, **Close**	To close the table.
2 Choose **File**, **Close**	To close the database.
3 Choose **File**, **Exit**	To close Access.

Topic C: Database tables

Explanation   The first objects to add in a new database are tables. The Table Wizard provides a quick and easy way to create tables. You can also create tables in Design view.

Database relationships

Tables within a database contain related data. For example, you wouldn't want to add a table that stores details about library books to a sales database. Instead, the tables in a sales database should be somehow related to each other—one might contain product information, another may contain customer information, and a third sales information.

Relationships are the connection between tables in a database. A *relationship* is an association set between common fields in two or more tables. Setting a relationship between two tables is a way of coordinating information.

For example, if you want to retrieve the values of the fields Product_desc and Unit_price from the Product table, as shown in Exhibit 15-5, and Qty_sold in the Transaction table, as shown in Exhibit 15-6, you have to set a relationship between the tables. To set a relationship, match the data in the fields' common to both tables. This field should have the same name in both tables.

As you can see, both the Product table and the Transaction table contain a Product_ID field, so you can use this field to establish a relationship.

Product : Table

Product_ID	Product_desc	Unit_price	Qty_available	Min_stock	Min_order
P001	Annatto Seed	1.23	1000	500	600
P002	Cinnamon Ground	2.29	1200	700	600
P003	Cinnamon (Ground) Extra High Oil(2X)	1.99	1000	300	800
P004	Asafoetida Powder	1.49	700	300	500
P005	Anise Seeds	1.49	900	500	500
P006	Basil Leaf (Whole)	1.89	1500	1000	700
P007	Carob Pods	2.49	800	300	600
P008	Carob Powder (Raw)	1.89	800	400	500
P009	Basil Leaf (Ground)	1.45	1000	600	500
P010	Caraway Seed	2.50	750	350	500

Record: 1 of 10

Exhibit 15-5: The Product_ID field in the Product table

Transaction : Table

Transaction_ID	Transaction_date	Product_ID	Qty_sold	Retailer_code
1	1/1/2002	P001	100	R001
2	1/1/2002	P003	400	R003
3	1/5/2002	P005	200	R009
4	2/1/2002	P002	200	R001
5	2/2/2002	P001	150	R002
6	2/2/2002	P004	110	R003
7	1/7/2002	P006	140	R004
9	3/1/2002	P002	100	R006
10	3/6/2002	P008	100	R007

Record: 10 of 10

Exhibit 15-6: The matching values of the Product_ID field in the Transaction table

Referential integrity

Referential integrity is a set of rules that ensures the relationships between tables are valid. Implementing referential integrity is important to verify that the relationship is always maintained. It also prevents the accidental deletion of data or the changing of data in one table so it no longer relates to data in other tables.

Primary key

A *primary key* is a field that uniquely identifies each record. For example, in an Employee table, the field Employee_name can potentially have duplicate values if two or more employees have the same name. You can use an Employee_code field to store a unique value for each employee. The Employee_code field, in this example, would be the primary key. In the Product table, as shown in Exhibit 15-5, Product_ID is the primary key.

Each primary key in a table is automatically indexed. *Indexing* is a feature to speed locating data and sorting tables.

The Table Wizard

The Table Wizard contains two categories of sample tables, one with 25 common business tables and the other with 20 common tables for personal use. For each sample table, there is a set of sample fields. You can create a table with the sample fields of your choice.

To create a table by using the Table Wizard:

1 Open the database for which you want to create a table.

2 Under Objects, select Table and then double-click "Create table by using wizard."

3 Select a table category to view the list of sample tables.

4 Select a sample table.

5 Select sample fields.

6 Set the primary key.

7 Finish the Table Wizard.

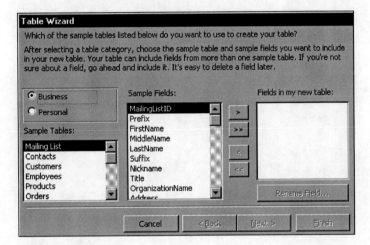

Exhibit 15-7: The Table Wizard

Do it!

C-1: Creating a table using the Table Wizard

Here's how	Here's why
1 Start Microsoft Access	
2 Open Employee	From the current unit folder.
Under Objects, verify that Tables is selected	
Select **Create table by using wizard**	To create the table by using the Table Wizard.
Click **Open**	The Table Wizard appears, as shown in Exhibit 15-7.
3 Observe the window	Business is selected by default.
From the Sample Tables list, select **EmployeesAndTasks**	To see a list of all the fields in the EmployeeAndTasks table.
Click ⧉	To add all fields to the Fields in my new table box.
Click **Next**	To see the next dialog box of the Table Wizard.
4 In the What do you want to name your table box, type **Employee_tasks**	This will be the name of the table.
Select **No, I'll set the primary key**	
Click **Next**	To see the next step of the Table Wizard.
5 From the What field will hold data that is unique for each record list, select **EmployeeID**	
Verify that the indicated option is selected	To generate Employee codes automatically.
Click **Next**	To see the next dialog box of the Table Wizard.

6	Verify that Enter data directly into the table is selected	
	Click **Finish**	To see the Employee_tasks table.
	Observe the screen	The Datasheet view of Employee_tasks. Notice that under Employee ID, AutoNumber appears. This implies that Access automatically generates consecutive numbers for new records.
7	Close the window	Choose File, Close.

Creating a table using Design view

Explanation

In Design view, you can create a table that is exactly designed to your needs. If you've already created a table by using the Table Wizard, you can modify it in Design view.

The Design view window is split horizontally into two panes, as shown in Exhibit 15-8. The upper pane contains rows and columns to hold the information about each field. Each row contains data under the columns, Field Name, Data Type, and Description. The row selector, as shown in Exhibit 15-8, indicates the active row that is being edited.

Enter the name of the fields under the Field Name column. In the Data Type column, specify the type of data to store in the field. You can do this by selecting a data type from a drop-down list, such as Number, Date/Time, Text, or Currency. The data type depends on the type of value you want to store in the field. For example, you can use the Text data type to store an employee name. Enter a description of the field in the Description column.

The lower pane is the Field Properties pane, which contains two tabs, General and Lookup. You can use the General tab for setting field properties like the size of a field.

Row selector

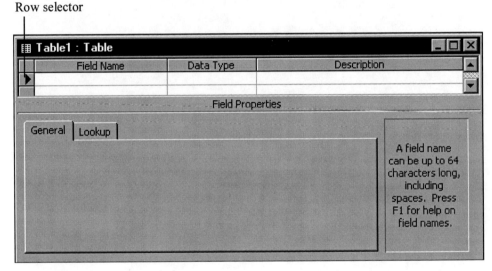

Exhibit 15-8: A table in Design view

Do it!

C-2:   Creating a table in Design view

Here's how	Here's why
1 Select **Create table in Design view**	
Click **Open**	To open the Design window.
2 Observe the window	Notice that Table1: Table appears in the title bar, and that the row selector is on the first record.
Observe the Field Properties pane	There are two tabs, General and Lookup. By default, the General tab is active.
3 Under Field Name, enter **Employee Name**	
Place the insertion point in the Data Type field	Notice that the Text data type appears. This is the default, but you can select a different data type from the drop-down list.
Under Description, type **Name of the employee**	

Saving and closing tables

Explanation

You can save a table by choosing File, Save As or by choosing File, Save. In the first method, you have the option of saving it as a table, a form, or a report. A prompt appears the first time you save it requesting the table name. After you save the table, you can start entering data.

To close a table, choose File, close.

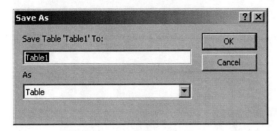

Exhibit 15-9: The Save As dialog box

Do it!

C-3:   Saving and closing a table

Here's how	Here's why
1 Choose **File, Save As...**	To open the Save As dialog box, as shown in Exhibit 15-9.
In the Save Table 'Table1' To box, type **Sales**	To save the table as Sales.
In the As box, verify that Table is selected	
Click **OK**	A message box appears prompting you to create a primary key.
Click **No**	Do not create a primary key.
2 Observe the title of the window	⊞ Sales : Table _ □ ✕
	The title of the Design window changes to Sales : Table.
Close the Design window	
Observe the Database window	In the list of tables, Sales table also appears.
3 Select **Sales**	
Click **Open**	To open the Sales : Table window in Datasheet view.

4 Observe the column heading	The column heading is the same as the field name you entered in Design view.
Observe the first row	The row selector is positioned to the left of the first row.
5 Close the table	

Deleting tables

Explanation

To delete a table:

1   Close the table that you want to delete.
2   In the database window, display the table objects.
3   Select the table you want to delete and press Delete.

Do it!

C-4: Deleting a table

Here's how	Here's why
1 Verify that Sales table is selected	
Press (DELETE)	A message box appears asking you to confirm that you want to delete the table "Sales."
Click **Yes**	To delete the table.
Observe the database window	The Sales table is not there.
2 Close the database	

Topic D: Getting help

Explanation

The Help system provides information on a topic or task. You can get help through the various tabs of the Help window, or by using the Office Assistant.

The Help window

There are three ways to open the Help window:

- Choose Help, Microsoft Access Help.
- Press F1.
- Click the Microsoft Access Help button on the toolbar.

Help window tabs

The Help window has three tabs that provide different ways of interacting with the Help system:

- Contents (shown in Exhibit 15-10)
- Answer Wizard
- Index

The Contents tab works through categories of information. The Answer Wizard enables you to look at topics that relate to questions you type, and the index shows topics based upon keywords.

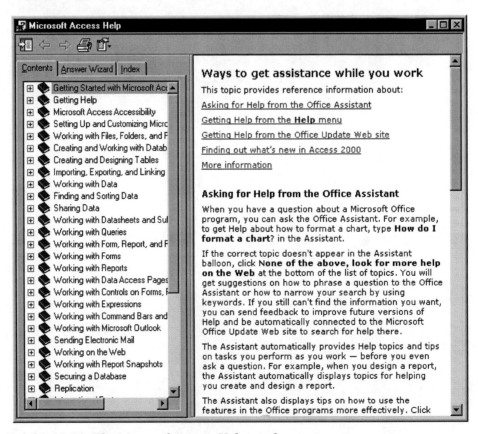

Exhibit 15-10: The Microsoft Access Help window

Do it!

D-1: Using the Help window to get help

Here's how	Here's why
1 Choose **Help**, **Microsoft Access Help**	(To open the Help window.) Notice that the Help window is spilt into two panes.
Observe the tabs on the left pane	To see that there are three tabs, as shown in Exhibit 15-10. The tabs are Contents, Answer Wizard, and Index.
Observe the right pane	The right pane displays the current Help topic.
Verify that the Contents tab is active	
2 Observe the Contents tab	
	The Contents tab displays a list of categories of Help topics, depicted by closed book icons.
In the Contents pane, locate Getting Started with Microsoft Access	It is at the top of the pane.
Click as shown	
	(This button is on the left side of the Getting Started with Microsoft Access topic.) To see a list of sub-topics.
Close the Microsoft Access Help window	

The Office Assistant

Explanation

The Office Assistant is an animated character that helps you to interact with the Help system. The character appears, by default, in the shape of a paper clip. Here's how you use it:

1   Choose Help, Show the Office Assistant.
2   Click the Office Assistant.
3   Type a question and click Search.

The Assistant will then guide you to relevant information in the Help system.

Do it!

D-2: Getting help through the Office Assistant

Here's how	Here's why
1 Choose **Help, Show the Office Assistant**	
	To display the Office Assistant.
Click the Office Assistant	
2 In the What would you like to do balloon, enter **What is a database?**	
Click **Search**	
Observe the Office Assistant	
	It shows a list of topics related to the question. You would select a topic to get more information.
3 Click **Options**	To display the Office Assistant options.
Clear **Use the Office Assistant**	To disable the Office Assistant.
Click **OK**	To close the Options window.
4 Choose **File, Exit**	To close Access.

Unit summary: Access basics

Topic A

In this topic, you learned what a **database** is, defined **database terminology**, including **field**, **record**, **data value**, and **table**. You also learned how to **plan a database**.

Topic B

In this topic, you learned how to **start Access** and **open**, **create**, and **save databases**. You also learned how to use **database templates** to create a database. Next, you learned about the available **views** for displaying database information. You also learned how to **add** and **remove toolbars** and **add commands** to a toolbar. Finally, you learned how to **close** a database and Access.

Topic C

In this topic, you learned how to **create a table** by using the **Table Wizard.** You also learned how to create a table in **Design view**. Then, you learned how to **save**, **close**, and **delete tables**.

Topic D

In this topic, you learned how to use get help by using the **Microsoft Access Help window**. You learned about the **Contents**, the **Answer Wizard**, and **Index** tabs, and how to use the **Office Assistant**.

Independent practice activity

1 Start Access.

2 Identify the toolbar, menu bar, and title bar of the Access window.

3 Open the Transaction database (from the current unit folder)/

4 Identify the objects of the database.

5 Open the Customer table. Identify the rows and columns.

6 Close the table.

7 Open the Create_table database.

8 Start the Table Wizard to create a table.

9 Select **Customers** as your sample table.

10 Add all the sample fields to fields in my new table.

11 Name the table **My customers**.

12 Set CustomerID as the primary key.

13 Finish the Table Wizard.

14 Close My customers.

15 Create a table in Design view with fields as follows:

- **Order_no** as Number
- **Product_id** as Number
- **Order_date** as Date/Time
- **Customer** as Text
- **Order_amt** as Currency
- **Dispatched** as Date/Time

16 Save the table as **Customer_order**. Don't set a primary key.

17 Close the table.

18 Open the table Customer_order.

19 Enter data in Customer_order, as shown in Exhibit 15-11.

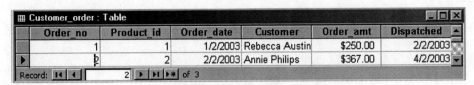

Exhibit 15-11: Records in Customer_order table

20 Close the table.

21 Display information on the topic "database templates" using Help.

22 Close the Help window.

23 Display the Office Assistant and search for help on the topic "database relationship."

24 Disable the Office Assistant.

25 Close the database and close Access.

Unit 16

Working with tables

Unit time: 60 minutes

Complete this unit, and you'll know how to:

A Insert, delete, move, and rename fields; edit field properties; set a primary key; and create a single or multiple field index.

B Add and delete records, find and replace data values, and undo the last change.

C Sort, filter, and navigate records; move columns; and modify column width.

D Create and delete relationships.

Topic A: Working with fields

Explanation

After creating a database and its related tables, you are ready to fill the table with data. Fields are the elements within tables that hold data. Some functions you can perform on fields include:

- Inserting
- Deleting
- Changing
- Moving
- Copying
- Setting properties
- Setting a primary key
- Creating an index

Inserting and deleting fields

You can insert a field anywhere in a table by selecting a row and then choosing Insert, Rows. For example, you can insert a field named qtr3 between qtr2 and qtr4. The new blank row is inserted above the selected row.

To delete a field in Design view, you have to select the row that contains the field and press the Delete key or choose Edit, Delete. Before deleting a field, a prompt appears to confirm the deletion

Selecting a row

To select a field row, point to the left of the record and click. The record selector will appear and the record will be highlighted, as shown in Exhibit 16-1.

Record selector

Field Name	Data Type	Description
SP_code	Text	Salesperson's code
SN	Text	Salesperson's name
Commission	Number	Commission on sales
qtr1	Number	Sales made in quarter 1
qtr2	Number	Sales made in quarter 2
qtr4	Number	Sales made in quarter 4

Exhibit 16-1: A selected field

Do it!

A-1:　Inserting and deleting fields

Here's how	Here's why
1 Start Access	
Open Working_with_records	From the current unit folder.
Open Quarterly_sales_analysis in design view	
2 Select the row for the field qtr4	You'll insert a field above this field.
Choose **Insert, Rows**	A blank row appears above the selected field.
Place the insertion point in the Field Name column, and type **qtr3**	(In the blank row.) To enter the field name.
Enter the rest of the field details as shown	qtr3 　Number 　Sales made in quarter 3
3 Insert a blank row above qtr3	(Select the field and choose Insert, Rows.) To insert a field above this field.
Fill in the new field as shown	DOJ 　Date/Time 　Date of Joining
4 Insert another field below DOJ as shown	STrgt 　Currency 　Sales Target
5 Point to the left of the field **Commission**, as shown	Commission 　Number 　Commission on sales
	An arrow appears.
Click the mouse button	To select the row.
Choose **Edit, Delete**	To delete the field Commission from the table.
6 Save the table as **My quarterly_sales_analysis**	A message appears prompting you to create a primary key.
Click **No**	

Changing field names

Explanation

It's a good practice to name fields so that the name suggests the type of data they contain. For example, it's unlikely anyone will be able to interpret the type of data contained by the field, STrgt. You can change field names to something more meaningful by simply replacing the old name with a new name. This does not affect the existing data in the table.

Do it!

A-2:   Modifying field names

Here's how	Here's why
1 Place the insertion point within the field SP_code	To change the name of the first field.
Type **Salesperson_code**	This will be the new name for the first field.
2 Change the field names for fields SN, qtr1, qtr2, DOJ, STrgt, qtr3, and qtr4 as shown	Salesperson_name Quarter1_sales Quarter2_sales Date_joining Sales_target Quarter3_sales Quarter4_sales
Observe the fields	The field names are more meaningful now.
3 Update the table	

Moving fields

Explanation

After you create several fields, you might find that you need to rearrange them. To move a field, select the row and drag it where you want it, as shown in Exhibit 16-2. The current field row automatically shifts to the next row.

	Field Name	Data Type	
🔑	SP_code	Text	Salesperson's code
	Salesperson_name	Text	Salesperson's name
	Quarter1_sales	Number	Sales made in quarter 1
	Quarter2_sales	Number	Sales made in quarter 2
▶	Date_joining	Date/Time	Date of Joining
	Sales_target	Currency	Sales Target

Exhibit 16-2: The pointer to move a field

Do it!

A-3:   Moving fields

Here's how	Here's why
1 Select the row for Date_joining	You'll move this field after the field Salesperson_name.
Point to the record selector for Date_joining	The pointer changes as shown in Exhibit 16-2. You can now drag the field.
Drag the row above Quarter1_sales	(While dragging, there will be an outline above the row for Quarter1_sales.) Notice that Quarter1_sales has shifted down.
2 Move Sales_target above Quarter1_sales	Select the row containing Sales_target and drag it above Quarter1_sales.
3 Update the table	

Field properties

Explanation

Each field has its own set of properties that determine either the way that values will be stored or the way they will appear. The General tab in the lower pane of Design view displays the field properties.

For example, if you want to change the default size of a text field, just modify the Field Size property.

Formatting text fields

To change the way a field is formatted, use the Format property. The following table shows some formatting characters for text fields.

Character	Description
@	At least one character or space must be entered.
<	Converts all characters to lowercase.
>	Converts all characters to uppercase.

Formatting other field types

You can also change the format of other field types, such as:

- Currency
- Date
- Number

To change the format of the currency field:

1 Select the field.

2 Display the Format list, as shown in Exhibit 16-3, and select a format.

Currency	▼
General Number	3456.789
Currency	$3,456.79
Euro	€3,456.79
Fixed	3456.79
Standard	3,456.79
Percent	123.00%
Scientific	3.46E+03

Exhibit 16-3: The formats available for the Currency and Number fields

To change the format of a number field, select the field, display the Format list, and then select a format. The options for a number field are the same as those for a currency field, shown in Exhibit 16-3.

To change the format of a Date field, select the field, display the Format list, and then choose a format. Options include long and short forms of the date and time, as shown in Exhibit 16-4.

dd-mmm-yyyy	▾
General Date	6/19/1994 5:34:23 PM
Long Date	Sunday, June 19, 1994
Medium Date	19-Jun-94
Short Date	6/19/1994
Long Time	5:34:23 PM
Medium Time	5:34 PM
Short Time	17:34

Exhibit 16-4: The formats available for the Date field

Validation rules

A *validation rule* is a constraint set on a field to ensure that the data entered in the field is valid. Consider Sales_target in the Quarterly_sales_analysis table. You want specify a range between $5,000 and $20,000, so that only the values in the specified range will be accepted. To set a validation rule on a field, you would do the following:

1 Switch to the Design view and select the field.

2 Activate the General tab.

3 Place the insertion point in the Validation Rule box.

4 Click the Build button next to the Validation Rule box.

5 Build the expression in the Expression Builder dialog box.

6 Click OK to close the Expression Builder box.

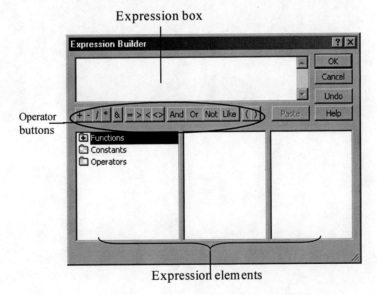

Exhibit 16-5: The Expression Builder dialog box

The Expression Builder builds an expression to validate the value entered in a field. An *expression* is a combination of values and operators. You can create an expression for any field. For the sales target example above, which is a number field, you would enter

```
> 5000 AND < 20,000
```

directly into the expression box. This would ensure that only numbers between 5000 and 20000 are entered. You can also build an expression by using the operator buttons, as shown in Exhibit 16-5, or by using the Operators folder from the left Expression elements box. After building the expression, click OK to close the Expression Builder dialog box.

You can also check the validity of date fields. For example, you want a hire date field to reject dates later than the current date. The built-in Now() function returns the current date. Follow the general steps above, and then enter the following into the expression box to ensure that only dates less than or equal to today are accepted:

```
<= Now()
```

Do it!

A-4: Editing field properties

Here's how	Here's why
1 Place the insertion point in the first field	In the first cell under Field Name.
Observe the Field Properties pane	There are two tabs, General and Lookup. The General tab is active.
Observe the Field Size box	The number 50 appears.
2 Edit the Field Size box to read **4**	Now, you won't be able to enter more than 4 characters in this field.
3 Place the insertion point anywhere in the second field row	
Edit Field Size for Salesperson_name to read **25**	To indicate that the salesperson's name can be no more than 25 characters long.
4 Place the insertion point in the Format box	
Enter **>**	To specify that all lowercase text be changed to uppercase while entering data.
5 Place the insertion point in the Validation Rule box	You'll enter a rule to ensure that this field is not empty.
Click as shown	
	To display the Expression Builder dialog box, as shown in Exhibit 16-5.
In the left Expression Elements box, select **Constants** as shown	
6 Click **Not**	
Select **Null**	
Double-click **Null**	To make "Null" appear in the Expression Builder box. This will ensure that this field is not empty during data entry.
Click **OK**	To close the Expression Builder dialog box.
7 Observe the Validation Rule box	"Not Null" appears in the box.

8	Place the insertion point anywhere in the fifth field	The Quarter1_sales field.
9	Place the insertion point in the Validation Rule box	You'll create a rule to ensure that the value entered in this field is greater than zero.
	Display the Expression Builder	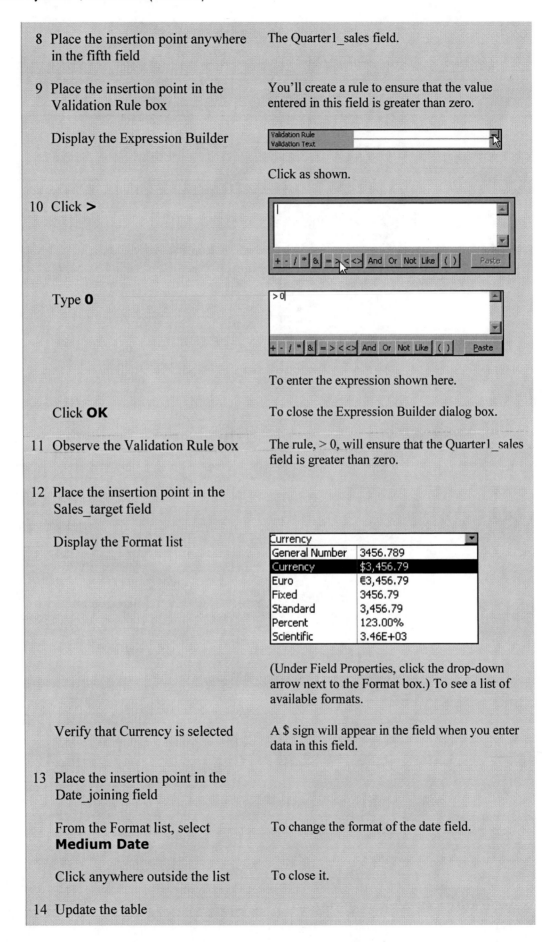 Click as shown.
10	Click **>**	
	Type **0**	To enter the expression shown here.
	Click **OK**	To close the Expression Builder dialog box.
11	Observe the Validation Rule box	The rule, > 0, will ensure that the Quarter1_sales field is greater than zero.
12	Place the insertion point in the Sales_target field	
	Display the Format list	(Under Field Properties, click the drop-down arrow next to the Format box.) To see a list of available formats.
	Verify that Currency is selected	A $ sign will appear in the field when you enter data in this field.
13	Place the insertion point in the Date_joining field	
	From the Format list, select **Medium Date**	To change the format of the date field.
	Click anywhere outside the list	To close it.
14	Update the table	

Primary keys

Explanation

The primary key is used to uniquely identify a row in a table. There are three different ways to set the primary key:

- Choose Edit, Primary Key.
- Click the Primary Key button on the Table Design toolbar.
- Right-click the field row and select Primary Key from the shortcut menu.

Do it!

A-5: Setting the primary key

Here's how	Here's why
1 Select the field Salesperson_code	You will set this field as the primary key for the table.
Right-click **Salesperson_code**	A shortcut menu appears.
Choose **Primary Key**	A key icon appears on the left side of Salesperson_code. This means that Salesperson_code is now the primary key.
2 Update and close the table	

Indexes

Explanation

An index is used to quickly sort and locate data for one or more specific fields. This makes the job of finding and sorting data in large tables quick and easy. A *single-field index* is created based on one field in a table. For example, you can create a single field index for Salesperson_name in the Quarterly_sales_analysis table to quickly sort and find data based on sales persons' names. A primary key is indexed by default.

To create a single-field index:

1 Open the table in Design view.
2 Choose View, Indexes to open the Indexes window.
3 In any cell under Index Name, enter a name for the index and press Tab.
4 From the list, select the field on which you want to create the index and press Tab.
5 Select a sort order.
6 Close the window.
7 Update and close the table.

You can also create a multiple-field index that is based on two or more fields in a table. For example, you can create an index based on the First_name and Last_name fields in the Employees table.

Do it!

A-6: Creating single and multiple field indexes

Here's how	Here's why
1 Under Objects, click **Tables**	If necessary.
2 Open SalesPerson_data in Design view	You'll add an index to this table.
3 Choose **View, Indexes**	To display the Indexes: SalesPerson_data window.
Place the insertion point in the first cell under Index Name	If necessary.
Enter **Sales person code**	This is the name of the new index.
Press (TAB)	To move the insertion point to the next column.
4 From the list, select **Salesperson_code**	To select the field on which you want to create the index.
Under Sort Order, verify that Ascending appears	
5 Place the insertion point in the Unique box	
From the drop-down list, select **Yes**	To avoid duplicate values in this field.
Close the window	

6 Update and close the table

7 Open Employee_data | (In the Design view.) You'll create a multiple-field index in this table.

Click ⚡ | (The Indexes button is on the Table Design toolbar.) To open the Indexes: Employee window.

Place the insertion point in the first cell under Index Name | If necessary.

Enter **Employee_name**

Press (TAB) | To select the field on which to base the index.

8 From the list, select **Last_name**

Verify that in the Unique box, No is selected | (In the Index Properties group.) To ignore duplicate values.

9 Click in the second cell under Field Name | (Leave the Index Name column empty because you are creating a multiple field index.) To select another field on which to base the index.

From the list, select **First_name**

In the first and second cells under Sort Order, verify that Ascending appears

10 Close the window

11 Update and close the table

Topic B: Manipulating records

Explanation

Now that you have created fields, you can begin to fill them with data. A record is a single set of related fields, and it is the object used to insert and retrieve data from a table. The following are actions that manipulate the data within a record:

- Add
- Modify
- Delete

If you accidentally modify or delete a record, you can use the Undo button on the toolbar to restore the original values.

Adding records in a table

You can add a new record to a table in either of these ways:

- Click the New Record button on the Table Datasheet toolbar.
- With the insertion point in the last field of the last record, press the Tab key.

You can add data to a new record by placing the insertion point in a field and typing. Navigate among the fields by using the Tab key.

P001	Annatto Seed	1.23	500	1000
P002	Cinnamon Ground	2.29	700	1200
P003	Cinnamon (Ground) Extra High Oil(2X)	1.99	300	1000
P004	Asafoetida Powder	1.49	300	700
P005	Anise Seeds	1.49	500	900

Exhibit 16-6: The sample records

Do it!

B-1:   Adding a new record to a table

Here's how	Here's why
1 Open Spices_data	(In the Datasheet view.) You'll add records to this table.
2 Place the insertion point in the Product_ID column	If necessary.
Type **P0001**	You cannot enter the code beyond P000, because the Product_ID that you are trying to enter contains five characters whereas the field size of Product_ID is 4.
Type **P001**	The value is accepted.
Press ⎡TAB⎤	To move to the next field.
3 Type **Annato Seed**	In the Product_description field.
Press ⎡TAB⎤	
4 Type **1.23**	In the Unit_price field.
Press ⎡TAB⎤	Notice that a $ sign automatically appears before the value. The $ sign appears when you specify the Format as Currency.
5 Type **500**	In the Minimum_quantity field.
Press ⎡TAB⎤	
6 Type **1000**	In the Qty_available field.
Press ⎡TAB⎤	
7 Add the remaining records	As shown in Exhibit 16-6.
8 Update and close the table	

Finding and replacing values

Explanation

Searching through a table for a specific data value can take a long time, especially if the table is large. For example, you might want to locate a particular employee in a table that contains over 2000 employees. Rather than finding the value manually, you can use the Find command to instantly find, and if necessary, replace the data.

To search for a value:

1   Click the Find button on the toolbar or choose Edit, Find. The Find and Replace dialog box appears, as shown in Exhibit 16-7.

2   On the find tab, specify the value you want to locate.

3   On the Replace tab, specify the value to replace the found value.

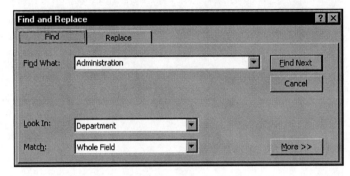

Exhibit 16-7: The Find and Replace dialog box

Do it!

B-2: Finding and replacing data

Here's how	Here's why
1 Open SalesPerson_data in Datasheet view	This table contains information about employees. You'll search this table for occurrences of the word "Administration" in the Department field, and replace them with "Customer Support."
2 Place the insertion point in the first row of the Department field.	When you search, Access will assume you want to search in the active field.
Click [binoculars icon]	(The Find button is on the Table Datasheet toolbar.) To open the Find and Replace dialog box. By default, the Find tab is active.
In the Find What box, type **Administration**	
In the Look In list, verify that Department is selected	To specify that you want to search in the Department field.
Click **Find Next**	The first occurrence of the word "Administration," corresponding to the employee Melinda McGregor, is highlighted.
3 Click the **Replace** tab	
In the Replace With box, enter **Customer Support**	
Click **Replace**	To replace the current instance of "Administration" with "Customer Support."
4 Observe the table	The next occurrence of "Administration," in the record for James Overmire, is highlighted.
Click **Replace**	To replace this occurrence of "Administration" with "Customer Support."
5 Click **Cancel**	To close the Find and Replace dialog box.
6 Update the table	

Deleting records

Explanation

There may be situations in which you need to delete records. For example, if an employee leaves the company, you might want to delete her record. To do this, select the record and either choose Edit, Delete or press the Delete key. You can also place the pointer anywhere in the record and choose Edit, Delete Record. A prompt appears to confirm the deletion. After a record is deleted, it cannot be restored.

Deleting field data

To delete field data in a record, point to the upper-left part of the field you want to delete, and click to select the data. When you're pointing to the right spot, the pointer takes the shape of a white cross, as shown in Exhibit 16-8. Delete the data by pressing the Delete key. You should be sure before you delete the data in a record, because there is no prompt asking you for confirmation. Deleting the data in a field can, however, be undone.

⬚Annie Philips	856-85-8586	West

Exhibit 16-8: The shape of the mouse pointer for selecting a field

Do it!

B-3: Deleting a record from a table

Here's how	Here's why
1 Place the insertion point in the Annie Philips's record	You'll delete this record because Annie Philips is leaving the company.
Choose **Edit**, **Delete Record**	A message box appears prompting you to confirm the deletion.
Click **Yes**	The record is deleted.
2 Point to the left corner of the field containing "Rita Greg," as shown	⬚Rita Greg 986-07-5705 East
	(The record with S009 as the Salesperson_code.) The pointer will take the shape of a white cross when you're pointing to the right spot.
Click to select the field	
Press (DELETE)	To delete the data.

Undoing changes

Explanation

You can restore deleted or modified values by clicking the Undo button on the Table Datasheet toolbar or by choosing Edit, Undo. You can undo only the most recently changed value.

Do it!

B-4: Undoing changes

Here's how	Here's why
1 Click [↶]	(The Undo button is on the Table Datasheet toolbar.) To restore the value before the last modification.
Observe the table	The data, "Rita Greg," is restored in the field.
2 In the Earnings column, select the first value	
Edit the value to read **0**	
3 Click [↶]	(To undo the change.) The older value is restored.
4 Update the table	

Topic C: Managing tables

Explanation

Managing tables means organizing data in a meaningful way so you can quickly retrieve accurate information. For example, if you want to view records in ascending order by employees' last names, you can sort the records based on the values in the last name field. You can also sort records based on more than one field.

Filtering means temporarily isolating a subset of records. For example, you can delete or edit Administration department records in Datasheet view without navigating through the records of all departments.

There are several navigational buttons to help you move quickly through the records, or you can adjust how the table appears aesthetically by moving columns or adjusting column width to better fit the data.

Sorting by a single field

Records in a table are automatically sorted based on the primary key field; however, you might want to sort the records based on a different field. The maximum number of characters for a sort field (or fields) is 255. You can sort in either ascending or descending order.

To sort on a single field in ascending order, you can do any of the following:

- Select the field, choose Records, Sort, and then choose either Sort Ascending or Sort Descending.
- Click the appropriate Sort button on the toolbar.
- Right-click the field and choose a sort command from the shortcut menu.

Ascending sort order rules are:

- Text values can be sorted alphabetically from A to Z.
- Date values can be sorted from earliest to latest.
- Number or currency values can be sorted from the lowest value to the highest.
- You cannot sort records based on memo fields.

Do it!

C-1: Sorting records by a single field

Here's how	Here's why
1 Place the insertion point anywhere in the Salesperson_name column	You will sort these records in ascending order based on the Salesperson_name field.
Choose **Records**, **Sort**, **Sort Ascending**	To sort the records in ascending order.
Observe the table	The records are sorted in ascending order based on the field Salesperson_name.
2 Update the table	

Sorting by multiple fields

Explanation

To sort by multiple fields:

1 Point to the column heading for one of the fields. The pointer changes to a downward-pointing arrow.

2 Drag over the headings for all the fields you want to sort. Both columns will be highlighted, as shown in Exhibit 16-9.

3 Choose Records, Sort, Sort Ascending.

Exhibit 16-9: The Salesperson_data table with multiple columns selected for sorting

Do it!

C-2:   Sorting records by multiple fields

Here's how	Here's why
1 Select the columns **Region** and **Department**	Drag the mouse pointer over the column labels of these two columns.
Choose **Records**, **Sort**, **Sort Ascending**	To sort records in ascending order of the two fields, Region and Department.
2 Select the column, **Salesperson_code**	
Sort the records in ascending order	Choose Records, Sort, Sort Ascending.
3 Update the table	

Filtering records

Explanation

The filtering feature displays only the records that you want to view. For example, if you want to view Human resources department records, you can apply a filter so that only records from the Human resources department appear in the table, as shown in Exhibit 16-10. To filter records you would:

1 Place the insertion point next to the specific value that you want to include.
2 Choose Records, Filter, Filter By Selection or click the Filter by Selection button on the toolbar.

You can remove a filter in either of the following ways:

- Click the Remove Filter button on the Table Datasheet toolbar.
- Choose Records, Remove/Filter Sort.

	Salesperson_code	Salesperson_name	SSN	Region	Department	Earnings
▶	S001	Malcom Pingault	816-17-3312	East	Human resources	$72,000.00
	S011	Paul Anderson	777-76-8856	East	Human resources	$72,000.00
	S019	Jamie Morrison	712-35-4665	East	Human resources	$72,000.00
	S020	Maureen O'Connor	189-85-3313	East	Human resources	$72,000.00

Exhibit 16-10: Records filtered on the Human resources department

Do it!

C-3: Filtering records

Here's how	Here's why
1 In the Department column, select the value **Human resources**	(In any row.) You'll filter the table to show only those records with this value in the Department field.
Choose **Records, Filter, Filter By Selection**	To shown only the records that contain the Department value "Human resources."
2 Choose **Records, Remove Filter/Sort**	To remove the filter and the sort.
Observe the table	The records are no longer sorted or filtered.
3 Update the table	

Navigating in tables

Explanation

Within Datasheet view, there are several navigational buttons located at the bottom of the window, as shown in Exhibit 16-11. You can also navigate through the records by using the record selector.

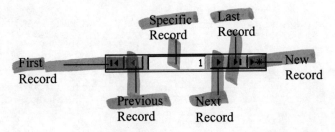

Exhibit 16-11: Navigation buttons in the Datasheet view

Record selector

The record selector selects a record. The symbol used to represent the record selector changes based on the record status. The following table explains these symbols.

Symbol	Description
▶	Represents the current record.
∗	Represents a new, blank record.
✎	Represents a record in Edit mode (not yet saved).

Do it!

C-4:   Navigating in a table

Here's how	Here's why
1 Select the row containing the Salesperson_code, **S001**	
Observe the Specific Record box	(On the Navigation bar.) This is record 1.
2 Click [▶]	(The Next record button is to the right of the Specific Record box, on the Navigation bar.) To move to the next record. Notice that the record selector is now on the second record.
3 Click [◀]	To move to the previous record. Notice that the record selector is on the first record.
4 Click [▶I]	To move to the last record. Notice that the record selector is on the record containing the data of Anna Morris.
5 Click [I◀]	To move to the first record.
Observe the Specific Record box	Record number 1 is once again active.
6 Edit the Specific Record box to read **5**	
Press (↵ ENTER)	To move to the fifth record.
7 Place the insertion point in the Department column of the last record	To edit the record.
Edit the department to read **Human resources**	[✎]
	Notice that the record selector symbol is changed to a pencil. This indicates that you are editing the record.
8 Update the table	

Modifying columns

Explanation

To modify the way a table appears within the Datasheet view, you can move columns to different locations or change their widths to better fit the data they contain.

Moving columns

To move columns:

1 Select a column or adjacent columns using the Field selector. A *field selector* is a downward-pointing arrow that appears at the top of a column when you point to it.

2 Press and hold the mouse pointer on the column labels. Notice that the shape of the mouse pointer changes.

3 Drag the columns where you want them.

Moving the columns to a new location does not reposition the fields in the actual table. You can confirm this by looking at the Design view for the table. By moving the columns of a table in the Datasheet view, you change only the appearance, and not the actual structure, of the table.

Change column widths

To change the width of a column:

1 Point the mouse over the right edge of the column. Notice that the insertion point turns to a double-headed arrow.

2 Drag the border of the column until it is the width you want.

Changing the width of a column doesn't change the size of the field. You are merely changing the appearance of the table, and not the size of the field, which you would do in Design view.

Do it!

C-5: Moving and resizing columns

Here's how	Here's why
1 Point as shown	Salesperson_code┼Salesperson_name
	(Between the Salesperson_code and Salesperson_name column labels.) You can resize a column by dragging its right border.
Drag to the left to narrow the column	

Sale	Salesperson_name
S001	Malcom Pingault
S002	Shannon Lee
S003	Melinda McGregor
S004	James Overmire
S005	Roger Williams

The exact size is not important.

2 Select the columns **SSN** and **Region**	Using the field selector.
Drag the columns to the left of the Earnings column	While dragging, notice a change in the mouse pointer.
Observe the table	

Sales	Salesperson_name	Department	SSN	Region	Earnings
S001	Malcom Pingault	Human resources	816-17-3312	East	$72,000.00
S002	Shannon Lee	Accounts	799-70-8097	South	$80,000.00
S003	Melinda McGregor	Customer Support	336-68-4467	South	$95,000.00
S004	James Overmire	Customer Support	312-71-3816	South	$90,000.00
S005	Roger Williams	Marketing	534-98-7549	East	$78,000.00

	The SSN and Region columns have been moved before Earnings.
3 Close the table	A message box appears asking you to save your changes.
Click **No**	As you don't need to resize or move the columns in this table.

Topic D: Relating tables

Explanation

After creating a database, tables, and fields, and filling the database with data, you are ready for normalization and creating table relationships. Normalizing a database eliminates data redundancy so you can store data more efficiently. The process of dividing a database into several related tables to reduce redundancy is called *normalization*.

A table is said to have a *relationship* with another table when there is a link between the common fields of these tables. In order to retrieve the data from these fields, you have to set a relationship between the tables.

Normalization

Normalization simplifies the database structure and increases the functionality of the data. To normalize tables follow the data design standards called normal forms. There are three normal forms, and each form requires that a table satisfy the preceding normal form. The three normal forms are:

- First normal form
- Second normal form
- Third normal form

First normal form

A table is in the first normal form when the following conditions are satisfied:

- It doesn't contain redundant data. For example, if you had fields called Project_number_1 and Project_number_2, both containing project numbers, those fields would be redundant.

- It doesn't contain fields that can be further broken down into smaller fields. For example, a field called Name can be broken into two fields, First_name and Last_name.

To convert a table to first normal form, break down the fields into the smallest possible parts and eliminate the fields that contain repetitive information.

Second normal form

Second normal form applies only to tables that have a composite (multiple-field) primary key. If a table has information that isn't related to the entire primary key, it is not in second normal form.

A table is in second normal form when the following conditions are satisfied:

- The table is in first normal form.
- All the fields in the table are related to all the fields of the composite primary key.

To convert a table to second normal form, you should find all the fields that are related to only a part of the composite primary key. Group these fields into another table, and then assign a primary key to the new table.

Third normal form

Third normal form applies to tables that have a single-field primary key. If a table contains fields that do not relate to the primary key, it is not in third normal form. For instance, consider an Order_details table that has the following fields:

- Order_ID
- Product_name
- Quantity
- Customer_ID
- Customer_address

Order_ID is the table's primary key. Notice that Customer_address is not related to the primary key. To put a table in third normal form, you remove all of the fields that do not relate to the primary key, and put them in a separate table.

Defining table relationships

While creating relationships you always work with two tables at a time. One table is called the *primary table* and the other table is called the *related table*. The primary and related tables are determined based on the kind of relationship. The tables are related based on a matching field, which is the primary key of the primary table. When the primary key exists in the related table, it is called the *foreign key*. Two tables can have one of the following relationships:

- One-to-one
- One-to-many
- Many-to-many

One-to-one relationships

Two tables have a *one-to-one relationship* when one complete record in the primary table is related to just one record in the related table and vice versa. For example, if for every employee record in the Employees table, there is just one corresponding record in the Employee_payroll table and vice versa. The tables would be said to have a one-to-one relationship. Usually the data in the related table is dependent on the data in the primary table, but in a one-to-one relationship both tables are equally dependent on each other.

One-to-many relationships

Two tables have a *one-to-many relationship* when one record in the primary table is related to one or more records in the related table. A record in the related table can have only one related record in the primary table. For example, an employee can belong to only one department, but a department can contain several employees.

To establish a table relationship:

1 In the Database window, choose Tools, Relationships to open the Relationships window.
2 On the Relationship toolbar, click the Show Table button to open the Show Table dialog box.
3 Select a table and click Add to add the table to the Relationships window.
4 Add any additional tables to the Relationships window, and then click close to close the Show Table dialog box.

5   In the Relationships window, drag a field from the first table to a field in the second table. This will open the Edit Relationships dialog box.

6   Click Join Type to open the Join Properties dialog box.

7   Select a Join option and click OK to return to the Edit Relationships dialog box.

8   Check Enforce Referential Integrity.

9   Click Create.

Exhibit 16-12: The Relationships window

Do it!   **D-1:   Creating relationships**

Here's how	Here's why
1 Choose **Tools,** **Relationships...**	(The Show Table dialog box appears.) To open the Relationships window. You will set a one-to-many relationship between Spices_data and Sales table.
Observe the dialog box	There are tabs for various database objects.
Verify that the Tables tab is active	It displays all the tables in the database.
2 From the list, select **Spices_data**	
Click **Add**	To add the table to the Relationships window.
3 Add Sales to the Relationships window	From the list, select Sales and click Add.
Click **Close**	To close the Show Table dialog box.
Observe the Relationships window	The field lists of both tables appear in the window.
4 Drag **Product_ID** from Spices_data to Product_id in Sales as shown	

Spices_data: Product_ID, Product_descripti, Unit_price, Minimum_quantity, Qty_available
Sales: Product_id, Salesperson, Sale_amount, Date_of_sale, Discount

The pointer changes to a field symbol while dragging. The Edit Relationships dialog box appears as soon as you drop the field.

5 Click **Join Type** — To open the Join Properties dialog box.

Observe the dialog box

Join Properties

○ 1: Only include rows where the joined fields from both tables are equal.

○ 2: Include ALL records from 'Sales_employees' and only those records from 'Sales_payroll' where the joined fields are equal.

○ 3: Include ALL records from 'Sales_payroll' and only those records from 'Sales_employees' where the joined fields are equal.

[OK] [Cancel]

The first option is selected by default. This option creates a one-to-one relationship between the tables.

Click **OK** — To close the Join Properties dialog box and come back to the Edit Relationships dialog box.

6	Check **Enforce Referential Integrity**	To ensure that data in the related tables matches.
7	Click **Create**	To create the relationship.
	Observe the Relationships window	(As shown in Exhibit 16-12.) A line appears between the Spices_data and Sales tables. Notice that 1 appears on one side of the line and an infinity symbol appears on the other side. This means that the tables have a one-to-many relationship.
8	Update the relationship	

Deleting relationships

To delete a table relationship, do the following:

1 Close all tables that are related to each other.

2 Switch to Design view and click the Relationships button on the Database toolbar. The Relationships window appears showing the relationships between tables.

3 Select the line depicting the relationship you want to delete, and then press the Delete key.

3 Click Yes to confirm the deletion and the relationship will be deleted permanently from the database

Cascading deletes

You can enforce referential integrity by performing cascading deletes. *Referential Integrity* is a set of rules to follow while inserting, updating, and deleting records from related tables so that the relationship remains intact.

When you use *cascading deletes* to delete a record from a primary table, it automatically deletes all related records from other related tables. This ensures that there are no orphan records in the related tables.

To enforce referential integrity with cascading deletes:

1 Open the Relationships window.

2 Double-click the line depicting the relationship for which you want to implement cascading deletes. This will open the Edit Relationships dialog box.

3 Check Enforce Referential Integrity.

4 Check Cascade Delete Related Records.

5 Click OK.

Do it!

D-2:   Deleting relationships

Here's how	Here's why
1 Double-click the line between Spices_data and Sales	To modify the relationship between these tables. The Edit Relationships dialog box appears.
From the Table/Query list, select **Spices_data**	(If necessary.) The field on which both the tables are related appears below. Notice that the options under Enforce Referential Integrity are now available.
Check **Cascade Delete Related Records**	To cascade deletes between the tables.
Click **OK**	To modify the relationship.
Update the relationship	
2 Close the window	
3 Open Spices_data in Datasheet view	You will delete one of these records to see how deletes are cascaded.
Delete the record containing data for **P003**	Select the record and press Delete.
Observe the message box	It prompts to cascade delete the corresponding record in the Sales table.
Click **Yes**	To confirm the deletion.
Close the table	
4 Open Sales in Datasheet view	
Verify whether the record is deleted from the table	Notice there is no record with Product_ID P003.
Close the table	
Close the database	

Unit summary: Working with tables

Topic A   In this topic, you learned how to **add** and **delete fields**, as well as how to **modify field names**. You also learned how to **rearrange** the fields in a table. Then, you learned how to **set field properties** to verify the validity of entered data. You also learned how to set a **primary key** for a table. Finally, you learned how to **create single-** and **multiple-field indexes** to quickly locate data.

Topic B   In this topic, you learned how to **add records** to a table. You also learned how to **find and replace** data values. Then, you learned how to **delete records** from a table. Finally, you learned how to **undo changes**.

Topic C   In this topic, you learned how to **sort records** on a **single field**. or by **multiple fields**. Then, you learned how to **filter records** to display only a subset of the records. You also learned how to **navigate** within a table. Finally, you learned how to **move** and **change the width** of **columns** to alter the appearance of a table.

Topic D   In this topic, you learned how to **normalize** a table and how to **create one-to-one** and **one-to-many relationships**. You also learned how to **delete relationships** and how to use **cascade deletes** to delete records from related tables.

Independent practice activity

1   Open Working_with_records_practice.

2   Open Product in Design view.

3   Insert the following fields before Min_stock:
   - **Date_Order** (Specify the data type as Date/Time.)
   - **Product_code** (Specify the data type as Text.)

4   Move **Product_code** before Product_desc.

5   Change the field size of Product_desc to **20**.

6   Change the format of Product_desc to **lowercase**.

7   Impose a validation rule on Date_Order such that the date entered must be less than the system's current date. (Hint: Use the `Now()` function.)

8   Set a primary key on Product_id.

9   Set an index on Product_code and ensure that the field doesn't accept duplicate values.

10   Save the table as **My product**. (If a message box appears, click Yes.)

11   Switch to Datasheet view.

12   Add records to the table, as shown in Exhibit 16-13.

13   Delete the record with Product_ID "P005."

14   Sort records in ascending order by Project_desc.

15   Filter records so that only those records whose **Qty_available = 1000** appears in the table.

16   Remove the filter.

17   Navigate to the last record using the navigation buttons.

18 Update the table.

19 Close Datasheet view.

20 Define a one-to-many relationship between **Kiosk** and **Transaction** based on **Kiosk code**.

21 Ensure that Referential Integrity and Cascading Deletes are maintained in the relationship.

22 Close the Relationship window.

23 Open the Kiosk table.

24 Delete the field starting with Kiosk code "K003."

25 Close the table.

26 Close the database.

Product_id	Product_code	Product_desc	Unit_price	Qty_available	Date_Order	Min_stock	Min_order
P001	OS_P01	anatto seed	1.23	1000	1/2/2003	500	600
P002	OS_P02	cinnamon ground	2.29	1200	1/2/2003	700	600
P003	OS_P03	cinnamon (ground) ex	1.99	1000	1/2/2003	300	800
P004	OS_P04	asafoetida powder	1.49	700	1/2/2003	300	500
P005	OS_P05	anise seeds	1.49	900	1/2/2003	500	500
P006	OS_P06	basil leaf (whole)	1.89	1500	1/2/2003	1000	700
P007	OS_P07	carob pods	1.33	600	1/2/2003	1110	300
P008	OS_P08	carob powder	2.45	1200	1/2/2003	330	100
P009	OS_P09	basil leaf (ground)	1.43	320	1/2/2003	650	250
P010	OS_P10	caraway seed	1.66	1220	1/2/2003	230	450

Exhibit 16-13: The records to be added in step 12 of Independent Practice Activity

Unit 17

Forms and queries

Unit time: 60 minutes

Complete this unit, and you'll know how to:

A Create forms by using AutoForm and the Form Wizard, and add or modify form headers and footers.

B Open and enter data in a form; modify form controls and properties; align form controls; use a form to modify data; and save, close or delete a form.

C Find, sort and filter records in forms.

D Create and run a simple query, save a query, modify a query to add fields, specify or modify criteria in a query, and close or delete a query.

Topic A: Creating forms

Explanation

A well-designed form adds to the effectiveness of a database management program. *Forms* are the primary objects used to enter and edit data. Forms are typically designed to correspond with a printed document for fast and accurate data entry. For example, a form can simulate a printed retailer card containing details, such as retailer code, retailer name, and contact name.

Forms have three different views:

- *Design view,* where you create the form
- *Datasheet view,* where you view records in a row and column format
- *Form view,* where you can view only one record at a time

To create a form, you can use the AutoForm or the Form Wizard.

AutoForm

AutoForm is the quickest way to create a form. You can either create a columnar or tabular form using the AutoForm. A *columnar form* displays the values in one or more columns. A *tabular form* displays the values in a row and column format.

To create a form by using the AutoForm feature:

1 Open the database.
2 Select the table on which you want to base the form.
3 Click the AutoForm button on the toolbar to create the form.
4 Save the form.

Navigate through a form by using the buttons on the Navigation bar.

Design view

When you create a form by using either the Form Wizard or AutoForm, you do not have the flexibility of customizing the form. With Design view, you have the flexibility to customize the form color or add, delete, move or resize controls.

The various sections in Design view include the:

- Header section
- Detail section
- Footer section

The header section contains a title, which appears at the top of every form record. The detail section contains the record data. The footer section contains information that appears at the bottom of every form record.

Form Header section   Field list

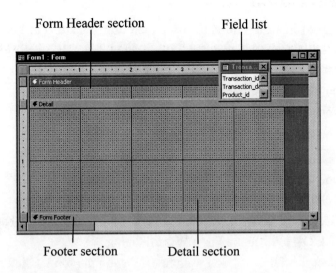

Footer section   Detail section

Exhibit 17-1: The Design view window

Do it!

A-1: Creating a form in Design view

Here's how	Here's why
1 Open Create_form	(From the current unit folder.) You'll create a form in this database.
Under Objects, select **Forms**	
Click **New**	(The New button is on the toolbar.) The New Form dialog box opens.
Observe the dialog box	Notice that Design View is selected by default.
2 From the drop-down list, select **Transaction**	You'll create a form based on this table.
Click **OK**	The Design view displays.
3 Choose **View, Form Header/Footer**	The header and footer sections display, as shown in Exhibit 17-1.
4 Close the form	A message box appears prompting you to save the form.
Click **No**	

The Form Wizard

Explanation

Another way to create a form is by using the Form Wizard. The Form Wizard guides you through all the steps to create a form. In the Form Wizard you can:

- Select fields
- Choose display order of fields
- Choose layout
- Choose style

To create a form using the Form Wizard you would:

1. Choose Form on the Objects bar in the Database window.
2. Click the New button to open the New Form dialog box.
3. Select Form Wizard, and then select the table on which to base the form.
4. Click OK to open the Form Wizard dialog box.
5. Select the fields that you want to display on the form. Click Next to move to the next dialog box.
6. Select a form layout and click Next.
7. Select a style for the form and click Next.
8. Enter a name for the form, then click Finish to close the dialog box and save the form.

Do it!

A-2: Creating a form using the Form Wizard

Here's how	Here's why
1 Under Objects, verify that Forms is selected	
Click **New**	The New Form dialog box opens.
2 Select **Form Wizard**	You'll create a form by using Form Wizard.
From the table list, select **Employee_tasks**	You'll create a form based on this table.
Click **OK**	The Form Wizard dialog box opens.
Observe the dialog box	Notice that under Tables/Queries, Employee_tasks is selected, and under Available Fields, all fields of the Employee_tasks table are listed.
3 Under Available Fields, verify that **EmployeeID** is selected	
Click ` > `	Adds EmployeeID to the Selected Fields list.
Click ` >> `	Adds all the fields to the Selected Fields list.
Click **Next**	The next dialog box appears.

4 Observe the dialog box

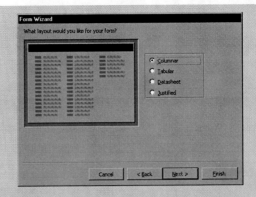

Notice the various form layout options.

Verify that Columnar is selected

You'll create a columnar form.

Click **Next**

The next dialog box opens.

5 Observe the dialog box

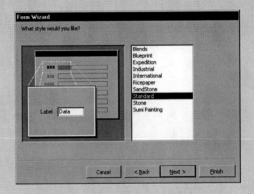

Notice the various styles of form.

Verify that **Standard** is selected

This will be the style of the form.

Click **Next**

The next dialog box opens.

6 In the What title do you want for your form box to read, type **My_employee_tasks**

This will be the title of the form.

Click **Finish**

The Form view appears.

7 Observe the form

The record appears in a columnar layout.

Form headers and footers

Explanation

Add a form header or footer, in Design view, by adding a label control. Use the formatting toolbar to modify the appearance of the text that is entered.

To add a header to a form:

1 Click the form header section.
2 Click the Toolbox button.
3 Select the label control from the toolbox.
4 Place the label control in the form header section.
5 Enter the heading in the label control.
6 Save the form.

Do it!

A-3: Adding and modifying headers and footers

Here's how	Here's why
1 Choose **View**, **Design View**	You'll add a header and footer.
Place the pointer as shown	
	Notice that the pointer changes to a double-headed arrow.
Drag down the Form Header	The header area of the form enlarges.
2 Click	(If necessary. The Toolbox button is on the Design toolbar.) The toolbox opens.
3 Click	(The Label button is on the toolbox.) Add a title to the form.
Point in the header area	Notice that the pointer changes to a crossbar with the letter A.
Drag towards lower-right as shown	
Type **Transaction**	This will be the title of the form.
Press ⏎ ENTER	
4 Click anywhere on the form	To deselect the title. Notice that the Formatting toolbar is not available.
Select **Transaction**	(This is the title you have just entered.) Notice that the Formatting toolbar is now available.

5	From the Font size list, select **12**	Increases the font size.
	From the Font style list, select **Arial**	Changes the font style.
	Click **B**	Makes the title bold.
6	Point to the Form Footer and drag down	Enlarges the footer area of the form.
7	Click **Aa**	The label control on the toolbox.
	Drag the footer area toward the lower-right	You will create a label here.
	Type **Page 1**	This text appears in the footer area.
	Press ⏎ ENTER	
8	Select **Page 1**	If necessary.
	Change the Font size to **10**	
	Click **I**	Makes the text italic.
9	Select **Transaction**	In the form header.
	Change the font size to **14**	
10	Close the toolbox	
11	Update and close the form	

Topic B: Modifying forms

Explanation

After creating a form, you can enter data by adding controls to it. A *control* is an object that:

- Shows data
- Edits data
- Performs actions

Opening an existing form

To open an existing form:

1   Choose Forms, under Objects in the Database window.
2   Select the form you want to open.
3   Click the Open button to open the form.

Do it!

B-1:   Opening an existing form

Here's how	Here's why
1 Under Objects, verify that Forms is selected	
Select **Retailerform**	To open this form.
Click **Open**	

Entering data

Explanation

Enter data to the form by clicking the New Record button.

To enter data in the form:

1 Click the New Record button.
2 Type data.
3 Press Tab to go to the next field.
4 Repeat steps 2 and 3 for remaining fields.
3 Save and close the form.

Do it!

B-2: Entering data in the form

Here's how	Here's why
1 Click ▶＊	(On the Navigation bar.) Notice that all the fields are blank.
Enter the details as shown	Retailer_code K016 Retailer_name Tremblay Contact_first_name Mary Contact_last_name Smith Address Seattle Phone_no 421161111
2 Update the form	

Controls

Explanation

All information on a form is stored in controls. Two of the most frequently used form controls include:

- *Label controls* display the name of the fields.
- *Text box controls* display the data corresponding to the fields.

In Design view you can change the appearance of the form by moving and resizing the controls.

To move or resize controls:

1 Select the fields.
2 Drag the controls to reposition them.
3 Save the form.

Form control properties

Each control on the form has a property sheet associated with it. The *property sheet* is a set of properties that determine the appearance and behavior of the control. For example, you can change the background color of the header section. You can also change the Special Effect of a text label to Raised and change the appearance of the text. The Property Sheet contains five tabs, as shown in Exhibit 17-2:

- Format
- Date
- Event
- Other
- All

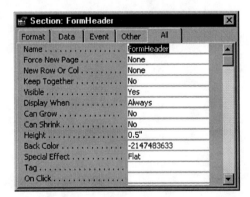

Exhibit 17-2: The Property Sheet

To modify form properties:

1 Select the form area to modify the properties.
2 Click the Properties button present on the Form View toolbar.
3 Change the properties.
4 Update the form.

Do it!

B-3: Modifying controls and form properties

Here's how	Here's why
1 Switch to Design View	
2 Expand the form header	If necessary.
Click anywhere in the form header section	You'll modify the properties of the form header section.
Click 🖺	The Properties button is on the Database toolbar.
Verify that the All tab is active	
Observe the Property Sheet	As shown in Exhibit 17-2.
3 Place the insertion point in Back Color	Notice that ellipses appear.
Click […]	The color palette appears.
Select the **blue color**	To change the background color of the form header section.
Click **OK**	
4 Place the insertion point in Special Effect box	A drop-down arrow appears.
Click the drop-down arrow	
From the list, select **Raised**	To change the appearance of the label control.
5 Close the Property Sheet	
6 Click any empty area within the Detail section	You'll modify the properties of the detail section.
Open the Properties sheet	
From Back Color list, select the **blue color**	To change the background color of the detail section.
7 Close the Property Sheet	
8 Click 🔲	(The View button is on the toolbar.) Switches to the Form view.
Observe the Form view	Notice that the modified form appears.
9 Click 🔲	Switches to Design view.
10 Update the form	

Controlling alignment

Explanation

To ensure that all controls are properly aligned, you can choose to align a control based on the alignment of all the other controls. You can align controls:

- Right
- Left
- Top
- Bottom
- To the design grid

To align controls in a form:

1 Open the form in Design view.

2 Select the controls that you want to align.

3 Choose Format, Align, and the required menu option to align the controls.

4 Update and close the form.

Do it!

B-4:   Aligning controls

Here's how	Here's why
1 Click the Retailer_code label control	
While holding (SHIFT) down, click all the other controls	All controls will be selected.
Choose **Format, Align, Right**	Aligns the controls to the right.
2 Update the form	
3 Switch to Form view	Notice that all the controls are aligned to the right.

Modifying data in a form

Explanation

You can modify or delete data that you have entered in a form.

To modify data:

1 Open the form in the Form view.

2 Place the insertion point in the field you want to modify. To edit the value, move the pointer to the extreme left in the field.

3 Type the text you want to insert.

To delete data:

1 Open the form in the Form view.

2 Place the insertion point in the record you want to delete.

3 Click Delete record present on the Form View toolbar.

Do it!

B-5: Using a form to modify data

Here's how	Here's why
1 In the Retailer_code box, type **K015**	This is the new retailer code.
2 In the Phone_no box, type **6366654582**	This is the new phone number.

Saving, closing, and deleting a form

Explanation   Save the form and close it after you make the necessary modifications.

To save a form:

1   Choose File, Save As to open the Save As dialog box.

2   Enter the name that to use for your form.

3   Click OK. If you click Cancel in the Save As dialog box, the form will not be saved.

To close a form, you can either choose File, Close or click the Close button in the form.

To delete a form:

1   Close the form that you want to delete.

2   Click Forms, in the Database window, under Objects.

3   Select the form that you want to delete.

4   Press Delete.

Do it!   ## B-6:   Saving, closing, and deleting a form

Here's how	Here's why
1 Choose **File**, **Save**	Saves the form.
Choose **File**, **Close**	Closes the form.
2 Under Objects, verify that Forms is selected	
Select **My_employee_tasks**	You'll delete the form.
Press (DELETE)	A message box appears confirming that you want to delete the form.
Click **Yes**	The form disappears.

Topic C: Finding, sorting, and filtering records

Explanation

The Find, Sort, and Filter features locate records. For example, you might want to view the retailer details, arranged in ascending order based on the field Retailer_name.

You may also want to restrict which records are made available for modifications. For example, filter the records to display only the records for the retailer names starting with S.

Using a form to locate information

You can search for a record by either clicking the Find button or by choosing Edit, Find. Before beginning the search, make sure that the insertion point is in the first record, because the search operation always starts from the current record.

To find a record:

1 Place the insertion point in the first field you want to search.
2 Click the Find button to open the Find and Replace dialog box. Verify that the Find tab is active.
3 Enter the data in the Find What box.
4 Click Find Next to display the required records.
5 Click OK to close the message box. Click Cancel to close the Find and Replace dialog box.

Do it!

C-1: Using a form to find records

Here's how	Here's why
1 Open Productform in Form View	You'll search for specific records in this form.
2 Place the insertion point in the Unit_price text box	You'll find records based on Unit_price.
Click 🔍	(The Find button is on the toolbar.) The Find and Replace dialog box opens. Notice that Find is active and the insertion point is in the Find What box.
In the Match box, verify that Whole Field is selected	Specify that the entire field has to be matched.
In the Find What box, enter **1.99**	Search records for this value.
Click **Find Next**	Display the result in Form view.
3 Observe Form view	A record with Unit_price of 1.99 appears.
Click **Find Next**	A message box appears informing you that the search item was not found.
Click **OK**	Closes the message box.
Click **Cancel**	Closes the Find and Replace dialog box.
4 Close the form	

Sorting records by using a form

Explanation

You can use a form to sort records either in ascending or descending order. To arrange the records in ascending order:

1 Select the field on which you want to sort.
2 Click the Sort Ascending button, to sort in ascending order, otherwise, click the Sort Descending button.

Do it!

C-2: Using a form to sort records

Here's how	Here's why
1 Open Retailerform in Form view	
2 Place the insertion point in the Retailer_name text box	Sorts records based on Retailer_name.
Click ▯	(The Sort Ascending button is on the toolbar.) Sorts records in ascending order.
Observe Form view	See the first record in the sorted set of records.

Filtering records by using a form

Explanation

The Filter By Form feature provides a way to selectively view specific records. For example, you can set the filter to view the products sold in a particular location. The Filter By Form window has two tabs: Look for and Or. The *Look for* tab is used to enter values to filter records, and the *Or* tab is used to enter alternate values.

To apply a filter:

1 Click the Filter By Form button, on the toolbar.
2 Select the field on which you want to set the filter.
3 Select the value for setting the filter from the available list.
4 Click Apply Filter.

To remove the filter, click the Remove Filter button on the Form View toolbar.

Do it!

C-3:   Using a form to filter records

Here's how	Here's why
1 Click 🔲	(The Filter By Form button is on the toolbar.) Displays a blank form.
Observe Form view	 A drop-down arrow appears next to the Retailer_code box. By default, the Look for tab is active.
2 Place the insertion point in the Retailer_name box as shown	 A drop-down arrow now appears next to the Retailer_name box.
Enter **S***	You'll view the records only for the retailer names starting with S.
Press (TAB)	In the Retailer_name box, Like "S*" appears.
3 Click 🔽	The Apply Filter button is on the toolbar.
Observe the form	The first record in the filtered set of records appears. Notice that at the bottom of the form, the total number of records filtered is shown.
4 Update and close the form, and close the database	

Topic D: Queries

Explanation

You can retrieve and analyze data from related tables by using a query. A *query* displays data based on a criterion. A *criterion* is a restriction or a condition to distinguish specific records you want to view. For example, you can use queries to see all the records in the Transaction table pertaining to product number P001.

You can use one or more tables in a query. You can also sort and filter query results.

Simple queries in Design view

Use the Design view window to create a simple query. The Design view, as shown in Exhibit 17-3, contains the Field list and a design grid. A query needs one or more data sources (table or another query).

To create a query in Design view:

1 Open the Database.
2 Under Objects, choose Queries.
3 Choose New to open the New Query dialog box.
4 Select Design View and click OK to open the Show Table dialog box.
5 Add the table from Show Table dialog box and click Close.
6 Select the fields that you want to appear in the query result.
7 Choose the Run button to display the results in the Datasheet view.

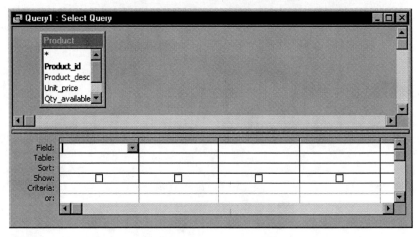

Exhibit 17-3: The query Design view

Do it!

D-1: Creating and running a simple query

Here's how	Here's why
1 Open Create_query	(From the current unit folder) You'll create a query in this database.
2 Under Objects, select **Queries**	You'll create a simple query.
Click **New**	(The New button is on the Database window.) Shows the New Query dialog box.
Verify that Design View is selected	
Click **OK**	View the Show Table dialog box.
3 Verify that the Tables tab is active	To view a list of tables.
Select **Product**	
Click **Add**	Adds the table to the Table pane of Design view.
Click **Close**	To close the Show Table dialog box. Notice that the Design view appears.
4 Observe Design view	(As shown in Exhibit 17-3.) Notice that the Table pane displays the Field list. The insertion point appears within the first cell of the Field row.
Click the arrow of the Field row	Product.* Product_id Product_desc Unit_price Qty_available Min_stock Min_order
	(In the design grid.) Notice that the list contains the table name with an * and the names of all the fields.
From the list, select **Product_id**	To add this field to the design grid.
Observe the design grid	Field: Product_id Table: Product Sort: Show: ☑ Criteria: or:
	The design grid displays Product_id in the first cell of the Field row. Notice that Product appears in the Table row and the check box in the Show row is checked.

5 Place the insertion point within the second cell of the Field row	Notice the second field list.
From the list, select **Unit_price**	To show Unit_price values in the query results.
Observe the design grid	Notice that the design grid displays two fields: Product_id and Unit_price.
6 Click ![Run button]	(The Run button is on the toolbar.) To run the query.
Observe the result	

Product_id	Unit_price
P001	1.23
P002	2.29
P003	1.99
P004	1.49
P005	1.49
P006	1.89
P007	2.49
P008	1.89
P009	1.45
P010	2.50

The Datasheet view displays the Product_id and Unit_price. The record selector is on the first record.

7 Click ![View button]	(The View button on the toolbar.) To return to Design view.

Two table queries

Explanation   To have a query with two (or more) tables, just add a second table from the Show Table dialog box. You can start with two tables when you first design the query, or add the second table later by clicking the Show Table button while in query design view.

After you add a second table, relationship lines will indicate the relationship between the tables, if there is one. You choose fields for the query as you do in a one-table query, except that the first time you look at the field list, each field name will be preceded by it's table name. You can show the fields of just one table by selecting that table in the table list, just below the field list, as shown in Exhibit 17-4.

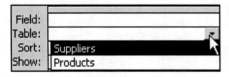

Exhibit 17-4: The table list in a two-table query

Sorting query output

You can quickly sort the results of a query on any field in ascending or descending order. In text fields, ascending means alphabetical order. In number or currency fields, ascending order is from the lowest to the highest number.

To sort the results of a query in ascending order:

1   Click anywhere in the field on which you want to sort, or on the field name.

2   Choose Records, Sort, Sort Ascending.

To sort on Descending order, choose Records, Sort, Sort Descending. Alternately, you can click on a field and click the Sort Ascending or the Sort Descending button. You can also right-click a field and choose Sort Ascending or Sort Descending.

Saving queries

You can save a one- or multiple-table query either by choosing File, Save As or by clicking on the Save button. When you choose File, Save As, the Save As dialog box appears, as shown in Exhibit 17-5.

Exhibit 17-5: The Save As dialog box

To save a query:

1   Choose File, Save As.

2   Enter the name of the query.

3   Click OK.

Do it!

D-2:   Saving a query

Here's how	Here's why
1 Choose **File**, **Save As...**	The Save As dialog box appears.
Observe the dialog box	As shown in Exhibit 17-5.
2 Edit the Save Query 'Query1' To box to read **Simplequery**	To save the query as Simplequery.
Click **OK**	
3 Observe the Title bar	Notice that Simplequery appears in the Title bar.

Adding, removing, and moving fields in a query

Explanation   You can change or refine the results of the query by:

- Adding fields
- Deleting fields
- Hide/Unhide fields
- Changing the field order

To add fields to the design grid:

1 Click within the cell of the Field row.
2 Select the field from the list.

Remove unwanted fields from a query by selecting the field on the query grid and then pressing the delete key. You can leave a field in a query but still hide it in the output by clearing Show checkbox for the given field. Check the box again to show the field in the query output.

To move a field in a query:

1 Highlight the entire field column by clicking at the top of the column, just above the field cell.
2 Drag the column to a new location.
3 A black bar will appear between fields until you drop the highlighted field, then the fields will be rearranged.

Do it!   ## D-3: Working with fields in a query

Here's how	Here's why
1 Place the insertion point within the third cell of the Field row	To add another field to the query.
From the list, select **Qty_available**	
2 Place the insertion point within the fourth cell of the Field row	To select one more field.
From the list, select **Product_desc**	
3 Place the insertion point within the fifth cell of the Field row	
From the list, select **Min_stock**	
4 Click ![!]	Run the query.
Observe the result	Notice that three more fields, Qty_available, Product_desc, and Min_stock appear in Datasheet view.
Return to Design view	
5 Update the query	

6 Under Product_id, clear the Show checkbox	You'll hide this field in the output, though it will still be part of the query.
7 Highlight the Product_desc field column	Click at the very top, just above the field cell (the pointer will turn into a down-pointing bold arrow).
Drag Product_desc between Product_id and Unit_price	To change the field order in the query.
8 Click [!]	Run the query.
Observe the result	Product_id is no longer visible, and the Product description is the first field in the query.
9 Switch to design view	
Highlight the Min_stock field and press (DELETE)	To remove this field from the query.
Move the Product_desc field back to the last place	(Highlight the field column and drag it after Qty_available.) To move the field to the last column in the query.
In the Product_id field, check the Show checkbox	To unhide this field in the query output.

Using criteria in queries

Explanation

In addition to running a simple query, you can specify criteria to create a more complex expression.

To enter criteria, click the Criteria cell for that particular field and enter an expression.

The AND condition in a query

Use the AND condition, when you specify more than one criteria, and you want all the conditions to be satisfied. For example, you can search for the products whose Unit_price is greater than 1.4 and less than 1.9. The result will show the records that satisfy both conditions.

The OR condition in a query

Use the OR condition, when you specify more than one criteria, and you want the result to include the records when any of these conditions are satisfied. For example, you want to see the records for Unit_price more than 2 or Qty_available equal to 700.

Product_ID	Unit_price	Qty_available	Product_desc
P010	2.50	750	Caraway Seed
P002	2.29	1200	Cinnamon Ground
P004	1.49	700	Asafoetida Powder
P007	2.49	800	Carob Pods
*			

Exhibit 17-6: The query result after using an OR condition

Do it!

D-4: Specifying criteria in a query

Here's how	Here's why
1 Switch to Design view	If necessary.
Place the insertion point within the second cell of the Criteria row	To enter a criterion for Unit_price.
Type **>2.0**	This will be the criterion for Unit_price.
2 Place the insertion point within the third cell of the or row	
Type **=700**	This will be the criterion for Qty_available.
3 Click ![!]	Run the query.
Observe the result	(As shown in Exhibit 17-6.) See all of the products with either a unit price greater than 2, or an available quantity of 700.
4 Switch to Design view	
5 Update the query	

Modifying and removing criteria

Explanation

You can refine the results of the query by:

- Adding fields
- Deleting fields
- Changing the field order
- Changing or removing the criteria

To change criteria:

1 Click the Criteria cell for that field.
2 Enter the new expression.
3 Run the query.

To remove the criteria, simply delete the contents of the Criteria cell.

Do it!

D-5: Modifying criteria in a query

Here's how	Here's why
1 Place the insertion point within the second cell of the Criteria row	To change the criteria for Unit_price.
In the Criteria box type **>3.0**	This will be the new criteria for Unit_price.
Click **!**	Runs the query.
Observe the result	Notice that only one product satisfies the criteria.
2 Switch to Design view	
3 Update the query	

Closing and deleting a query

Explanation

There are various ways to close a query:

- Choose File, Close.
- Choose Close on the Control menu of the query.
- Click the Close button of the query.

To delete a query:

1 Close the query that you want to delete.
2 Click Query, in the Database window, under Objects.
3 Select the query you want to delete.
4 Press Delete.

Do it!

D-6: Closing and deleting a query

Here's how	Here's why
1 Choose **File**, **Close**	Closes the query.
Select **Simplequery**	To delete this query.
Press (DELETE)	A message box appears confirming that you want to delete the query.
Click **Yes**	The Simplequery disappears
2 Close the database	

Unit summary: Forms and queries

Topic A   In this topic, you learned how to **create** a **form** in **Design View.** You learned how to **create** a form using the **Form Wizard.** You also learned how to **add** and **modify headers** and **footers** on a form.

Topic B   In this topic, you learned how to **open** an **existing form.** You learned how to **enter data** in a form. You learned how to **modify controls** and **form properties.** You learned how to **align controls.** You learned how to use a form to **modify data.** Finally, you learned how to **save, close,** and **delete** a form.

Topic C   In this topic, you learned how to use a **form** to **find records.** You learned how to use a form to **sort records.** Finally, you learned how to use a form to **filter records.**

Topic D   In this topic, you learned how to **create** and **run** a **simple query.** You learned how to **save** a query. You learned how to **modify** a query by **adding more fields.** You learned about using **criteria** in a query. You also learned how to **modify criteria** in a query. Finally, you learned how to **close** and **delete** a query.

Independent practice activity

1   Open the Employees database.

2   Using the Form Wizard, create a form based on the Employee_information table.

3   Select the **Employee_code, First_name, Last_name, Region, Department,** and **Earnings** fields to create a Tabular form based on the Industrial style.

4   Save the form as **Employee_form.**

5   Enter a new record for Megan Reid as shown in Exhibit 17-7.

6   Update and Close **Employee_form.**

7   Create a new form. Select the **Quarterly_sales_analysis** table and use Design View.

8   Enter the label **Sales** as the form title. The size and font of the label should be 14 and Arial Black.

9   Save the form as **Sales_analysis.**

10 Close the form.

11 Create a query in **Design View** based on **Employee_information** table.

12 Display all the records with **Earnings** greater than **$50.00.**

13 Save the query as **Earnings.**

14 Close the query.

15 Close the database.

Employee_	First_name	Last_name	Region	Department	Earnings
S014	Michael	Lee	West	Sales	$85,000.00
S015	Sandra	Lawrence	North	Sales	$85,000.00
S016	Kendra	James	North	Accounts	$80,000.00
S017	Kevin	Meyers	North	Administration	$95,000.00
S018	Adam	Long	North	Administration	$95,000.00
S019	Jamie	Morrison	East	Human resourc	$72,000.00
S020	Maureen	O'Connor	East	Human resourc	$72,000.00
S021	Michelle	Washington	North	Sales	$85,000.00
S022	Stuart	Young	North	Customer supp	$86,000.00
S023	Jesse	Bennet	South	Sales	$85,000.00
S024	James	Owens	West	Marketing	$78,000.00
S025	Pamela	Carter	West	Accounts	$80,000.00
S026	Anna	Morris	West	Accounts	$80,000.00
S028	Megan	Reid	East	Human resourc	$75,000.00

Exhibit 17-7: A sample of Employee_form after step 5 of the Independent Practice Activity

Unit 18

Reports

Unit time: 60 minutes

Complete this unit, and you'll know how to:

A Create a report using either the Report Wizard or a query.

B Group and sort records, summarize information, modify report appearance, add headers and footers, delete a report.

C Use the Page Setup dialog box, and print reports.

Topic A: Creating reports

Explanation

Reports are a method to communicate information contained in a database in a meaningful way. You can create reports by using the following methods:

- Design View
- Report Wizard
- AutoReport
- Chart Wizard
- Label Wizard

You can select which records a report contains by using a query. For example, to prepare a weekly report showing the products with a quantity sold of less than 200, just create a report based on this query. The following table describes each of the four methods to create reports.

Methods	Description
Design View	Provides the report layout, you must insert the components of the report manually.
Report Wizard	Guides you through every step of designing a report, from selecting fields to choosing a style for the printed page.
AutoReport	Creates a columnar or tabular report.
Chart Wizard	Assists you in creating all kinds of graphs from pie charts to 3-D bar graphs.
Label Wizard	Creates reports that print labels.

Using the Report Wizard

Using the Report Wizard, you can:

- Specify the type of report you need
- Select fields from one or more tables
- Sort records
- Show summary calculations

To create a report by using the Report Wizard:

1 Select Reports, from the Objects bar and click the New button to open the New Report dialog box.
2 Select Report Wizard, then select a table to base report and click OK to open the Report Wizard.
3 Add fields to the report, from the Available Fields list and click Next.
4 Select the options of your choice from the remaining steps of the Report Wizard.
5 Save the report.
6 Choose Finish to exit the wizard and create the report.

Transaction Report

Product_ID	Transaction_date	Transaction_ID	Qty_sold	Retailer_code
P001				
	1/1/2003	1	100	R001
	2/2/2003	5	150	R002
P002				
	2/1/2003	4	200	R001
	3/1/2003	9	100	R006
P003				
	1/1/2003	2	400	R003
P004				
	2/2/2003	6	110	R003
P005				
	1/5/2003	3	200	R009

Exhibit 18-1: A sample report preview

Do it!

A-1: Creating a report using the Report Wizard

Here's how	Here's why
1 Open Create_report	(From the current unit folder.) To create a report using this database.
2 Under the Objects bar, click **Reports**	If necessary.
Click **New**	Opens the New Report dialog box.
Observe the dialog box	By default, the Design View is selected.
Select **Report Wizard**	To create a report using the Report Wizard.

3 Display the data source list as shown	*(drop-down list showing:)* Customers Order_detail Product Retailer Sales_query Transaction
	A list of tables and queries appears.
From the drop-down list, select **Transaction**	Create a report based on this table.
Click **OK**	Opens the first step of the Report Wizard.
Observe the dialog box	In the Tables/Queries list, Transaction is selected.
4 In the Available Fields list, verify that Transaction_ID is selected	This field will appear in the report.
Click `>`	Adds Transaction_ID to the Selected Fields list.
Observe the Selected Fields list	*(dialog box showing Available Fields: Transaction_date, Product_ID, Qty_sold, Retailer_code and Selected Fields: Transaction_ID)*
	Transaction_ID now appears in the Selected Fields list.
5 Click `>>`	(Add all the fields.) Now all the fields appear in the Selected Fields list.
Click **Next**	Moves to the next step of the Report Wizard.
6 Observe the dialog box	This dialog box groups records based on a specific field. Notice that Grouping Options is not available, because you have not yet selected any field for grouping.
Select **Product_ID**	To group records based on this field.
Click `>`	Adds Product_ID to the grouping levels.
Observe the dialog box	Product_ID appears in a separate box in the top pane. Grouping Options is now available.
Click **Next**	Moves to the next step in the Report Wizard. Use this dialog box to specify the field on which you want to sort the records in the report.

7	Observe the dialog box	The insertion point is in the first list.
	From the first list, select **Transaction_date**	To sort records by Transaction_date in ascending order.
	Click **Next**	Moves to the next step in the Report Wizard.
8	Observe the dialog box	The previews of various report layouts appear.
	Under Layout, verify that Stepped is selected	Specifies a layout for the report.
	Under Orientation, verify that Portrait is selected	Specifies the orientation of the report.
	Verify that Adjust the field width so all fields fit on a page is checked	Ensures that the field widths are adjusted to fit on a page.
	Click **Next**	Moves to the next dialog box.
9	Observe the dialog box	The different report styles appear.
	Select **Corporate**	(If necessary.) Specifies a style for the report.
	Click **Next**	Moves to the next dialog box.
10	Edit the What title do you want for your report box, to read **Transaction Report**	This is the title for the report.
	Verify that Preview the report is selected	To preview the report on the screen before printing it.
	Click **Finish**	Preview the report, as shown in Exhibit 18-1.
11	Observe the preview	The title of the report is Transaction Report. It contains records that are grouped on Product_ID and sorted by Transaction_date.
	Update the report	Choose File, Save.
	Choose **File**, **Close**	Closes the report.

Creating reports based on queries

Explanation

To base a report on a query, either select an existing query or create a new one. Then use AutoReport to create the report.

To create a report query:

1 Choose Queries, under the Objects bar.

2 Select the query to base report.

3 Open the query in Design view.

4 Click the down arrow next to the New Object button. From the list, select Report to open the New Report dialog box.

5 Select one of the AutoReport options: Tabular or Columnar.

6 Click OK to create the report.

Do it!

A-2: Creating a report by using a query

Here's how	Here's why
1 Under the Objects bar, choose **Queries**	
Open Sales_query in Design view	To create a report based on the query.
Observe the design of the query	

Field:	Transaction_date	Transaction_ID	Product_ID	Qty_sold
Table:	Transaction	Transaction	Transaction	Transaction
Sort:				
Show:	☑	☑	☑	☑
Criteria:				<200

Notice that the query is based on the table Transaction. There are four fields in the design grid, and the Criteria cell of Qty_sold is <200. This implies that the query will display records containing values < 200 in the Qty_sold field.

2 Click as shown

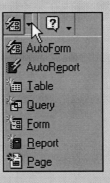

(The New Object button is on the Query Design toolbar.) Displays the drop-down list.

3 From the list, select **Report**	(To create a report based on the query Sales_query.) Opens the New Report dialog box.
Observe the dialog box	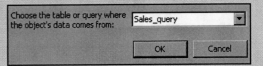
	Sales_query appears in the drop-down list.
4 Select **AutoReport: Tabular**	To create a tabular report.
Click **OK**	Creates and displays the report.
Observe the report	

Sales_query

Transaction_date	Transaction_ID	Product_ID	Qty_sold
1/1/2003	1	P 001	100
1/1/2003	2	P 003	400
1/5/2003	3	P 005	200
2/1/2003	4	P 002	200
2/2/2003	5	P 001	150
2/2/2003	6	P 004	110
1/7/2003	7	P 006	140
3/1/2003	9	P 002	100
3/6/2003	10	P 008	100
3/6/2003	11	P 009	170

	The records that meet the criterion appear in the report. Notice that the report heading is automatically placed and is the same as the source query name. You can modify this later in the Design view.
Click **Close**	(On the Print Preview toolbar.) Returns to Design view.
5 Save the report as **My sales_report**	

Topic B: Working with reports

Explanation

Group records based on a specific field, so the report organizes the records accordingly. Similarly, you can sort records in a particular order based on a specific field. In addition, you can place an appropriate group name above each group or place a field showing total quantity sold at the end of each group.

Grouping and sorting records

Grouping records helps improve the readability of the report. For example, you can group data in the report by Transaction_date, so that all records of a Transaction_date are collated in a group, as shown in Exhibit 18-2.

Sales Report

Transaction_date	Transaction_ID	Product_ID	Qty_sold
1/1/2003	2	P003	400
1/1/2003	1	P001	100
1/5/2003	3	P005	200
1/7/2003	7	P006	140
2/1/2003	4	P002	200
2/2/2003	6	P004	110
2/2/2003	5	P001	150

Exhibit 18-2: A report sorted and grouped on Transaction_date

To group records, click the Sorting and Grouping button on the Report Design toolbar. In the upper pane of the Sorting and Grouping window, specify the field to group and the sort order, as shown in Exhibit 18-3.

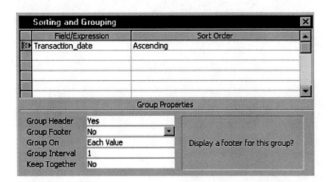

Exhibit 18-3: The Sorting and Grouping window

If you set either the Group Header or Group Footer fields to Yes, a separate section appears in Design view to place this additional information.

Do it!   **B-1:   Grouping and sorting records in a report**

Here's how	Here's why
1 Click [icon]	(The Sorting and Grouping button is on the Database toolbar.) Opens the Sorting and Grouping window.
Observe the window	[image of Sorting and Grouping window with Field/Expression and Sort Order columns, Group Properties section: "Select ascending or descending sort order. Ascending means sorting A to Z or 0 to 9"]
Place the insertion point in the first cell under Field/Expression	If necessary.
From the drop-down list, select **Transaction_date**	Groups records, first by Transaction_date.
In the Sort Order column, verify that Ascending appears	Sorts records in ascending order based on the values in the Transaction_date field.
2 Place the insertion point in the Group Header box	Under Group Properties.
From the drop-down list, select **Yes**	The Group Header section will be included in Design view, where you can add information about the group. If you do not add anything , a blank line will appear before each group.
3 Place the insertion point in the second cell under Field/Expression	
Select **Product_ID**	Now, group the records by Product_ID.
In the Sort Order column, select **Descending**	Records are then sorted in descending order based on the values in the Product_ID field.
Close the Sorting and Grouping window	
4 Click [icon]	Opens the Print Preview window.
Observe the preview	The records are first sorted in ascending order based on the field Transaction_date and then descending order of Product_ID.
Click **Close**	(On the Print Preview toolbar.) Closes the Print Preview window.
5 Update and close the report	
6 Close the query	

Adding summary information

Explanation

It is sometimes necessary to show the totals for a group of records. For example, in a report containing daily sales of various products, you might want to show the weekly total and weekly average sales for each product. You can perform these types of calculations by using various summary functions such as Sum, Avg, Min, and Max.

To use a summary function in a report:

1   Choose New to open the New Report dialog box.
2   Select Report Wizard and then select the table on which to base the report and click OK.
3   Select the fields of your choice and click Next.
4   Add a field to the grouping level and click Next.
5   Specify the sort order.
6   Choose Summary Options to open the Summary Options dialog box.
7   In the dialog box, check the summary value you would like to calculate.
8   Click OK to close the dialog box and return to the Report Wizard.

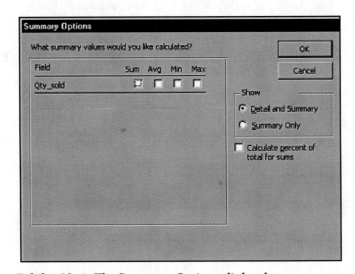

Exhibit 18-4: The Summary Options dialog box

Do it!   **B-2: Summarizing information**

Here's how	Here's why
1 Under Objects bar, choose **Reports**	You'll create a report with summary information.
Click ⬛ New	Opens the New Report dialog box.
Select **Report Wizard**	
From the Choose the table or query where the object's data comes from list, select **Order_detail**	To create a report based on this table.
Click **OK**	Opens the Report Wizard dialog box.
2 Move all the fields from the Available Fields list to the Selected Fields list	View all of the fields in the report.
Click **Next**	Moves to the next dialog box. In this dialog box, you can specify the fields on which you want to group records.
3 Select **Customer_ID**	To group records based on this field.
Click >	Groups records based on Customer_ID.
Click **Next**	Moves to the next dialog box. In this dialog box, you can specify the field to sort the records.
4 From the first list, select **Product_description**	Sorts records by Product_description.
Click **Summary Options**	Opens the Summary Options dialog box.
Under Qty_sold, check **Sum**	Calculates the sum on Qty_sold.
Under Show, verify that Detail and Summary is selected	
Click **OK**	Returns to the Report Wizard dialog box.
5 Click **Next**	Moves to the next dialog box.

Changing the layout and style of a report

Explanation

The arrangement of data and labels on a report is referred to as the *layout*. The *style* of a report refers to the appearance of the title and other information on the report. When you create a report using the Report Wizard, you can specify both a layout and a style.

To change the layout and style of a report by using the Report Wizard:

1 Select the layout from the Report Wizard dialog box, as shown in Exhibit 18-5, and click Next.
2 Select the style of your choice. Click Next.
3 Enter the title that you want to give to your report.
4 Click Finish.
5 Preview the report.

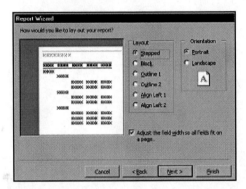

Exhibit 18-5: The Report Wizard layout dialog box

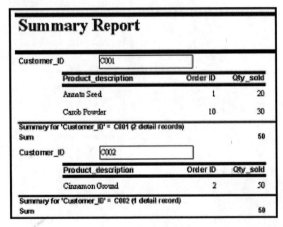

Exhibit 18-6: A sample formatted report with summary fields

Do it!

B-3: Modifying the appearance of a report

Here's how	Here's why
1 Verify that the Report Wizard dialog box is open	(As shown in Exhibit 18-5.) The current layout of the report, Stepped, is the default layout of the Report Wizard.
Under Layout, select **Outline 1**	This will be the new report layout.
Under Orientation, verify that Portrait is selected	
Verify that Adjust the field width so all fields fit on a page is checked	This will ensure that all fields in the report fit on one page.
Click **Next**	Moves to the next dialog box.
2 Select **Bold**	
Click **Next**	Moves to the next dialog box.
3 In the What title do you want for your report box, enter **Summary Report**	
Verify that Preview the report is selected	
4 Click **Finish**	Preview the report, as shown in Exhibit 18-6.
Observe the preview	A summary of Qty_sold per Customer_ID appears.
5 Click **Close**	(On the Print Preview toolbar.) Closes the Preview window.
Update the report	
Close the report	

Adding headers and footers

Explanation
You can include a variety of information in different sections of a report. For example, you can include the company logo in the report header section and the page numbers in the report footer section. A report can have the following sections:

- Report header
- Page header
- Group header
- Detail
- Group footer
- Report footer
- Page footer

Report headers and footers

The report header section appears only on the first page of a report. The report header is printed before the page header section. You can include information such as a logo image and a report title. For example, the report, Customers by city, could have the report title and the logo of Outlander Spices. The report footer section appears only once on the last page of the report. You can include details such as report totals.

To add a report header:

1 Open the report in Design view.
2 Choose View, Report Header/Footer.
3 Drag the Report Header or the Report Footer section to a desired size.
4 Add the controls.
5 Update and close the report.

Do it!
B-4: Adding headers and footers

Here's how	Here's why
1 Open Customers by city in Design view	To add a report header to this report.
Choose **View**, **Report Header/Footer**	Displays the report header and footer sections.
Verify that the Toolbox is open	
Maximize the window	
Drag the Report Header section as shown	

2 Click 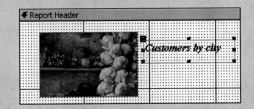	(The Image button is on the Toolbox.) To insert an image in the header section.
Place the insertion point in the left-most grid	(In the header section.) The Insert Picture dialog box appears.
Select **Outlander-logo**	From the current unit folder.
Add a label control with the caption **Customers by city** as shown	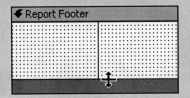
	From the toolbox, using the Label button.
Click anywhere outside the label control	
3 Drag the Report Footer section as shown	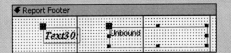
Click **abl**	(From the Toolbox.) Inserts a text box.
4 Create a text box as shown	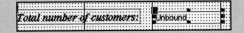
In the label, type **Total number of customers:**	(The label has blue text in it.) Notice that the label overlaps the neighboring box.
Drag the box to the right and place it next to the label as shown	
5 Resize the label	If necessary.
6 Place the insertion point as shown	
Right-click the text box control	
Choose **Properties**	From the shortcut menu.
Place the insertion point in the Control Source box	
Click the button with the ellipses.	Opens the Expression Builder dialog box.

7   Type **=Count(**

   Double-click **Tables**

   Double-click **Customers** as
   shown

   Double click **CustomerID**

   In the Expressions box, type **)**

8   Click **OK**

   Close the window

9   Click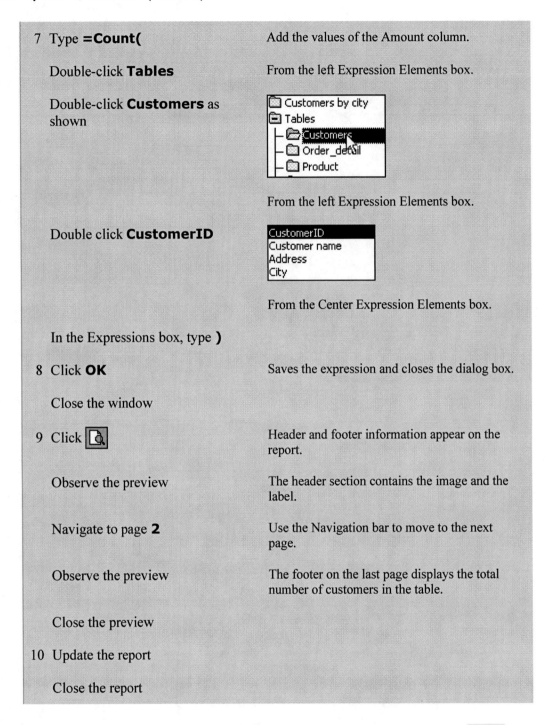

   Observe the preview

   Navigate to page **2**

   Observe the preview

   Close the preview

10 Update the report

   Close the report

Add the values of the Amount column.

From the left Expression Elements box.

From the left Expression Elements box.

From the Center Expression Elements box.

Saves the expression and closes the dialog box.

Header and footer information appear on the
report.

The header section contains the image and the
label.

Use the Navigation bar to move to the next
page.

The footer on the last page displays the total
number of customers in the table.

Arranging fields and headings

Explanation

After you run a report, you might decide to change the arrangement of data fields and headings. To change the arrangement of a report you've already created:

1 Open a database.
2 On the objects bar, click Reports.
3 Select the report you want to modify and click the design button.
4 Expand the report to see more of the report design, if necessary.
5 Click on a field and drag to move it. Drag the handles to resize it. You can also use the format toolbar to modify the properties of the selected text.
6 Switch to report view to see your changes.
7 Update and close the report when you are done.

Deleting a report

To delete a report:

1 Selecting the report.
2 Choose Delete.
3 A message appears to confirm deletion. Click Yes to delete the record.

Do it!

B-5: Deleting a report

Here's how	Here's why
1 Under the Objects bar, verify that Reports is selected	If necessary.
Select **Retailer**	
Press DELETE	A message appears prompting you to confirm the deletion.
Click **Yes**	Deletes the report.

Topic C: Printing

Explanation

The Page Setup dialog box modifies print options before printing the report. The Page Setup dialog box offers options to:

- Change the orientation of the report
- Change the paper size

Preview the report to see how the options will look on the printed report.

The Page Setup dialog box

To set the Page Setup options, you would do the following:

1   Choose File, Page Setup to open the Page Setup dialog box, as shown in Exhibit 18-7.
2   Activate the Page tab.
3   Select the preferred orientation from the Orientation group.
4   Select a paper size, using the Size list.

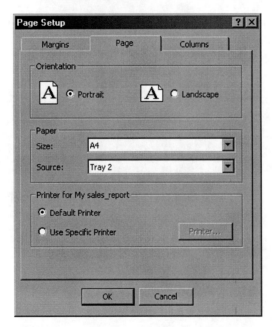

Exhibit 18-7: The Page Setup dialog box

Do it!   **C-1: Using Page Setup**

Here's how	Here's why
1 Open My sales_report	
2 Choose **File**, **Page Setup...**	Displays the Page Setup dialog box.
Click the **Page** tab	(If necessary.) The tab will look like Exhibit 18-7, although the specific options depend on the printer you are using.
Under Orientation, select **Landscape**	Specify a landscape orientation for the printout.
In the Size list, verify that Letter is selected	(Under the Paper group.) Letter is the default paper size.
Click **OK**	Closes the Page Setup dialog box.

Printing reports

Explanation

To print database objects, such as tables, forms, and queries, simply open the object you want to print and do any one of the following:

- Choose File, Print
- Click the Print button.
- Press Ctrl+P to open the Print dialog box, shown in Exhibit 18-8.

Printing specific pages

You can print a specified range of pages from a report, table, form or query. To do so:

1 Open the object you want to print.
2 Choose File, Print.
3 Under Print Range, select Pages.
4 Enter the starting page number in the From box and the ending page number iin the To box.
3 Click OK. Only the pages you specified will print.

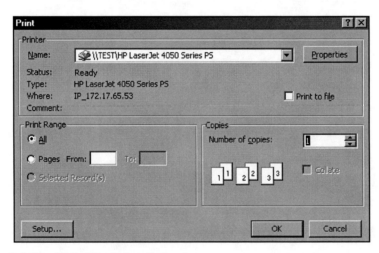

Exhibit 18-8: The Print dialog box

Printing from a table

Although you will usually print data in the form of reports, you can get printed data quickly by printing records directly from a table. To do so:

1 Open a table in datasheet view.
2 If you don't want to print the whole table, select the record or records you want to print.
3 Choose File, Print. The print dialog box will open, as shown in Exhibit 18-8, except now the Selected Records option will be available under Print Range.
4 Under Print Range, select All to print the whole table, select Pages to enter specific pages to print, or select Selected Records to print only those records you selected in step 2.
2 Click OK.

Do it!

C-2: Printing a report

Here's how	Here's why
1 Choose **File, Print...**	Opens the Print dialog box.
Verify that the default printer is selected	
Under Print Range, verify that All is selected	
Click **Cancel**	Cancels printing.
2 Close the database	

Unit summary: Reports

Topic A   In this topic, you learned how to **create** a **report** using the **Report Wizard**. You also learned how to create reports based on **queries**.

Topic B   In this topic, you learned how to **group** and **sort records** in a **report**. You learned how to **add summary information**. You also learned how to **change** the **layout** and **style** of a report. You learned how to add **headers** and **footers**. Finally, you learned how to **delete** a report.

Topic C   In this topic, you learned how to use the **Page Setup** dialog box to **change** the **orientation** and **paper size** of the report. Finally, you learned how to **print** a report.

Independent practice activity

1 Open Emp.

2 Create a report based on the **Employee_list** table using the Report Wizard with the following settings:

   Display all the fields of the table

   Group by **Department**

   Sort **Earnings** in ascending order

   Summarize by calculating the **Avg** of **Earnings**

   Use **Outline1** layout

   Use **Soft Gray** style

   Specify **Employee Details** as the title

3 Close the preview.

4 Add the image, **Logo practice**, from the current unit folder to the Report Header and the label, **Outlander Spices** to Report Footer.

5 Save the report as **My employee details**.

6 Preview the report.

7 Close the preview.

8 Close the report.

9 Delete the report, **Employee Temp**.

10 Create a query based on the **Quarterly_sales_analysis** table displaying the **Salesperson_name** and **Quarter1_sales** fields. Specify the following criterion: **Quarter1_sales>10000**.

11 Save the query as **My sales_query**.

12 Create a columnar report based on this query.

13 Open the Page Setup dialog box.

14 Change the Orientation to **Landscape**.

15 Print the report.

16 Close the preview.

17 Save the report as **My query_report**.

18 Close the report and the database.

19 Close Access.

Unit 19

PowerPoint basics

Unit time: 30 minutes

Complete this unit, and you'll know how to:

A Start PowerPoint, open and run a presentation, examine the PowerPoint environment, and change display modes.

B Use Office Assistant and find help on the Web.

C Save a presentation in an existing folder or create a new folder, and update an existing presentation.

D Close a presentation and close PowerPoint.

Topic A: Getting started

Explanation

PowerPoint is a software program that creates presentations using a combination of text, graphics, charts, clip art, and WordArt. The resulting presentations can then be shown at professional business meetings, sales calls, and training events. You can also post a PowerPoint on either the Internet or a company intranet.

The delivery of presentations can be through a variety of media, including timed shows on a computer, slides, overheads, printouts with notes, and the Web.

The easiest way to start PowerPoint is to click the Start button, then choose Programs, Microsoft PowerPoint. The Microsoft PowerPoint window with the PowerPoint dialog box appears, as shown in Exhibit 19-1.

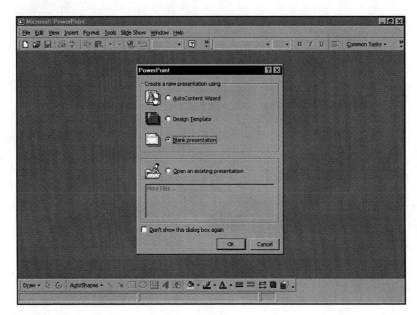

Exhibit 19-1: The PowerPoint window

Opening presentations

The PowerPoint dialog box provides the option to either create a new presentation or open an existing one. By default, the Blank presentation option is selected.

To open an existing presentation:

1 In the PowerPoint dialog box, Select Open to open an existing presentation.
2 Click OK and the Open dialog box appears, as shown in Exhibit 19-2.
3 Select the folder and the file name of the presentation that you want to open.
4 Click Open.

To open a presentation when PowerPoint is running:

1 Choose File, Open, or click the Open button on the Standard toolbar.
2 Select the folder and the file name of the presentation you want to open.
3 Click Open.

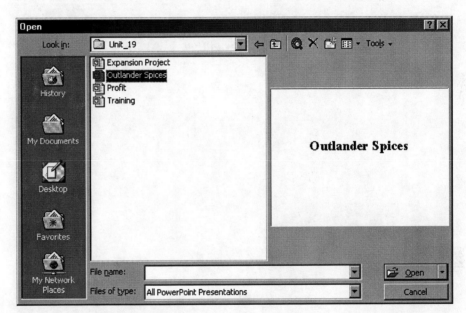

Exhibit 19-2: The Open dialog box

Opening multiple presentations

When you open more than one presentation, each one opens in its own window. All the open presentations are listed in the Window menu. To switch between presentations, just choose Window, and the presentation you want to view.

Running a presentation

In order to display a presentation to an audience, you need to run a slide show. When running a slide show, only one slide displays at a time.

Manually advance through the slides, or setup the presentation to automatically advance. To manually move to the next slide either click the mouse or use the Page Down key. To move to the previous slide, you can use the Page Up key. To end the slide show at any time, press the Esc key.

Normally, you will start running a presentation from the first slide, but you don't have to. You can start a slide show from any slide. To start a slide show from a specific slide, select the slide and clicking the Slide Show button, which is located in the bottom left corner of the PowerPoint window as shown in Exhibit 19-3.

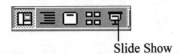

Slide Show

Exhibit 19-3: The Slide Show button.

Do it!

A-1:   Opening and running a presentation

Here's how	Here's why
1 Click **Start**, then choose **Programs**, **Microsoft PowerPoint**	Starts Microsoft PowerPoint.
Observe the screen	The PowerPoint dialog box appears within the Microsoft PowerPoint window. By default, the Blank presentation option is selected.
2 Select **Open an existing presentation**	
Click **OK**	The Open dialog box displays.
From the Look in list, select the current unit folder	Notice the list of presentations.
Select **Outlander Spices**	
Click **Open**	The presentation opens. The first slide appears in the PowerPoint window.
3 Choose **Slide Show**, **View Show**	The slide show starts.
4 Click the mouse button	The next slide appears.
Observe the slide	Notice the bulleted slide titled "Project Justification."
5 Click the mouse button	A slide with formatted text appears.
6 Move to the next slide	(Click the mouse button.) This is the fourth slide containing drawing objects.
7 Move to the next slide	The fifth slide contains Clip Art and WordArt.
8 Press (PAGE UP)	(To move to the previous slide.) Use the Page Up and Page Down keys to navigate through the slide show.
9 Press (PAGE DOWN)	The next slide appears which is the fifth slide.
10 Press (PAGE DOWN)	A slide containing a table appears.
11 Move to the next slide	A slide containing a chart appears.
12 Move to the next slide	(The slide show ends.) A black screen with "End of slide show, click to exit." appears.
13 Click the mouse button	Exits the slide show and returns to the first slide.

The PowerPoint environment

Explanation   The PowerPoint environment, as shown in Exhibit 19-4, contains several elements that are common to other Windows applications. These elements interact with the PowerPoint application to perform operations, such as editing a presentation or viewing a slide show.

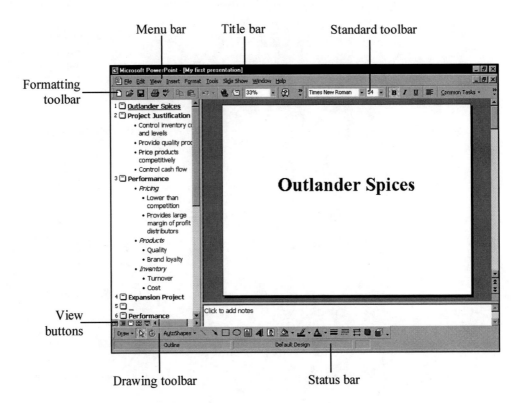

Exhibit 19-4: The components of a PowerPoint window

Item	Description
Title bar	Displays the name of the application and the name of the presentation file.
Menu bar	Provides menus containing PowerPoint commands. For example, the Edit menu contains commands to edit text.
Toolbars	Perform common tasks without using the menus. By default, PowerPoint displays the Standard, Formatting, and Drawing toolbars.
Status bar	Provides information, such as the slide number and the name of the design template.
View buttons	View slides using one of five different views.

Do it!

A-2:   Examining the PowerPoint environment

Here's how	Here's why
1 Observe the title bar	Notice the name of the presentation file, "Outlander Spices."
2 Observe the menu bar	The menu bar provides options that you can use to work with PowerPoint.
3 Observe the toolbars	By default the Standard, Formatting, and Drawing toolbars appear.
4 Observe the Outline pane	This is the left pane of the PowerPoint window. It displays the contents of the slides in the presentation.
5 Observe the Slide pane	This is the right pane of the PowerPoint window.
6 Observe the status bar	The slide number of the current slide appears on the left side of the status bar.
7 Observe the view buttons	There are five view buttons that you can use to switch between different views.

Display modes

Explanation There are five different views, as shown in Exhibit 19-5, to view your slides. They are:

- Normal
- Outline
- Slide
- Slide Sorter
- Slide Show

You can switch between views by clicking the buttons in the lower-left corner of the window.

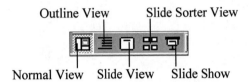

Exhibit 19-5: The View buttons

Item	Description
Normal	Contains three panes: the Outline pane, the Slide pane, and the Notes pane.
Outline	Arranges all the slides in a tree-like structure.
Slide	Work with only one slide at a time to add text, graphs, charts, organization charts, Clip Art, and WordArt.
Slide Sorter	View all the slides in the presentation at the same time to arrange and move the order.
Slide Show	Display presentation on a full screen and shows any special effects, such as transitions and timings.

Do it!

A-3:   Changing display modes

Here's how	Here's why
1 Click 🔳	(The Outline View button is the second button on the lower-left corner of the window.) Changes to Outline view.
Observe the Outline pane	1 ▢ **Outlander Spices** 2 ▢ **Project Justification** • Control inventory costs and levels • Provide quality products • Price products competitively • Control cash flow 3 ▢ **Performance** (The Outline pane is on the left side of the screen.) View an overview of all the text in the presentation.
2 Click 🔳	(The Slide View button is the third button on the lower-left corner of the window.) Switches to the Slide view. Notice you can only view one slide view at a time.
3 Click 🔳	Switches to the Slide Sorter view to see all the slides in the presentation. You can use this view to rearrange the slides.
4 Click 🔳	Runs the slide show. Notice the slides displayed on the full screen.
Press (PAGE DOWN)	Moves to the next slide.
Press (ESC)	Exits the slide show.
5 Click 🔳	Switches back to Normal view.

Topic B: Getting help

Explanation

You can use the Help system to get assistance with questions.

There are several ways to access Help:

- Choose Help, Microsoft PowerPoint Help.
- Press F1 on the keyboard.
- Use the Office Assistant.

You can also get help from Microsoft through their Web page.

The Help database

The Help database is a collection of topics. It contains answers to frequently asked questions about Microsoft PowerPoint and its interactions with other Office programs. If you want to use this database without the Office Assistant, you must first turn the Office Assistant off.

Index

The Help database is divided into three tabs: Contents, Answer Wizard, and Index. By default, when you access help, the Index tab is displayed. You'll see two panes. The left pane allows you to search for a help topic and select the related topics by typing or selecting a keyword and clicking Search. A list of topics appears in the lower portion of the left pane. The right pane then displays the information on the topic you've selected.

Answer Wizard

The Answer Wizard uses plain language to find an answer to your question. Like the Index, you'll see a left and right pane. You type a question in the text box of the left pane and click Search. A list of topics appears in the lower portion of the pane. You can then select a topic and the contents will appear in the right pane. The Answer Wizard is really the Office Assistant without the animated character.

Contents

The Help Contents tab also has two panes. The left pane lists the various topics available by category. Double-clicking on a category displays the information documents related to that category. You may then select a document. The information and a list of any related topics appear in the right pane.

The Office Assistant

The Office Assistant is an animated Help system to answer your questions while you work. Just type your questions and the Assistant displays the appropriate Help topics. If there is no information related to the question, the Assistant gives you suggestions on how to phrase a question. To show the Office Assistant, choose Help, Show the Office Assistant. To hide it, choose Help, Hide the Office Assistant.

To locate help on a topic:

1 Click the Office Assistant.
2 Type your question in the "What would you like to do?" balloon.
3 Click Search.

Exhibit 19-6: The Office Assistant

Do it!

B-1: Using the Office Assistant

Here's how	Here's why
1 Choose **Help, Show the Office Assistant**	The Office Assistant appears, as shown in Exhibit 19-6.
Click the Office Assistant	The "What would you like to do?" balloon appears on the screen. The balloon contains a text box where you can type questions.
In the Office Assistant text box type **edit**	
Click **Search**	Help topics that pertain to editing appear.
2 Click **Edit a picture**	Microsoft PowerPoint Help window appears with the information on editing a picture.
Maximize the window	
Close the Help window	The close button is in the upper-right corner of the Help window.
3 Choose **Help, Hide the Office Assistant**	Hides the Office Assistant.

Help on the Web

Explanation

If you don't find relevant information within the Office Assistant, you have the option of connecting to the Web to locate additional information. Connect to the Microsoft Office Web site directly from PowerPoint to access technical information and download product enhancements.

To use Help on the Web:

1 Choose Help, Office on the Web. This opens Internet Explorer and the Microsoft Office Update site.

2 Use this as a starting point to find answers to your questions regarding Microsoft Office and PowerPoint.

Do it!

B-2: Using Help on the Web

Here's how	Here's why
1 Choose **Help, Office on the Web**	Gets Help from the Web. This starts Internet Explorer and opens the Microsoft Office Update site.
2 Select **Downloads**	Downloads PowerPoint enhancements.
Choose **File, Close**	Exits the browser.

Topic C: Saving presentations

Explanation

You need to save your presentations to prevent loss of content. After you save a presentation once, you can modify it at any time and retain those changes by saving it again.

Saving presentations in existing folders

The first time you save a presentation; you must assign a file name and select a folder in which to store the file.

To save a presentation in an existing folder:

1   Choose File, Save As to display the Save As dialog box, as shown in Exhibit 19-7.
2   Select the drive and folder where you want to save the presentation, from the Save in list.
3   Type a name for the presentation in the File name box.
4   From the Save As type list, select the format according to your requirement. You can select different file formats, such as RTF, Web Page and Design template.
5   Click Save.

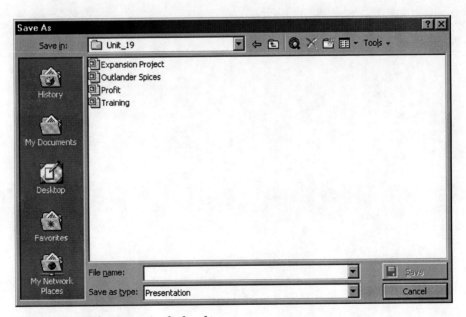

Exhibit 19-7: The Save As dialog box

Do it!

C-1: Saving a presentation in an existing folder

Here's how	Here's why
1 Choose **File**, **Save As...**	Displays the Save As dialog box.
Navigate to the current unit folder	(If necessary.) Saves your presentation in the existing folder.
In the File name box, edit to read **First Presentation**	This will be the new presentation name.
Observe the Save as type box	By default, PowerPoint shows the type as Presentation.
2 Click **Save**	Saves the presentation in the existing folder.
Observe the title bar	Microsoft PowerPoint - [First presentation]
	See that the file name appears in the Title bar.

Saving presentations in new folders

Explanation

To save a presentation in a new folder:

1 Choose File, Save As to open the Save As dialog box.
2 Select the appropriate location, from the Save in list.
3 Click the Create New Folder button to open the New Folder dialog box.
4 Specify a folder name, in the Name box. Click OK.
5 Verify that the Save in list displays the name of the new folder.
6 Type a name for the presentation, in the File name box.
7 Click Save.

Saving presentations in other versions of PowerPoint

After saving a presentation, you might decide to share the file with some coworkers. But what if those individuals have an older version of PowerPoint? To deal with this obstacle, you'll need to save your presentation in another format. To do this:

1 Open the Save As dialog box and navigate to the desired folder location. In the File name box, enter the name of the file.
2 In the Save as type list, select one of the PowerPoint file formats. The following table explains the various PowerPoint formats.
3 Click Save.

Save as type	Description
Presentation (*.ppt)	Saves the presentation in the PowerPoint 2000 format and is the default option.
PowerPoint 95 (*.ppt)	Saves the presentation in the PowerPoint 95 format.
PowerPoint 97-2000 & 95 Presentation (*.ppt)	Saves the presentation in format that can be opened in PowerPoint 95, PowerPoint 97, and PowerPoint 2000.
PowerPoint 4.0 (*.ppt)	Saves the presentation in the PowerPoint 4.0 format.

Saving a presentation in an image file format

Once you've saved a presentation in the native PowerPoint 2000 format, you can also save it in one of the many image-based formats. To do this:

1 Open the Save As dialog box and navigate to the desired folder location. In the File name box, enter the name of the file.

2 In the Save as type list, select one of the image file formats. The following table describes the available image formats.

3 Click Save.

4 You are prompted with a message box that asks "Do you want to export every slide in the Presentation?" Click Yes to save every slide in the image file format and click No to save only the first slide in the presentation.

Save as type	Description
GIF Graphics Interchange Format (*.gif)	Saves the slide(s) in the GIF file format. This is a file format normally used for Web and on-screen images that have less that 256 colors.
JPEG File Interchange Format (*.jpg)	Saves the slide(s) in the JPEG file format. This file format is normally used for Web and on-screen images that have more than 256 colors, such as photographs and artwork with lots of detail.
PNG Portable Network Graphics Format (*.png)	Saves the slide(s) in the PNG file format. This is also a Web and on-screen image format, similar to GIF.
Device Independent Bitmap (*.bmp)	Saves the slide(s) in the BMP file format. This is a common Windows-based format. Images are saved in this file format when they are to be printed.
Windows Metafile (*.wmf)	Saves the slide(s) in the WMF file format. This is a Microsoft specific format.
Tag Image File Format (*.tif; *.tiff)	Saves the slide(s) in the TIF file format. This is one of the most widely used and support file formats. Images are saved in this file format when they are to be printed.

Saving a presentation in a rich text format

You can also save just the text of a presentation in the RTF file format. To do this:

1 Open the Save As dialog box and navigate to the desired folder location. In the File name box, enter the name of the file.

2 In the Save as type list, select Outline/RTF (*.rtf).

3 Click Save.

Do it!

C-2: Saving a presentation in a new folder

Here's how	Here's why
1 Choose **File, Save As...**	Displays the Save As dialog box.
Navigate to the current unit folder	(If necessary.) To create a folder within the current unit folder to save your presentation.
Click	(The Create New Folder button is in the Save As dialog box.) The New Folder dialog box appears.
In the Name box, enter **My folder**	This will be the folder's name.
Click **OK**	Notice that in the Save in list, My folder appears.
2 In the File name box, edit to read **My first presentation**	
Click **Save**	Saves the presentation in the new folder.

Updating presentations

Explanation

Each time you save a presentation, the file updates with your latest changes.

To update the presentation, do any of the following:

- Choose File, Save.
- Click the Save button on the Standard toolbar.
- Press Ctrl+S.

Once a presentation is saved, you can save it with a different name. You do this by choosing File, Save As to open the Save As dialog box. In the File name box, enter the new name and click Save.

Do it!

C-3: Updating a presentation

Here's how	Here's why
1 Place the insertion point at the end of the second bullet	To add more bullet items to the slide.
Press (↵ ENTER)	Adds a bullet item to the slide.
Type **Progress to date**	
2 Press (↵ ENTER)	
Type **Outstanding issues**	
3 Click outside the bullet placeholder	Deselects it.
Observe the slide	You have added 2 bulleted items to the slide.
4 Click 🖫	Saves the presentation.

Topic D: Closing presentations and closing PowerPoint

Explanation

There are multiple ways to close a PowerPoint presentation:

- Choose File, Close.
- Click the Close button in the top-right corner of the menu bar, as shown in Exhibit 19-8.
- Double-click the Control menu icon in the top-left corner of the menu bar, as shown in Exhibit 19-8.
- Click the Control menu icon and choose Close.

Control menu   Close button

Exhibit 19-8: The Control menu icon and the Close button

Closing PowerPoint

To close the PowerPoint program do any of the following:

- Choose File, Exit.
- Click the Close button in the top-right corner of the title bar.
- Double-click the Control menu icon in the top-left corner of the title bar.
- Press Alt+F4.

Do it!

D-1: Closing a presentation and closing PowerPoint

Here's how	Here's why
1 Choose **File**, **Close**	Closes the presentation.
2 Choose **File**, **Exit**	Closes PowerPoint.

Unit summary: PowerPoint basics

Topic A In this topic, you learned how to **start PowerPoint** and then **open** and **run** a **presentation**. You learned how to examine the various **components** of the PowerPoint **environment**. You also learned how to **change** the various presentation **views**.

Topic B In this topic, you learned how to access the **Help features**, including the **Office Assistant**. You also learned how to **find help** using the **Web**.

Topic C In this topic, you learned how to **save** a presentation in an **existing folder**. You learned how to **create** a **new folder** to **save** a presentation. Finally, you learned how to **update** a presentation after making changes.

Topic D In this topic, you learned how to **close** a **presentation**. You also learned how to close **PowerPoint**.

Independent practice activity

1 Start PowerPoint.

2 Open Profit. (From the current unit folder.)

3 Switch to the Slide Sorter view.

4 Switch back to the Normal view.

5 Save the presentation as **My profit**. (In the current unit folder.)

6 Close the presentation and close PowerPoint.

Unit 20

Building new presentations

Unit time: 45 minutes

Complete this unit, and you'll know how to:

A Create a new PowerPoint presentation, add text to slides, and add or delete slides.

B Use the formatting toolbar, change the font size and type, change bullet styles, apply numbered lists, change case and magnification.

C Move or copy text to another slide, change text alignment, and use the undo or redo commands.

Topic A: Creating new presentations

Explanation

Create a new blank presentation using the New Presentation dialog box. After you create the presentation, you can:

- Enter text in a slide
- Add new slides
- Delete Slides

The New Presentation dialog box

To create a new presentation, choose File, New. The New Presentation dialog box contains the following options:

Option	Description
Blank presentation	Creates a new presentation with default settings for text and colors.
AutoContent Wizard	Creates a presentation based on the content, purpose, style, handouts, and output you provide.
Design Templates	Select from a collection of templates that you apply to your presentation.
Presentations	Select from twenty-four pre-designed presentations.

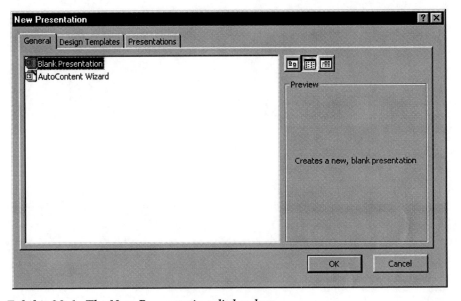

Exhibit 20-1: The New Presentation dialog box

Slide layouts

When you create a new presentation, it contains only one slide. The slide has the Title Slide layout applied; you can select a different layout from the New Slide dialog box, as shown in Exhibit 20-2. This dialog box provides twenty-four AutoLayouts or formats for slides.

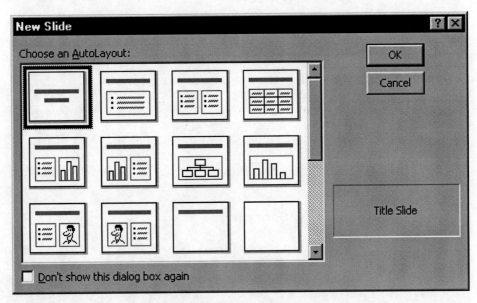

Exhibit 20-2: The New Slide dialog box

Do it!

A-1:   Creating a new presentation

Here's how	Here's why
1 Start PowerPoint	The PowerPoint dialog box appears.
Select **Design Template**	You will create a new presentation from a design template.
Click **OK**	The New Presentation dialog box appears, as shown in Exhibit 20-1.
2 Select **Bold Stripes**	The template design appears in the Preview area.
3 Choose the **Presentations** tab	A collection of presentations appears.
Select **Business Plan**	The template design appears in the Preview area.
4 Choose the **General** tab	
Select **Blank Presentation**	To create a new, blank presentation.
Click **OK**	(The New Presentation dialog box closes.) The New Slide dialog box opens.
5 Observe the New Slide dialog box	By default, the first AutoLayout is selected. Notice the description for the selected AutoLayout, "Title Slide," in the lower-right corner of the dialog box.
Click **OK**	Creates a presentation with the Title Slide AutoLayout.
Observe the window	By default, the slide opens in Normal view.

Entering text in slides

Explanation

After you create a presentation and select a slide layout, you can begin to enter text on the slide. The Title Slide AutoLayout contains two placeholders for text: one placeholder for the title, and one for the subtitle, as shown in Exhibit 20-3. To enter text, place the insertion point in the placeholders and start typing.

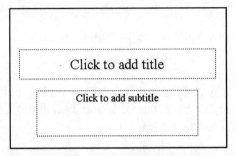

Exhibit 20-3: The Title Slide layout

Do it!

A-2:   Entering text in a slide

Here's how	Here's why
1 Place the insertion point in the title placeholder	
Type **Outlander Spices**	This will be the title of the slide.
2 Place the insertion point in the subtitle placeholder	
Type **Expansion project**	
3 Click anywhere outside the placeholder	Deselects it.

Adding, editing and deleting slides

Explanation

You will need to add more slides to your new presentation, since it only contains one slide. To add a slide, you can use any one of these methods:

- Choose Insert, New Slide.
- Click the New Slide button on the Standard toolbar.
- Press Ctrl+M.

When you add a slide, the New Slide dialog box appears.

Adding bullet slides

The New Slide dialog box provides multiple layouts for adding bullet slides to a presentation, as shown in Exhibit 20-4. The Title and Text slides have two placeholders: one for the title and a second for the bulleted items.

To insert text in the Bulleted list placeholder:

1 Click the Bulleted List placeholder.
2 Type the text for the first bullet.
3 Press Enter to display a second bullet.
4 Type the text for the second bullet, and press Enter.
5 Continue this process to add text for additional bullets.
6 After adding bulleted items, click outside the placeholder to deselect it.

Exhibit 20-4: The layouts for bullet slides

Editing text in a slide

After creating a slide, you can edit any word or phrase by selecting the text and typing. As you type, the selected text is removed.

Deleting slides

You can delete slides when you no longer need them. To delete a slide:

1 Select it in the Outline view or in the Slide Sorter view.
2 Choose Edit, Delete Slide or press the Delete key.

To delete multiple slides, select adjacent slides by pressing the Shift key and then pressing the Delete key. To delete non-adjacent slides, select the slides by pressing the Ctrl key and then pressing the Delete key.

Changing the slide layout

If you want to use a different layout for a slide, you can apply another layout style using the Slide Layout dialog box. To change the layout of a slide:

1 Select a slide. You will apply a new layout to this slide.
2 Choose Format, Slide Layout.

3 Select a new layout style.

4 Click Reapply.

Do it!   **A-3:   Adding, editing and deleting slides**

Here's how	Here's why
1 Choose **Insert, New Slide...**	The New Slide dialog box opens.
Observe the New Slide dialog box	By default, the Bulleted List AutoLayout is selected because it's a logical choice after a Title Slide.
Click **OK**	Inserts a Bulleted List slide.
2 Place the insertion point in the title placeholder	To add a title to the slide.
Type **Web Initiative**	
3 Place the insertion point in the text placeholder	Adds a bulleted list.
Type **Launch online store**	This will be the first item in the bulleted list.
4 Press ⏎ ENTER	Adds the second item to the bulleted list.
Type **Redesign site**	
5 Choose **Format, Slide Layout**	To open the Slide Layout dialog box.
Under Reapply the current master styles, select **2 Column Text**	Select the preview image in the first row, third column.
Click **Reapply**	To change the Bulleted List layout to the 2 Column Text layout.
6 Select **Web**	You'll replace "Web" with "Online."
Enter **Online**	Typing replace selection.
7 Switch to the Slide Sorter view	The second slide is selected.
Press DELETE	Deletes the slide.
8 Switch back to the Normal view	
9 Save the presentation as **My new presentation**	In the current unit folder.

Creating a slide in Outline view

Explanation

PowerPoint 2000 provides you with many views in which you can review your slides. You also can create new slides or an entire presentation in any of these views. The two main views are Normal view and Slide Sorter view. You can switch to other views by clicking the buttons in the lower left corner of the PowerPoint window (as shown in Exhibit 20-5).

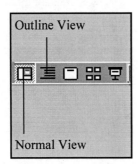

Exhibit 20-5: The View buttons

Outline view helps you to organize and develop the contents of your presentation. This view has three panes: the Outline pane, the Color Preview pane, and the Notes pane. The *Outline pane* is on the left side of the window and shows the title and text for each slide. A slide icon and number appear to the left of each slide title. You can use the Outline pane to rearrange text within a slide and to move slides from one position in the presentation to another.

In Outline view, the text is arranged into five levels, each of which is indented from the left margin. The title appears at the leftmost level; bulleted items and other elements appear at subsequent levels.

To insert a new slide in Outline view:

1 Select the slide icon after which you want to insert the new slide.
2 Click the New Slide button on the Standard toolbar.
3 Choose an AutoLayout for the slide.
4 Click OK.

Exhibit 20-6 shows a new slide in Outline view. You can see what the slide will look like in the Color Preview pane in the upper right corner of the window. A number and a slide icon denote the new slide in the Outline pane. You'll see that Outline view is nearly the same as Normal View, except that the Outline and Notes panes in Outline view are larger than they are in Normal View.

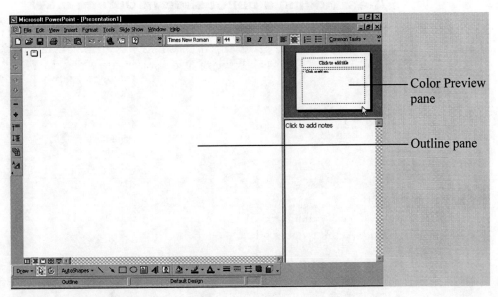

Exhibit 20-6: Outline view

Do it!

A-4: Adding a bullet slide in Outline view

Here's how	Here's why
1 Click the Outline View button	(In the lower left corner of the PowerPoint window, as shown in Exhibit 20-5.) To switch to Outline view.
2 Click the first slide	You'll insert a new slide at the end of the presentation.
3 Click [icon]	(On the Standard toolbar.) To open the New Slide dialog box.
4 Verify that the Bulleted List AutoLayout is selected	You'll insert a bullet slide in the presentation.
Click **OK**	To insert the new slide. The insertion point appears next to the slide icon in the Outline pane.
5 Select the title placeholder	(In the Color Preview pane.) To add a title to the slide.
Type **Performance**	The text, "Performance" appears in the Outline pane as you type it in the Color Preview Pane.
6 Select the bullet-list placeholder	To add items to the bulleted list.
7 Type **Pricing**	The Pricing bullet appears in both the Color Preview pane and the Outline pane.
Press (↵ ENTER)	To add a second bullet.
8 Type **Lower than competitors**	
9 Click the Normal View button	(In the lower left corner of the PowerPoint window, as shown in Exhibit 20-5.)
10 Update and close the presentation	

Topic B: Formatting

Explanation

You can apply formatting to draw the user's attention to specific text on a slide. You can format the text by:

- Applying bold
- Applying italics
- Applying underline
- Changing the font
- Changing the background colors
- Aligning the text
- Applying bulleted or numbered lists
- Changing the case of text

The Formatting toolbar

Select the text and then use the Formatting toolbar to change:

- Font
- Font size
- Type style (Type styles include bold, italics, and underlining.)

Some of the buttons available on the Formatting toolbar are shown in Exhibit 20-7.

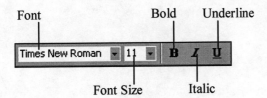

Exhibit 20-7: The Formatting toolbar

Displaying toolbars

PowerPoint 2000 has many toolbars in addition to the Standard, Formatting and Drawing toolbars. These additional toolbars are used for specific tasks, such as reviewing comments, and they can be shown on the screen when needed.

You can display any toolbar by choosing View, Toolbars and then selecting a toolbar from the submenu. To hide a toolbar, choose View, Toolbars and select the toolbar you want to hide.

Customizing toolbars

Many of the toolbars have additional buttons that you can add based on your needs. A small downward-pointing triangle at the right end of the toolbar indicates that more buttons are available. Here's how you modify a toolbar:

1 Click the More Buttons button (the downward-pointing triangle).

2 Click Add or Remove Buttons. Then:

- Click a button you want to add or remove.

- Choose Reset Toolbar to reset a toolbar to its original state.

Do it!

B-1: Using the Formatting toolbar

Here's how	Here's why
1 Open Project Phase One	(From the current unit folder.) To format the text in this presentation.
2 Double-click **Outlander**	(In the title placeholder.) Selects the word, "Outlander" to format the title of the first slide.
Click **B**	(On the Formatting toolbar.) Applies bold formatting to the word.
Apply bold formatting to the word spices	Double-click the word and click the Bold button.
3 Double-click **Project**	(In the subtitle placeholder.) To italicize this word.
Click **I**	(On the Formatting toolbar.) Applies italics to the word.
4 Apply italics to the words Phase One	Select the words and click the Italic button.
5 Select **Project Phase One**	To underline these words.
Click **U**	
6 Save the presentation as **My project phase one**	

Changing font type and size

Explanation
You can change the appearance of text by changing its attributes. For example, it's a good idea to increase the font size of titles and subtitles to make them stand out and readable from a distance.

Changing font and background color

To change the font color:

1 Select the text.
2 Click the drop-down arrow by the Font Color to display the Font Color menu.
3 Select a color from the menu and it will be applied to the selected text.

Change the background color of a slide by:

1 Choosing Format, Background. You have the option of applying the background selected to one or all slides of the presentation.

Apply a shadow effect to the text by:

1 Selecting the text.
2 Clicking the Shadow button on the Drawing toolbar
3 Selecting a shadow effect of your choice.

Do it!

B-2: Changing the font type and font size

Here's how	Here's why
1 Select **Outlander spices**	(In the title placeholder.) To make the title larger.
From the Font Size list, select **60**	(On the Formatting toolbar.) Increases the font size of the word.
From the Font list, select **Courier New**	(On the Formatting toolbar.) Changes the font type.
2 Click as shown	
	(On the Drawing toolbar.) Opens the color palette.
Select as shown	
	Changes the font color to blue.
3 Click as shown	
	(On the Drawing toolbar.) To apply shadow effect to the text.
Select as shown	
	Applies a shadow effect to the text.
Deselect the text	(Click anywhere else on the slide.) Observe how the text has changed.

4 Choose **Format**, **Background...**	The Background dialog box appears.
Click as shown	
Select as shown	
Click **Apply**	Applies the background color to the current slide.
5 Scroll through the presentation and observe the slides	Notice that the background color of other slides hasn't changed.
Place the insertion point on the first slide	
6 Choose **Format**, **Background...**	To change the background color of all slides in the presentation.
Click **Apply to All**	
Scroll through the presentation and observe the slides	Notice that the background color of all slides has changed.
7 Update the presentation	

Changing bullet styles

Explanation

You can change bullet styles to emphasize a bulleted list by performing the following steps:

1 Select the text.

2 Choose Format, Bullets and Numbering.

3 Select one of the available bullet styles, from the Bullets and Numbering dialog box, and click OK.

Line spacing

Another way to emphasize a bulleted list is to increase or decrease the spacing between bullets. In order to do this:

1 Choose Format, Line Spacing.

2 Select the line spacing of your choice from the Line Spacing dialog box, and click OK.

Do it!   **B-3:   Changing the bullet style**

Here's how	Here's why
1 Move to the second slide	View the bulleted list slide.
2 Select the text as shown	

Outlander spices

• Project justification
• Performance
• Progress to date
• Outstanding issues

	To change the bullet style.
Choose **Format, Bullets and Numbering...**	The Bullets and Numbering dialog box opens.
Observe the dialog box	By default, the previously applied bullet style is selected.
Select the style as shown	

➢ ___
➢ ___
➢ ___

Click **OK**	Applies the bullet style.
3 Observe the slide	The bullet style changes.
4 Select the bulleted text	If necessary.
Choose **Format, Line Spacing...**	The Line Spacing dialog box opens.
Under Line Spacing, edit the value to read **.75**	Changes the spacing between lines.
Click **OK**	Closes the Line Spacing dialog box and accept the line spacing to be .75.
5 Observe the new line spacing	There's less space between the lines.
6 Update the presentation	

Numbered lists

Explanation

You can apply automatic numbering to a list so any item you add is automatically numbered sequentially. To use the Numbered list:

1   Select the text.

2   Choose Format, Bullets and Numbering to open the Bullets and Numbering dialog box.

3   Click the Numbered tab.

4   Select the numbering style you want.

5   Click OK.

Do it!

B-4: Applying a numbered list

Here's how	Here's why
1 Move to the seventh slide	The slide with the title, Outstanding issues.
2 Select the bulleted text	
Choose **Format, Bullets and Numbering...**	The Bullets and Numbering dialog box opens.
Click the **Numbered** tab	
Select the Number style as shown	
Click **OK**	The dialog box closes.
3 Observe the slide	The bulleted list has become a numbered list.
4 Place the insertion point at the end of the fifth bullet	Click after the word "program."
Press (← ENTER)	Creates a new line.
Observe the slide	The new line is numbered accordingly.
Type **Recruiting new employees**	
5 Press (← ENTER)	
Type **Training**	(Adds a seventh item in the numbered list.) The text size adjusts to fit the additional text.
6 Select the sixth numbered item	The item containing the text, "Recruiting new employees."
Press (DELETE)	Deletes this item from the list.
Observe the list	The numbering adjusts automatically.
7 Update the presentation	

Changing case and magnification

Explanation

You can change the case of text using the Change Case dialog box, as shown in Exhibit 20-8. The following table describes the options the Change Case dialog box provides.

Option	Description
Sentence case	Capitalizes the first letter of the selected text.
Lower case	Doesn't capitalize any letter of the selected text.
Upper case	Capitalizes all the letters of the selected text.
Title case	Capitalizes the first letter of every word in the selected text.
Toggle case	Inverts the casing of the selected text.

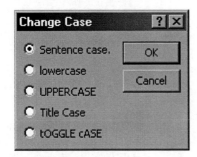

Exhibit 20-8: The Change Case dialog box

To change the casing:

1 Choose Format, Change Case to open the Change Case dialog box.
2 Select the case of your choice.
3 Click OK.

Changing magnification

The page magnification feature adjusts your text to appear either smaller or larger. Using this feature you can focus on just one part or the entire presentation.

To adjust the page magnification either:

• Use the Zoom list on the Standard toolbar.
• Choose View, Zoom to open the Zoom dialog box.

Do it!

B-5:   Changing case and magnification

Here's how	Here's why
1 Select **Outstanding issues**	The title of the slide.
Choose **Format**, **Change Case...**	The Change Case dialog box appears.
Select **UPPERCASE**	Case changes to uppercase.
Click **OK**	(The Change Case dialog box closes.) Notice that the title has changed to uppercase.
2 Open the Change Case dialog box	Choose Format, Change Case.
Select **Title Case**	Case changes to title case.
Click **OK**	Change Case dialog box closes.
3 Deselect the text	Click anywhere on the slide.
Observe the slide	The text, Outstanding Issues, appears in title case.
4 From the Zoom list, select **150%**	(On the Standard toolbar.) To change the display of the slide to 150%.
Observe the slide	The slide has zoomed in so that only a part of the slide is visible.
Zoom the slide to **50%**	From the zoom list.
Observe the slide	The entire slide is visible.
5 Update the presentation	

Topic C: Working with text

Explanation

You can move and copy text from one slide to another or from one presentation to another. These features are a significant time saver as you reorganize a presentation. It's also useful if you want to use a portion of a presentation in another one.

When you move or copy text, the selected text is placed in the Clipboard. The *Clipboard* is a temporary storage area that holds the text until you specify where to place it. If you mistakenly place the text in the wrong area, the Undo command cancels the action.

Cutting and Pasting commands

When you want to move text from one location to another, use the Cut command. The *Cut* command removes the selected text from the current slide and places it on the Clipboard. To place the text in a new location on the same slide, on another slide, or in a different presentation, use the Paste command. The *Paste* command takes the text from the Clipboard and inserts a copy of it wherever you position the insertion point.

To move text:

1 Select the text you want to move.

2 Choose Edit, Cut or click the Cut button on the Standard toolbar, or press Ctrl+X.

3 Place the insertion point wherever you want to insert the text.

4 Choose Edit, Paste or click the Paste button on the Standard toolbar, or press Ctrl+V.

Do it!

C-1: Moving text to another slide

Here's how	Here's why
1 At the end of the presentation, insert a new Bulleted List slide	Move to the last slide, and click the New Slide button. In the New slide dialog box, select the Bulleted List auto layout.
2 Move to the second slide	
Select **Outlander spices**	The title of the slide.
Click [✂]	(The Cut button is on the Standard toolbar.) To remove the title from the slide and place the text on the Clipboard.
3 Move to the last slide	
Click in the title placeholder	
Click [📋]	(The Paste button is on the Standard toolbar.) To paste the text from the Clipboard to the title placeholder.
Observe the slide	The title text is inserted from the Clipboard.
4 Update the presentation	

Copying command

Explanation

When you want to copy text from one location to another, use the Copy command. The *Copy* command creates a copy of the selected text in the Clipboard. This is different from the Cut command because the Copy command does not remove the selected text from the slide; however, you still use the Paste command to complete the copy procedure.

To copy text:

1   Select the text you want to copy.
2   Choose Edit, Copy or click the Copy button on the Standard toolbar.
3   Place the insertion point wherever you want to insert the text.
4   Choose Edit, Paste or click the Paste button on the Standard toolbar.

Copying between presentations

To copy text or an object from one presentation to another:

1   Select the text or object.
2   Copy it using the method of your choice.
3   Display the Window menu and choose an open presentation.
4   Place the insertion point wherever you want to insert the text or object.
5   Paste it using the method of your choice.

Do it!

C-2:   Copying text to another slide

Here's how	Here's why
1 Move to the second slide	
Select the bulleted text	Click once to select the bulleted area, then drag to select all the bullets.
Click 📋	(The Copy button is on the Standard toolbar.) Copies the selected text to the Clipboard.
2 Move to the last slide	
Click the bullet list placeholder	
Paste the copied text	Click the Paste button.
Observe the slide	The bullet items you copied from the second slide are inserted.
3 Switch to Slide Sorter view	
Select the second slide	
Press (DELETE)	Deletes the second slide.
4 Switch to Normal view	
5 Update the presentation	

Setting alignment

Explanation

The alignment features determine how text is positioned on the slides. Text is *left-aligned* when the lines of text are aligned along the left side of the text placeholder, and the right side of the paragraph appears ragged. Text is *right-aligned* when the lines of text are aligned along the right side, and the left side looks ragged. You can *justify* text to align it so that the lines end evenly at the left and right sides.

Aligning text

To align text:

1   Place the insertion point in a line of text, or select the text.

2   Choose Format, Alignment, and one of the submenu items:

- Align Left
- Align Right
- Center
- Justify

You can also use the alignment buttons on the Formatting toolbar.

Do it!   ## C-3: Changing text alignment

Here's how	Here's why
1 Move to the fourth slide in the presentation	A slide titled "Performance."
Select the left-side text	To change the alignment of the entire left side of the slide.
Click [≡]	The Align Right button is on the Formatting toolbar.
Deselect and observe the text	

Performance

Our pricing typically undercuts our competitors, yet still provides a large margin of profit for distributors.
Our products are manufactured for quality, and have earned end-user loyalty resulting in repeat sales.

Our products move! Inventory typically turns over 50 percent faster than competitive products.
Our customers have saved up to 14% of inventory cost while improving productivity and cost flow.
Sales to restaurants have never been better.

The left-side text is aligned to the right, and the right-side text is still aligned to the left.

2 Select the left-side text	
Click [≡]	(The Center button is on the Formatting toolbar.) Aligns the left-side text to the center.
3 Align the right-side text to the center	Select the text, and click the Center button.
Deselect the text	
Observe the slide	

Performance

Our pricing typically undercuts our competitors, yet still provides a large margin of profit for distributors.
Our products are manufactured for quality, and have earned end-user loyalty resulting in repeat sales.

Our products move! Inventory typically turns over 50 percent faster than competitive products.
Our customers have saved up to 14% of inventory cost while improving productivity and cost flow.
Sales to restaurants have never been better.

Both text boxes have centered text.

4 Update the presentation	

The Undo and Redo command

Explanation

PowerPoint provides an easy way to undo, or reverse, many of the actions that you enter when editing slide content. It also provides an easy way to redo any actions you've mistakenly undone.

The Undo command

The *Undo command* reverses one or more of the most recent actions. You can undo an action in one of the three ways:

- Choose Edit, Undo.
- Click the Undo button on the Standard toolbar.
- Press Ctrl+Z.

The Redo command

The *Redo command* reverses one or more of the actions you've recently undone. You can redo an action in one of the three ways:

- Choose Edit, Redo.
- Click the Redo button on the Standard toolbar.
- Press Ctrl+Y.

You can undo or redo several actions at one time by clicking the down arrow next to the Undo or Redo button to display a list recently performed actions. Drag the mouse pointer over the items in the list to select. Keep in mind, when you select from the list, all the actions listed above the one you select will be undone or redone as well.

Do it!

C-4: Using the Undo and Redo commands

Here's how	Here's why
1 Select **Performance**	The title of the fourth slide
Click **B**	Applies bold formatting to the text.
Click ↺	(The Undo button is on the Standard toolbar.) The formatting is undone.
Click ↻	(The Redo button is on the Standard toolbar.) Retains the formatting.
2 Select the left-side text	
Press (DELETE)	Deletes the text.
Undo the delete	Press the Undo button on the Standard toolbar.
3 Update and close the presentation	

Unit summary: Building new presentations

Topic A   In this topic, you learned how to **create a new presentation** by using the **File, New command** and the **New Presentation dialog box**. You also learned how to **enter text** in slides. Next, you learned how to **add slides** to your presentation and **select different slide layouts** from the **New Slide** dialog box. You also learned how to **delete** slides by using the **Delete** key or by choosing **Edit, Delete**.

Topic B   In this topic, you learned how to use the **Formatting toolbar** and how to apply **bold** and **italics** to text. You also learned how to increase the **font type, font size**, change the **font color**, apply **shadow effects**, and change the **background color**. You learned how to **change bullet styles** and **adjust** the **spacing** between bulleted lines. You also learned how to create a **numbered list**. You learned how to **format text** by **changing** the **case**. Finally, you learned how to use the **magnification tools** to **zoom in** and **out** on a slide.

Topic C   In this topic, you learned how to use the **Cut**, and **Paste commands** to **move** text to another slide. You learned how to use the **Copy** and **Paste commands** to copy text to another slide. You learned to **align text** within a slide. Finally, you learned how to use the **Undo** and **Redo commands** to undo and redo the changes made to the slides.

Independent practice activity

1 Create a new Blank Presentation with the title layout.

2 Add the text, as shown in Exhibit 20-9 to the slide.

3 Add a Bulleted List slide and enter text in it, as shown in Exhibit 20-10.

4 Save the presentation as **My practice presentation**. (In the current unit folder.)

5 In the first slide, do the following changes:

   Apply bold format to **Outlander Spices**

   Underline **Progress Report**

6 In the second slide, change the text format to:

   Font: **Arial**

   Font type: **Italics**

   Font size: **36**

7 In the second slide, change the bullet style to the one of your choice.

8 Adjust the Line spacing of the bullets to **1**.

9 Add another Bulleted List slide to the end of the presentation.

10 Create a numbered list in the third slide, as shown in Exhibit 20-11.

11 Change the Font color of the text in the third slide to any shade of blue.

12 Apply shadow effects to the title in the third slide.

13 In the second slide, change the title to Title Case.

14 Zoom the slide to **150%**.

15 Zoom the slide to **50%**.

16 Change the background color of the presentation to a color of your choice. (Hint: In the Background dialog box, click Apply to All.)

17 Insert a bulleted list at the end of the presentation and move the content of the second slide to the last slide.

18 Copy the title from the first slide to the last slide.

19 Change the alignment of the text in the last side to the center.

20 Undo the last action.

21 Update and close the presentation.

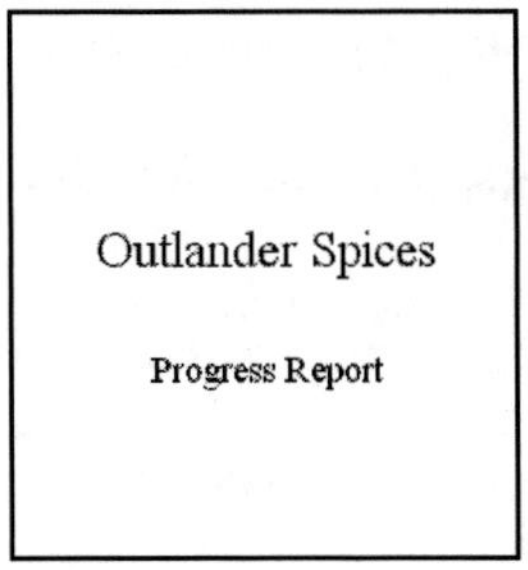

Outlander Spices

Progress Report

Exhibit 20-9: The slide after step 2 of the Independent Practice Activity

Progress to date

• Assembled internal team
• Retained a project management consultant
• Market analysis and research
• Preliminary plans for expansion
• Specifications for successful Web initiative

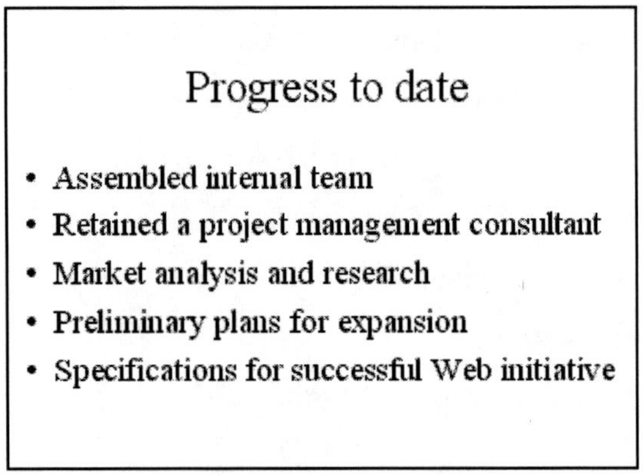

Exhibit 20-10: The slide after step 3 of the Independent Practice Activity

Outstanding issues

1. Selecting internal service provider
2. Identifying stores in East and Midwest markets
3. Building Web site
4. Creating a sales rollout plan
5. Developing a training program

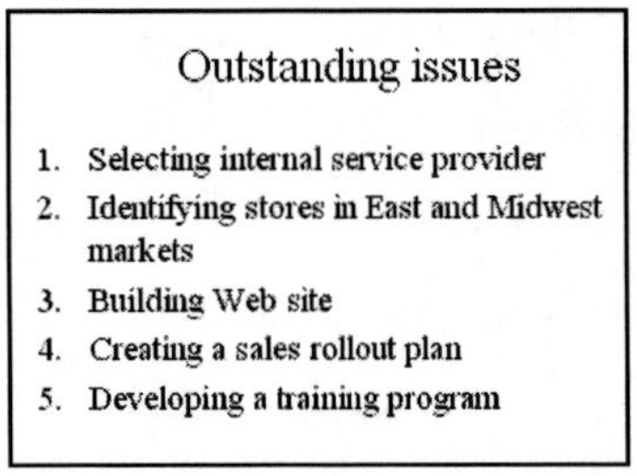

Exhibit 20-11: The slide after step 12 of the Independent Practice Activity

Unit 21

Using drawing tools

Unit time: 60 minutes

Complete this unit, and you'll know how to:

A Create objects by using the Drawing toolbar; and duplicate, move, resize, delete, and align objects.

B Add and format AutoShapes.

C Add and adjust text in objects, and modify the text by using the Formatting toolbar.

D Insert images and clipart, and apply color effects.

Topic A: Drawing objects

Explanation

The use of drawing objects, such as rectangles, ovals, lines, and other shapes, enhances presentations. The tools necessary to create these objects are located on the Drawing toolbar. Once you create an object, you can do any of the following with it:

- Duplicate
- Move
- Resize
- Rotate
- Delete
- Align

The Drawing toolbar

The Drawing toolbar adds AutoShapes, WordArt, and clip art to your presentations. By default, the Drawing toolbar is located above the Status bar. The Drawing toolbar, as shown in Exhibit 21-1, contains buttons to draw and modify objects.

In addition, the toolbar contains options to, order, flip, and rotate objects, as well as move objects in front of or behind each other. You can also apply shadow and 3-D effects to the drawn objects.

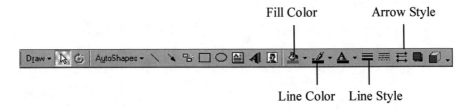

Exhibit 21-1: The Drawing toolbar

To create an object using the Drawing toolbar:

1 Choose a drawing button, such as the rectangle, oval, or line.
2 Point to the location where you want to begin drawing. The pointer changes to a crossbar.
3 Drag until the drawing object reaches the desired size and shape.
4 Release the mouse button, and the object is automatically selected.

Exhibit 21-2 shows the slide that you will be creating in this unit.

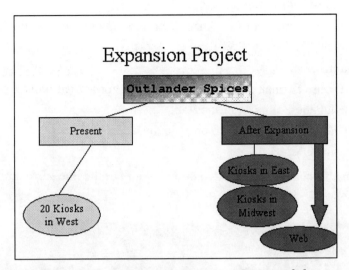

Exhibit 21-2: The completed Expansion Project slide

Drawing a free form line

To draw a free form line:

1 On the Drawing toolbar, click Autoshapes and choose Lines to open a submenu.
2 Select the Scribble tool.
3 Drag on the slide to draw a line.
4 Release the mouse button to stop drawing.

Drawing shapes

You can draw basic shapes like a circle or a square by using the appropriate tools on the Drawing toolbar. To draw a circle, select the Oval tool and place the pointer on the slide. Press and hold the Shift key, and drag to draw the circle. Release Shift and the mouse button to stop drawing.

To draw a square, select the Rectangle tool and place the pointer on the slide. Press and hold the Shift key, and drag to draw the rectangle. Release Shift and the mouse button to stop drawing.

Drawing a text box

To create a custom text box, select the Text Box tool from the Drawing toolbar. Place the pointer on the slide and drag to draw the text box. When you release the mouse button, the text box is placed on the slide and the insertion point is ready for you to add text.

Using the Fill Color

Fill the objects with color to enhance your presentation. By default, a fill color is applied to all objects you create.

To add a fill color:

1 Choose Format, AutoShape to open the Format AutoShape dialog box.
2 Click the Colors and Lines tab.
3 Under Fill, select the color from the Color list.
4 Click OK.

You can also change the style, color, and width of the line surrounding the object by using the Line Color and Line Style lists.

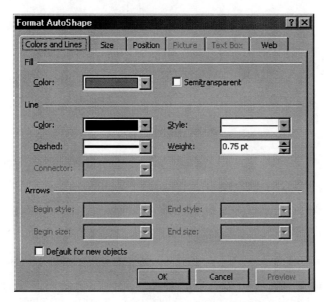

Exhibit 21-3: The Colors and Lines tab of the Format AutoShape dialog box

Change the order of objects

When objects overlap, you might want to change the order in which they appear. For example, let's say you have two objects on a slide, an image of a plate and an image of an apple. The images overlap so that the plate is on top of the apple, and you want to switch them. To bring the apple image to the front, select the the object you want to move (in this case, select the apple). If the object is hidden, press Tab or Shift+Tab until it's selected. On the Drawing toolbar, choose Draw, Order, Bring to Front.

There are also three other options available in the Order submenu. Depending on how you want to change the order of the selected object(s), you can also choose Send to Back, Bring Forward, or Send Backward.

Do it!

A-1: Using the drawing tools

Here's how	Here's why
1 Open Expansion project	From the current unit folder.
2 Click ▢	The Rectangle button is on the Drawing toolbar.
Move the pointer inside the slide	The pointer changes to a crossbar.
Drag to create a rectangle as shown	

Expansion Project

3 Select the rectangle	(If necessary.) To change the default fill color.
4 Choose **Format, AutoShape...**	The Format AutoShape dialog box, as shown in Exhibit 21-3, opens.
Verify that the Colors and Lines tab is active	
Under Fill, click the drop-down arrow	The color palette appears.
From the palette, select Pale Blue as shown	

No Fill

Automatic

More Colors...
Fill Effects...
Background

	The rectangle will fill with pale blue color.
Click **OK**	Applies the color and close the dialog box.
5 Observe the rectangle	The rectangle appears in Pale Blue color.

6 Click ⬭ (The Oval button is on the Drawing toolbar.) To draw an oval.

Drag to create an oval as shown

Expansion Project

Open the Format AutoShape dialog box Choose Format, AutoShape.

Under Fill, from the Color palette select **No Fill** Removes the default fill color.

Check **Default for new objects** This option is in the lower-left corner of the dialog box.

7 Click **OK** (The dialog box closes.) The default color no longer appears in the oval.

8 Click ◺ (The Line button is on the Drawing toolbar.) To draw a line.

Create a line as shown

Expansion Project

9 Save the presentation as **My expansion project** In the current unit folder.

Duplicating an object

Explanation

Duplicating an existing object ensures that similar objects are of uniform size and shape. For example, if your presentation contains multiple oval objects, you can make them all the same size by duplicating the original oval.

To duplicate an object, such as a drawn object, choose Edit, Duplicate or press Ctrl+D.

Copying an object between presentations

To copy an object from one slide to another:

1 Select the object.
2 Choose Edit, Copy or press Ctrl+C.
3 Move to the appropriate slide.
4 Choose Edit, Paste or press Ctrl+V.

To copy an object from one presentation to another:

1 Select the object.
2 Choose Edit, Copy or press Ctrl+C.
3 Choose Window and the name of an open presentation.
4 Navigate to the appropriate slide.
5 Choose Edit, Paste or press Ctrl+V.

A-2:   Duplicating objects

Here's how	Here's why
1 Select the rectangle	
Choose **Edit, Duplicate**	Duplicates the selected rectangle.
2 Create another duplicate of the rectangle	(Select the rectangle, if necessary.) Choose Edit, Duplicate.
Observe the slide	The duplicates are placed one after the other on top of the original rectangle.
3 Change the color of both the duplicate rectangles from Pale Blue to No Fill	(Select the rectangles. Choose Format, AutoShape, and then select No Fill.) Removes the color from both the rectangles that you've just created.
4 Select the oval	To create a duplicate of the oval.
Press (CTRL) + **D**	Duplicates the oval.
5 Create three more duplicates of the oval	You should now have five ovals.
6 Duplicate the line four times	You should now have five lines.
Update the presentation	

Moving objects

Explanation

To move or rearrange the objects on a slide:

1 Select the object. Selection handles will appear around it.
2 Point to the edge of the selected object but not to any of the selection handles. The mouse pointer changes to a four-headed arrow.
3 Drag the object to a new position.
4 Release the mouse button.

Moving filled objects

To move a fill object, you have to place the pointer inside the object and not on the object's edges. When you place the pointer inside the object, it changes to a four-headed arrow. You can then drag it to a new position.

Moving an object between presentations

To move an object from one presentation to another:

1 Select the object.
2 Choose Edit, Cut or press Ctrl+X.
3 Choose Window and the name of an open presentation.
4 Navigate to the appropriate slide.
5 Choose Edit, Paste or press Ctrl+V.

Resizing objects

You may want to resize an object after you move it. To do so you would:

1 Select the object. Selection handles will appear around it.
2 Point to a horizontal or vertical selection handle, if you want to increase the width or height of the object. To keep the same proportions while increasing or decreasing the size, press the Shift key.
3 Drag the selection handle until the object reaches the desired size.
4 Release the mouse button.

Do it!

A-3: Moving and resizing objects

Here's how	Here's why
1 Select the last duplicated rectangle	To move the selected rectangle. The small squares around the rectangle resize, move, delete, or duplicate the rectangle.
2 Point to the edge of the rectangle as shown	
Observe the pointer	The pointer changes to a four-headed arrow, which indicates that you can drag to move the selected object.
Drag to reposition the rectangle as shown	
3 Point to the horizontal resize handle as shown	
	The pointer changes to a two-headed arrow.
Drag as shown	
	Increases the width of the rectangle.
4 Select the second copy of the rectangle	To move the duplicate.
Move the rectangle as shown	

5 Select the blue rectangle

   Point inside the rectangle

   To move the blue rectangle.

   Move the rectangle under the text
   Expansion Project, as shown

   Change the color of the rectangle
   from Pale Blue to No Fill

   (Use the Format AutoShape dialog box.)

6 Move the duplicate ovals as
   shown

7 Select the last duplicate line

   To resize and move the line.

   Drag one end of the line to the left
   oval, as shown

   Drag the other end of the line to
   the left rectangle

   Move the other lines as shown

   Update the presentation

Deleting objects

Explanation   You can delete an object that is no longer needed. To delete an object, select the object and press the Delete key.

Do it!   ## A-4:   Deleting an object

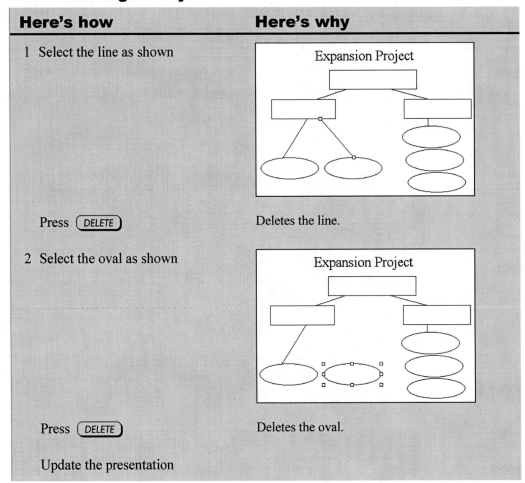

Here's how	Here's why
1 Select the line as shown	
Press (DELETE)	Deletes the line.
2 Select the oval as shown	
Press (DELETE)	Deletes the oval.
Update the presentation	

Aligning objects

Explanation   You can align all or some of the objects on a slide. To align objects:

1 Select the object you want to align.
2 Press the Shift key and select the other objects.
3 Choose Draw, Align or Distribute, and the align option you want.

To align objects in relation to the slide, choose Draw, Align or Distribute, Relative to Slide. Then, select the object(s) and choose Draw, Align or Distribute, and the align option you want.

Adding arrowheads

You can add different types of arrows to your presentation by:

1 Selecting the object to add an arrowhead.
2 Click the Arrow Style button on the Drawing toolbar.
3 Choose the style you want, or click More Arrows to choose a different one.

Do it!   ## A-5:   Aligning objects

Here's how	Here's why
1 Select the rectangle on the left side of the slide	
Press (SHIFT) and select the rectangle on the right side	Aligns these two objects.
Release (SHIFT)	
2 Click **Draw**	The Draw button is on the Drawing toolbar.
Choose **Align or Distribute**, **Align Middle**	
Observe the slide	The two rectangles are aligned.
Deselect the rectangles	
3 Update the presentation	

Topic B: AutoShapes

Explanation

The AutoShapes menu on the Drawing toolbar includes multiple categories of shapes that you can insert directly into a presentation. For example, you can insert a flow chart by using the drawing objects available on the Auto Shapes, Flowchart submenu. After you insert the object, you can resize it or make other formatting changes.

Inserting AutoShape objects

The AutoShapes menu contains submenus of various shape categories. To insert an AutoShape, choose one from the submenus. After you insert a shape you can edit it.

To draw an AutoShape:

1   Click AutoShapes on the Drawing toolbar.

2   Expand a submenu category.

3   Choose an AutoShape from the submenu.

4   Point to where you want to insert the AutoShape; then drag to draw the object.

Applying a shadow to an object

To add a shadow to an object:

1   Select an object.

2   From the Drawing toolbar, click the Shadow tool to open a submenu.

3   From the submenu, select the shadow option of your choice.

To remove the shadow, select the object and click the Shadow tool. From the submenu, choose No Shadow.

Do it!   **B-1:   Using AutoShapes**

Here's how	Here's why
1 Click **AutoShapes**	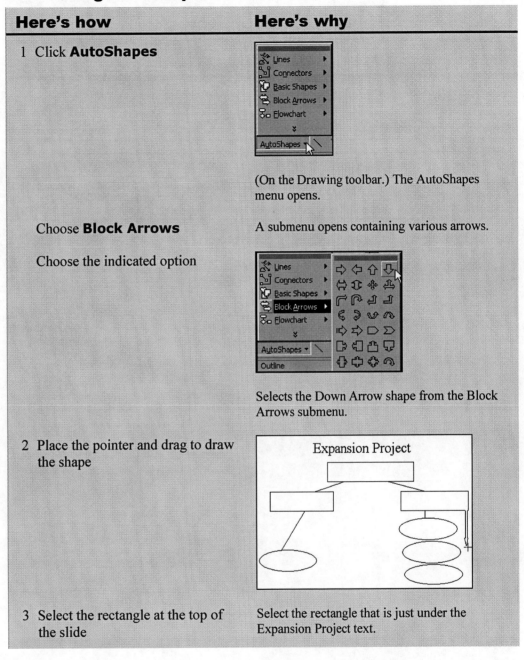
	(On the Drawing toolbar.) The AutoShapes menu opens.
Choose **Block Arrows**	A submenu opens containing various arrows.
Choose the indicated option	
	Selects the Down Arrow shape from the Block Arrows submenu.
2 Place the pointer and drag to draw the shape	
3 Select the rectangle at the top of the slide	Select the rectangle that is just under the Expansion Project text.

4 Click   (Select the Shadow tool from the Drawing toolbar.) To display the submenu.

Select the shadow option as shown

5 Observe the rectangle   It now has the Shadow Style 1 applied to it.

6 Select the Shadow tool

Choose **No Shadow**   To remove the shadow.

7 Update the presentation

Formatting AutoShapes

Explanation

You can change the shape's appearance, after you insert an object. For example, you can resize, add a shadow effect, or rotate the object.

Rotating or flipping

The Rotate Left and Rotate Right commands rotate the object in 90-degree increments. The Free Rotate command allows you to manually rotate the object by dragging the rotation handles. Flipping an object horizontally or vertically actually inverts the object. Any text in the object is also inverted.

To rotate or flip an object you would:

1 Select the object.
2 On the Drawing toolbar, click Draw.
3 Choose Rotate or Flip.
4 Choose the desired option.

B-2: Formatting an AutoShape

Here's how	Here's why
1 Select the down arrow object	(If necessary.) To make changes to the down arrow.
Drag the resize handle horizontally

Increases the width of the block arrow. |
| Drag the resize handle vertically as shown |

Increases the length of the down arrow. |
2 Click **Draw**	
Choose **Rotate or Flip, Rotate Left**	
Observe the down arrow	Notice that the arrow turns towards its left.
3 Rotate it back to its original position	Click Draw. Choose Rotate or Flip, Rotate Right
Update the presentation	

Topic C: Working with text in objects

Explanation

The addition of text provides information about the object. After you add text, you can modify the text and adjust it to fit within the object.

Adding text to objects

When you add text to an object, the text becomes part of the object and moves along with it. If you resize the object, the text is not automatically resized.

By default the text you add to an object is centered. You can change the text to be either right or left aligned.

Do it!

C-1: Adding text to an object

Here's how	Here's why
1 Select the rectangle on the top	(Located under the Expansion Project text.) You'll add text to it.
2 Type **Outlander Spices**	
Observe the rectangle	The text is centered within the rectangle.
3 Select the left rectangle	To add text to the left rectangle.
Type **Present**	
4 In the right rectangle, type **After Expansion**	Select the rectangle and type the text.
5 In the left oval, type **20 Kiosks in West**	Select the oval and type the text.
Observe the text in the oval	The text flows outside the oval's boundaries.
Update the presentation	

Adjusting text in objects

Explanation

The text you enter in an object does not automatically move to the next line when it reaches the edge of the object. The text is written outside the object's boundaries. To fit text within an object, you can either resize the object or wrap the text to fit.

The word-wrap feature adjusts text so that when it reaches the border, the text moves to the next line.

To wrap text in an object:

1   Select the object.

2   Choose Format, AutoShape to open the Format AutoShape dialog box.

3   Click the Text Box tab.

4   Check Word wrap text in AutoShape.

5   Check Resize AutoShape to fit text.

6   Click OK.

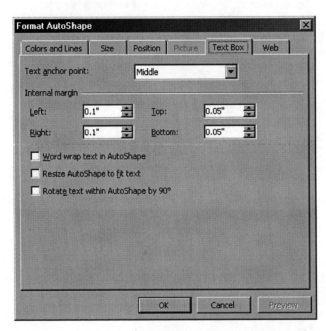

Exhibit 21-4: The Text Box tab of the Format AutoShape dialog box

Do it! **C-2: Adjusting text in an object**

Here's how	Here's why
1 Select the left oval or the text inside it	(If necessary.) You can select either one for text wrap.
2 Choose **Format, AutoShape...**	The Format AutoShape dialog box opens.
Click the **Text Box** tab	The Text Box tab appears, as shown in Exhibit 21-4.
Check **Word wrap text in AutoShape**	Wraps text in the object.
3 Check **Resize AutoShape to fit text**	Resizes the object so that it accommodates the text.
Click **OK**	

Applies the settings. The text wraps, and the object resize to fit the text.

4 Add text to the other ovals as shown

Wrap text wherever necessary

5 Update the presentation

Modifying text in objects

Explanation

You can modify the text to improve the look of your presentation. You can make any of the following changes using the Formatting toolbar:

- Bold
- Italic
- Underline
- Color
- Font type
- Font size

Do it!

C-3: Modifying text in an object

Here's how	Here's why
1 Select Outlander Spices	To highlight this text.
Click **B**	Makes the text bold.
From the Font list, select **Courier New**	Changes the font style.
From the Font Size list, select **28**	Increases the font size.
2 Increase the width of the rectangle	If necessary.
Update the presentation	

Topic D: Working with graphics

Explanation

The addition of images or clip art, such as company building, photographs of employees or meetings, and celebrations, can make your presentation more meaningful and appealing. You can also increase their visual appeal by changing their color.

Inserting images

To add an image:

1   Choose Insert, Picture, From File to open the Insert Picture dialog box.
2   Select a picture.
3   Click Insert.

Do it!

D-1:   Inserting an image

Here's how	Here's why
1 Insert a new slide with a Blank layout	Choose Insert, New Slide.
2 Choose **Insert**, **Picture**, **From File...**	Opens the Insert Picture dialog box.
Select **SpicePicture**	(From the current unit folder.) To add this image to the slide.
Click **Insert**	The image appears on the slide.
3 Deselect the image	Click anywhere on the slide.
Update the presentation	

Adding color effects

Explanation

You can apply various color effects by using the Image Control button on the Picture toolbar. This button includes the following list of effects:

- Black & White
- Grayscale
- Watermark

To apply a color effect to an image:

1 Select the image.
2 Click the Image Control button on the Picture toolbar, as shown in Exhibit 21-5.
3 Apply the relevant effect to the image.

Image Control

Exhibit 21-5: The Picture toolbar

Do it!

D-2: Applying color effects

Here's how	Here's why
1 Select the image	To change the appearance of this image.
Click ▦	The Image Control button is on the Picture toolbar.
Choose **Grayscale**	Changes the appearance of the image from color to grayscale.
2 Deselect the image	
Update the presentation	

Adding clip art

Explanation

Clip art is another way to enhance the visual impact of your presentation. Clip art images are stored in PowerPoint's Clip Art Gallery. You can access additional clip art images on the Web.

To add clip art to a slide:

1 Choose New Slide from the Insert menu.
2 Select an AutoLayout that accepts clip art. AutoLayouts that accept clip art show a picture of a person's head.
3 Click OK.
4 Double-click the clip art icon in the content placeholder.
5 Select a clip art image you want to add, from the Microsoft Clip Gallery.
6 Click the Insert clip button.

You can also open the Clip Gallery by choosing Insert, Picture, Clip Art.

Do it!

D-3:   Inserting clip art

Here's how	Here's why
1 Insert a third slide with Clip Art & Text layout	 **Click to add title** • Click to add text Double click to add clip art
Double-click the clip art icon	The Microsoft Clip Gallery opens.
2 Under Categories 1-51, select **Business**	View the various graphics available in Business category.
Select the indicated image	
	Click the graphic to select it.
From the pop-up menu, choose as shown	
	This is the Insert clip button.
Observe the slide	The clip art you selected appears in the clip art placeholder. The Picture toolbar appears.
3 Click the title placeholder, type **Annual Revenue**	Enters the title.
4 Click the bullet placeholder, type **Meeting our goals**	
Deselect the bullet placeholder	
Observe the slide	The slide contains a title, clip art, and a bulleted item.
5 Update and close the presentation	

Unit summary: Using drawing tools

Topic A
In this topic, you learned how to insert **drawing objects** by using the **Drawing toolbar**. You learned how to **duplicate objects**. You learned how to **move** and **resize objects**. You learned how to **delete an object**. Finally, you learned how to **align** one or more objects on a slide.

Topic B
In this topic, you learned how to insert **AutoShapes using the Drawing toolbar**. You also learned how to **format** the AutoShapes by **rotating or flipping** it.

Topic C
In this topic, you learned how to **add text** to objects. You learned how to **adjust text** within an object so the **line wraps**. You learned how to modify text using the **Formatting toolbar**.

Topic D
In this topic, you learned how to **insert** an **image** in a slide. You learned how to apply **color effects** to the image. You also learned how to **insert clip art** from the Clip Art Gallery.

Independent practice activity

1 Create a new presentation with a blank slide layout.

2 Select the Horizontal Scroll AutoShape. (From the Stars and Banners submenu.)

3 Drag to draw the AutoShape on the slide as shown in Exhibit 21-6.

4 Change the fill color to **No Fill**.

5 Make no fill the default for all new objects.

6 Add **Explosion 2** and **5-Point Star** AutoShapes (from the Stars and Banners submenu), as shown in Exhibit 21-6.

7 Use the Drawing toolbar to draw an oval, as shown in Exhibit 21-6.

8 Add text to objects, as shown in Exhibit 21-6.

9 Wrap the text and resize objects wherever necessary.

10 Make the Web initiatives text bold. Set the font size to **32**.

11 Add different fill colors to the objects.

12 Compare your work to Exhibit 21-7.

13 Insert a new slide with Clip Art & Text layout.

14 Insert the first clip from the Communications category.

15 Add **Communication** as the title and **Letters** as the bulleted item to the slide.

16 Save the presentation as **My drawing** in the current unit folder.

17 Close the presentation.

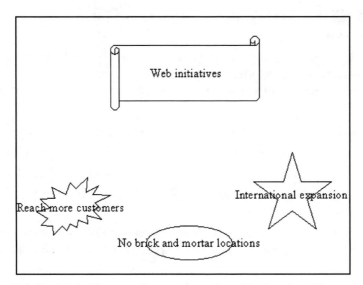

Exhibit 21-6: The text that needs to be added to AutoShapes in step 8 of the Independent Practice Activity

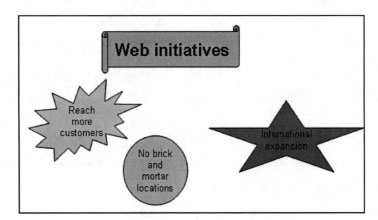

Exhibit 21-7: The slide after step 11 of the Independent Practice Activity

Unit 22

Modifying presentations

Unit time: 60 minutes

Complete this unit, and you'll know how to:

A Create a presentation based on a template and apply a template to an existing presentation.

B Identify the elements of the slide master, modify the slide master, add and delete a picture in the master, and add text to the footer.

C Set transitions and timings, animate objects, reorder animation effects, setup a slide show, create a custom slide show, hide and unhide slides.

D Customize the toolbar and use the options dialog box.

E Add notes to a presentation and add headers and footers to notes.

Topic A: Using templates

Explanation

PowerPoint presentations are based on *templates*. A template contains pre-designed formats to build presentations. The formats include color schemes, slide masters, and title masters that provide a consistent look for a presentation.

PowerPoint comes with a wide variety of professionally designed templates. The appearance of a presentation changes by applying a template. After applying a template, each new slide you add to the presentation will have the same customized look.

To create a new presentation based on a blank template:

1　Choose File, New.
2　Select Blank Presentation and click OK. You can also modify an existing template to suit your requirements.

Creating a presentation based on a template

To create a new presentation based on a template:

1　Choose File, New to open the New Presentation dialog box.
2　Click Design Templates, in the New Presentation dialog box.
3　Select a template, from the list.
4　Click OK.

You can also apply a different design template to an existing presentation.

Do it!

A-1:   Creating a presentation based on a template

Here's how	Here's why
1 Choose **File, New...**	The New Presentation dialog box appears.
Click the **Design Templates** tab	Various design templates that can be used for your presentation appear.
Select **Bold Stripes**	Notice the preview of the design template in the Preview area.
Click **OK**	Opens the New Slide dialog box.
2 Click **OK**	Selects the default AutoLayout for the first slide in your presentation.
Observe the slide	The slide has the selected template applied to it. Notice that the first slide in a presentation is the Title Slide, by default.
3 In the title placeholder, type **Outlander Spices**	Select the title placeholder and start typing.
4 Insert a new Bulleted List slide	The new slide has the same design template applied to it.
5 Save the presentation as **My design**	In the current unit folder.

Applying a design template to an existing presentation

Explanation

When you apply a design template to an existing presentation, PowerPoint automatically updates the text styles, graphics, and color scheme for the entire presentation.

To apply a design template to an existing presentation:

1 Open the presentation.
2 On the Formatting toolbar, click Common Tasks.
3 Choose Apply Design Template, from the menu.
4 Select a design template from the list.
5 Click Apply.

You can also change the design template by choosing Format, Apply Design Template.

Do it!

A-2: Applying a design template to an existing presentation

Here's how	Here's why
1 Click **Common Tasks**	(On the Formatting toolbar.) A submenu appears.
Choose **Apply Design Template...**	The Apply Design Template dialog box opens.
From the list, select **Blends**	
Click **Apply**	Applies the template to your presentation.
2 Scroll through and observe the presentation	Notice that the entire presentation has been updated with the design template you selected.
3 Update the presentation	

Topic B: Working with the slide master

Explanation

All presentations have a slide master that controls:

- Text characteristics
- Background color
- Shadowing
- Bullet styles
- Headers and footers

If you change the formatting in the slide master, the formatting for the entire presentation is affected.

Elements of a slide master

The *Master Title Area* of the slide master controls the following in the title object area:

- Font type
- Font size
- Font color
- Font style
- Alignment of text

The *Master Object Area* controls the very same elements for the text object area.

You can add background items to the slide master, such as the date and time, slide numbers, stamps, company logos, and borders. These items, if added to the master, will appear on every slide.

To display the slide master, as shown in Exhibit 22-1, choose View, Master, and Slide Master. This view is also called the *Master view* and includes the Master Toolbar.

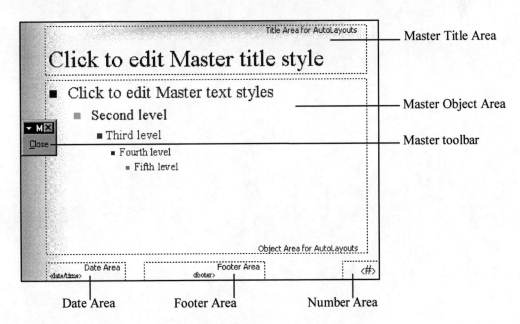

Exhibit 22-1: The elements of the slide master

Do it!

B-1: Examining the elements of a slide master

Here's how	Here's why
1 Choose **View**, **Master**, **Slide Master**	(To display the slide master.) The Master toolbar appears.
2 Observe the Master Title Area	The Master Title Area controls the formatting of the title placeholder on the slide.
Observe the Master Object Area	The Master Object Area controls the formatting of the text object area on the slide.
Observe the Date Area	The Date Area controls the formatting of the date and time.
Observe the Footer Area	The Footer Area controls the formatting of the footer.
Observe the Number Area	The Number Area controls the formatting of the slide numbers.

Changing the slide master

Explanation

When you want a format to be applied throughout the presentation, you don't have to make the change on every slide of the presentation. You can modify the entire presentation by changing the format in the slide master. For example, you might want all the bulleted lists in the presentation to be Arial Black with a font size of 24. To reflect this change throughout the presentation, change the font style and font size in the Master Object Area.

Other elements you can modify in the Master Object Area include:

- Text formatting
- Bullet style
- Line spacing

To change the master slide format:

1 Open the Slide master and select the Master Title Area.
2 Change the font type, size, or color.
3 Select the Master Object Area.
4 Change the font type, size, or color.
5 Change the bullet style.
6 Switch to Normal view.
7 Update the presentation.

Do it!

B-2:   Modifying the slide master

Here's how	Here's why
1 Select the Master Title Area	
2 From the Font list, select **Arial**	(On the Formatting toolbar.) Changes the font of the title. Notice that the font for the title has changed.
From the Font Size list, select **40**	(On the Formatting toolbar.) Changes the font size of the title. Notice that the font size has changed.
3 Select the Master Object Area	
From the Font list, select **Courier New**	(Changes the font of the text.) Notice that the font for the text has changed.
From the Font Size list, select **32**	The font size has changes.
4 Select the first line of text	To format the text.
5 Choose **Format, Bullets and Numbering...**	Displays the Bullets and Numbering dialog box.
Verify that the Bulleted tab is active	
Select as shown	Changes the shape of the first level bullet style.
Click **OK**	To return to the Slide master.
Observe the Master Object Area	The shape of the first level bullet has changed.

```
> Click to edit Master text
  styles
  ■ Second level
     ■ Third level
        ■ Fourth level
          ■ Fifth level
```

6 Select the second line of text

Open the Bullets and Numbering | Choose Format, Bullets and Numbering.
dialog box

Select as shown

Click **OK** | To return to the Slide master.

7 Click **Close** | (On the Master toolbar.) To switch to Normal View.

8 In the Bulleted List slide, enter as shown

Observe the second slide | Notice that the shape of the bullets for both the first and second levels has changed.

9 Insert a Bulleted List slide

Enter as shown

10 Update the presentation

Adding and deleting a picture from the slide master

Explanation

You can add graphic elements to a slide master. For example, you might want every slide to contain the company's logo. Instead of manually placing a logo in every slide, you can modify the slide master to contain the logo. To add a picture to a slide master:

1 Choose Insert, Picture, From File.

2 Select a picture of your choice from the Insert Picture dialog box.

3 Click Insert to insert the picture to the slide master.

You can delete a picture from the slide master by selecting the picture and pressing the Delete key.

Do it!

B-3:   Adding and deleting a picture from the slide master

Here's how	Here's why
1 Switch to the slide master view	Choose View, Master, and Slide Master.
2 Choose **Insert**, **Picture**, **From File...**	To open the Insert Picture dialog box.
Observe the Files of type list	By default, this dialog box displays a list of all picture files stored in the selected folder.
Select **SpicePicture**	(From the current unit folder.) Notice that a preview of the selected picture appears on the right side of the dialog box.
Click **Insert**	(To insert the graphic into the slide master.) The Picture toolbar appears.
3 Drag the graphic to the upper right corner of the slide	
4 Click **Close**	(On the Master toolbar.) To switch to the Normal view.
Scroll through and observe the presentation	Notice that the picture has been added to all the bulleted slides in the presentation.
5 Switch to the slide master view	Choose View, Master, and Slide Master.
Select the picture	
Press ⟨ DELETE ⟩	To delete the picture.

6	Click **Close**	(On the Master toolbar.) To switch to the Normal view.
	Scroll through and observe the presentation	The picture has been deleted from the presentation.
7	Update the presentation	

Adding footers to the slide master

Explanation   You can use *footers* at the bottom of each slide to display information common to the entire presentation, such as:

- Date and time
- Slide or page number
- Occasion for the presentation
- Company name
- Copyright information

The footer information in the slide master displays across all bulleted slides. To add a footer to the slide master you would:

1   Switch to the slide master view.

2   Place the insertion point in the Date Area.

3   Choose Insert, Date and Time and select a date format from the Date and Time dialog box. Check the Update automatically box to automatically update the date information on all slides.

4   Place the insertion point in the Footer Area.

5   Enter text in the Footer text box.

6   Place the insertion point in the Number Area.

7   Choose Slide number.

The footer information is visible by choosing View, Header and Footer. The Header and Footer dialog box, as shown in Exhibit 22-2, includes the option of displaying the information in one or all slides.

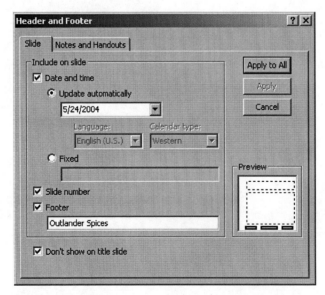

Exhibit 22-2: The Header and Footer dialog box

Adding footers to specific slides

To apply footer information, such as slide numbers and dates, to specific slides, select the specific slides in before choosing View, Header and Footer.

Do it!

B-4:   Adding text to the footer

Here's how	Here's why
1 Switch to the slide master view	
2 In the Date Area, select **<date/time>**	
Choose **Insert, Date and Time...**	The Date and Time dialog box appears.
From the Available formats list, select as shown	Available formats: 10/24/2003 Friday, October 24, 2003 24 October 2003 October 24, 2003
	You will see the current date as an example for the formats.
Click **Cancel**	(To Close the Date and Time dialog box.) You'll insert the date another way..
3 Choose **View, Header and Footer...**	Displays the Header and Footer dialog box. There are options to include the date, slide number, and text in the header and footer area
4 Verify that the Slide tab is active	
Under Include on slide, check **Date and time**	If necessary.
Select **Update automatically**	Displays the current date.
Check **Slide number**	Displays the number of the slide.
Check **Footer**	If necessary.
In the Footer box, type **Outlander Spices**	To specify a footer.
Check **Don't show on title slide**	You don't want the footer to appear on the title slide.
5 Click **Apply to All**	Applies the Header and Footer settings to all the bulleted slides in the presentation.
6 Click **Close**	(On the Master toolbar.) To switch to the Normal view.
Scroll down and observe the slides	The footer information is visible on the bulleted slides.
7 Update and close the presentation	

Topic C: Working with slide shows

Explanation   Setup a slide show presentation to view slides in succession. Slide show presentations include, in addition to the slides, any special effects, such as transitions and animations.

Transitions are special effects that can be used, for example, to indicate a new section or to emphasize a certain slide. There are a variety of transitions to choose from.

You can also set timings for your presentation, so that you can run a slide show without using your mouse or keyboard. Each slide displays automatically at specified time intervals.

Moving and copying slides

Before setting the transitions and timings, you need to make sure the slides are in the correct order. If you need to move a slide, the easiest way to do it is in Slide Sorter view. Once in Slide Sorter view, select the slide you want to move. Drag the slide to its new location and release the mouse button.

To copy a slide:

1   In Slide Sorter view, select the slide or slides you want to copy.

2   Choose Edit, Copy or press Ctrl+C.

3   Determine where you want the copied slide to go. Once you've determined that location, select the slide in front of it.

4   Choose Edit, Paste or press Ctrl+V.

To copy a slide from one presentation to another:

1   In Slide Sorter view, select the slide or slides you want to copy.

2   Choose Edit, Copy or press Ctrl+C.

3   Choose Window, and the name of the open presentation.

3   Determine where you want the copied slide to go. Once you've determined that location, select the slide in front of it.

4   Choose Edit, Paste or press Ctrl+V.

To move a slide from one presentation to another:

1   In Slide Sorter view, select the slide or slides you want to copy.

2   Choose Edit, Cut or press Ctrl+X.

3   Choose Window, and the name of the open presentation.

3   Determine where you want the copied slide to go. Once you've determined that location, select the slide in front of it.

4   Choose Edit, Paste or press Ctrl+V.

Setting transition effects and timings

You can apply different transition effects to each slide, or you can set the same transition effect for all slides. To set a transition:

1   Select the slide in either Normal or Slide Sorter view.
2   Choose Slide Show, Slide Transition to open the Slide Transition dialog box.
3   Select the transition option.
4   Click Apply to set the transition effect for one slide or Apply to All to set the transition effect for all slides.

Set timings for a slide show

Timings are useful when you want the audience to spend more time reading a specific slide. You can set timings manually for each slide, and then run the slide show to review them. To set the timings for a slide show:

1   Select a slide.
2   Choose Slide Show, Slide Transition to open the Slide Transition dialog box as shown in Exhibit 22-3.
3   Under Advance, check Automatically after.
4   In the Automatically after box, enter 00:04.
5   Click Apply to set timings for one slide or Apply to All to set timings for all slides in the presentation.

Exhibit 22-3: The Slide Transition dialog box

Do it!

C-1: Setting transitions and timings

Here's how	Here's why
1 Open Training	From the current unit folder.
2 Switch to the Slide Sorter view	
3 Select the first slide	If necessary.
Choose **Slide Show**, **Slide Transition...**	Display the Slide Transition dialog box, as shown in Exhibit 22-3.
Under Effect from the list, select **Blinds Vertical**	Notice the preview of the effect in the Effect box.
Select **Medium**	Change the speed at which the transition occurs.
4 Under Advance, check **Automatically after**	
In the Automatically after box, enter **00:04**	Set the timing to four seconds between slides. You can use the spinner controls or your keyboard to enter the time interval.
5 Under Sound, from the list, select **Applause**	
Click **Apply**	Add the specified transition effect to the first slide.
Observe the slide	

The Transition icon appears under slide 1.

6 Click 🖼	View the Blinds Vertical transition and hear the applause.
7 Open the Slide Transition dialog box	Choose Slide Show, Slide Transition.
Under Effect from the list, select **Box In**	Notice the preview of the effect in the Effect box.
Select **Medium**	(If necessary.) Change the speed at which the transition occurs.
Click **Apply to All**	Apply the transition effects to the entire presentation. ·

8 Click 🖳	(In the bottom left pane of the window.) Watch the slide show. Notice that the Box In effect occurs on all slides during transition.
Switch to Normal view	
9 Save as **My training**	In the current unit folder.

Animations

Explanation

Animation effects include the illusion of movement on a slide. For example, you can have bulleted items displayed one at a time or "fly in" from any side of the slide.

Presetting Animations

The Preset Animation option provides an easy way of using the animation effects, but you don't have control over the timing.

Custom Animations

A custom animation enables you to add animations, control timings, and synchronize all effects. You can add animation effects to a single object or multiple objects. For example, you can animate bulleted text to appear one letter at a time, one word at a time, or one paragraph at a time. You can also specify the order and timing of animations. For example, you can set the animations to occur automatically at regular intervals or only after you click the mouse. After you define the custom animation, preview it to see how it plays. To set custom animations:

- Choose Slide Show, Custom Animation to open the Custom Animation dialog box as shown in Exhibit 22-4.
- Click Effects.
- Under the Entry animation and sound box, in the first list, choose an animation effect of your choice, say Fly.
- Click OK to close the dialog box.

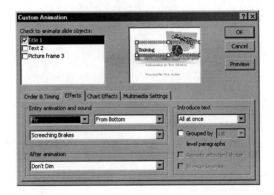

Exhibit 22-4: The Custom Animation dialog box

Do it!

C-2:   Animating objects

Here's how	Here's why
1 Move to the title slide	(If necessary.) To apply animation effects to the objects in this slide.
2 Choose **Slide Show, Custom Animation...**	Open the Custom Animation dialog box as shown in Exhibit 22-4.
Under Check to animate slide objects, check **Title 1**	Apply animation effects to the title.
Click the **Effects** tab	If necessary.
Under Entry animation and sound, select as shown	
Under Entry animation and sound, select as shown	
3 Click the **Order & Timing** tab	To set timing for the animation.
Under the Start animation, select **Automatically**	If necessary.
In the Automatically box, enter **00:02**	Sets timing for the animation.
4 Activate the Effects tab	To apply animation effects on Text 2.
Under Check to animate slide objects, check **Text 2**	
Select **Blinds**	From the first list under the Entry animation and sound group.
Select **Vertical**	From the second list under the Entry animation and sound group.
Select **Whoosh**	(From the third list under the Entry animation and sound group.) Add a sound effect to the animation.

5 Under After animation, select as shown

After animation

☐ Follow Title Text Scheme Color

More Colors...
Don't Dim
Hide After Animation
Hide on Next Mouse Click

Change the color of the text to blue after animation.

6 Click the **Order & Timing** tab

To set the timing for Text 2.

Under the Start animation, select **Automatically**

If necessary.

Set the timing of the animation to **00:02**

(If necessary.) Enter 00:02 in the Automatically box from the Click Order & Timing tab.

7 Under Check to animate slide objects, check **Picture frame 3**

To set an animation effect to the picture.

8 Activate the Effects tab

Select **Checkerboard**

From the first list under the Entry animation and sound group.

Set the timing of the animation to **00:02**

(If necessary.) Enter 00:02 in the Automatically box in the Order & Timing tab.

9 Click **Preview**

Preview the animation effects on the slide.

Click **OK**

Closes the Custom Animation dialog box.

10 Run the slide show

Choose View, Slide Show.

11 Update the presentation

Organizing animation effects

Explanation

A slide consists of a title, a bulleted list, and graphics. You can reorder animation effects to change the display sequence. You may want to order the sequence so the graphic appears first, followed by the title and then the bulleted list. For example, running a business presentation, you can have the company's logo appear first, followed by the title and then the text.

To reorder the effects:

1 Click the Orders & Timing tab in the Custom Animation dialog box.
2 Click the Up or Down arrow buttons.

Do it!

C-3:   Reordering the effects in a slide

Here's how	Here's why
1 Open the Custom Animation dialog box	Choose Slide Show, Custom Animation.
2 Activate the Order & Timing tab	If necessary.
From the Animation order list, select **Picture frame 3**	
Click ⬆ twice	Rearranges the animation so that the picture object is the first to be animated.
3 From the Animation order list, select **Text 2**	
Click ⬆	Animate the text object after animating the picture.
4 Click **Preview**	Preview the reordered animation effects.
Click **OK**	Close the Custom Animation dialog box.
5 Click 🖵	Run the presentation and notice the effects on the Title Slide. Notice that the picture appears first followed by the text and the title.
6 Update the presentation	

Setting up slide shows

Explanation

There are multiple options for running a presentation. You can set up slide shows for different audience and situations, such as a kiosk, at trade show. For such situations, you can use the various options in the Set Up Show dialog box.

To set up a slide show:

1 Choose Slide Show, Set Up Show to open the Set Up Show dialog box, as shown in Exhibit 22-5.
2 Under Show type, select the option(s) of your choice.
3 Under Slides, select the range of slides you want to include in the slide show.
4 Under Advance slides, select the options for controlling the pace of the presentation.
5 Click OK.

Slide shows for speakers

A speaker can narrate a presentation while advancing slides automatically or manually, and he can take time to handle queries. To set up a slide show for a speaker you would:

1 Choose Slide Show, Set Up Show to open the Set Up Show dialog box.
2 Under Show type, select Presented by a speaker (full screen).
3 Under Slides, select the range of slides you want to include in the slide show.
4 Under Advance slides, select the options for controlling the pace of the presentation.
5 Click OK.

Setting slide shows for kiosks

You can customize slide shows to run on a kiosk or for a situation like a convention. In this type of situation, you need to consider several things:

- Will a person be there to monitor the kiosk?
- Will you use transition effects in your presentation?
- Should the user be given control of the slide show?

To set up a slide show for a kiosk:

1 Choose Slide Show, Set Up Show to open the Set Up Show dialog box.
2 Under Show type, select Browsed at a kiosk (full screen.)
3 Under Slides, select the range of slides you want to include in the slide show.
4 Under Advance slides, select the options for controlling the pace of the presentation.
5 Click OK.

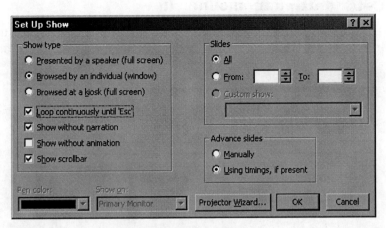

Exhibit 22-5: The Set Up Show dialog box

Do it!

C-4: Setting up a slide show

Here's how	Here's why
1 Move to the first slide	(If necessary.) Set up a slide show for this presentation.
2 Choose **Slide Show, Set Up Show...**	Open the Set Up Show dialog box.
3 Under Show type, select **Browsed by an individual (window)**	
Observe the dialog box	The Show scrollbar option is checked automatically and the Pen color option is no longer available.
4 Check **Loop continuously until 'Esc'**	Specify that the presentation should run continuously until the user presses the Esc key.
5 Check **Show without narration**	Run the slide show without narration.
Under Slides, verify that All is selected.	This setting means that the entire presentation will be displayed during the slide show.
Under Advance slides, verify that Using timings, if present is selected	With this setting, the slide show will advance according to the specified timings.
6 Click **OK**	Apply the settings and close the dialog box.
7 Run the presentation	Click the Slide Show button on the bottom left corner of the window.
Observe the screen	Notice that the presentation runs within the PowerPoint window rather than in Full Screen view. You can navigate the slide show by using the scroll bar. Also, the Web toolbar is visible.
Press (ESC)	Stops the slide show loop and switch to Normal view.
8 Open the Setup Show dialog box	Choose Slide Show, Set Up Show.
Select **Presented by a speaker (full screen)**	
Clear **Loop continuously until 'Esc'**	

9	Click **OK**	Closes the Set Up Slide Show dialog box.
10	Run the presentation	Click the Slide Show button on the bottom left corner of the window.
	Observe the screen	Notice that the presentation runs within the Full Screen view and stops after running the presentation once.
11	Update the presentation	

Creating custom slide shows

Explanation   You can create a custom slide show, for instances such as including only a few slides in
your presentation. You can create multiple custom shows with different names and run
them when needed.

To create a custom slide show:

1   Choose Slide Show, Custom Shows to open the Custom Shows dialog box as
shown in Exhibit 22-6.

2   Click the New button to open the Define Custom Show dialog box as shown in
Exhibit 22-7.

3   Enter a name for the custom slide show, in the Slide show name box.

4   Select a slide you want to include in the custom slide show, from the Slides in
presentation list, and then click the Add button. Repeat this step for each
additional slide you want to include.

5   Click OK to close the Define Custom show dialog box.

6   Click Show to close the Custom Shows dialog box and run the custom slide
show.

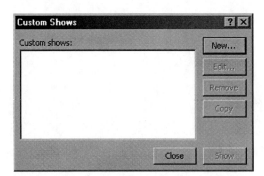

Exhibit 22-6: The Custom Show dialog box

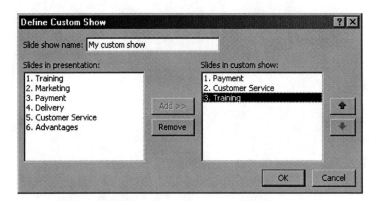

Exhibit 22-7: The Define Custom Show dialog box

Do it!

C-5: Creating a custom slide show

Here's how	Here's why
1 Choose **Slide Show, Custom Shows...**	Opens the Custom Shows dialog box. Create a custom show based on this presentation.
Observe the dialog box	Notice that only the New and Close buttons are active, as shown in Exhibit 22-6. This is because there are no existing custom shows to edit, remove, copy, or show.
2 Click **New**	Opens the Define Custom Show dialog box.
In the Slide show name box, type **Customized show**	This will be the name of the custom show.
From the Slides in presentation list, select **4. Delivery**	To add this slide to your custom show.
Click **Add**	Add the fourth slide to your custom show.
Add slides 5 and 6 to the custom show	Select the slides and click the Add button.
3 Click **OK**	Closes the Define Custom Show dialog box.
Observe the dialog box	Notice that all the buttons are now active.
4 Click **Show**	Runs the presentation.
5 Update the presentation	

Hiding and unhiding slides

Explanation

Some slides you may want to hide during the slide presentation. For example, you may not want to show the information contained in a slide to a particular audience. So, rather than deleting the slide from the presentation, you can hide it.

To hide a slide:

1 Select it and choose Slide Show, Hide Slide or click the Hide Slide button on the Slide Sorter toolbar.

The Hide Slide button works as a toggle. When you want to show a hidden slide again, select the slide and click the Hide Slide button.

Do it!

C-6: Hiding and unhiding slides

Here's how	Here's why
1 Click 🔲	
2 Select the third slide	To hide this slide.
Click 🔲	The Hide Slide button is on the Slide Sorter toolbar.
Observe the slide	The Hide Slide icon appears under the slide. Notice the line drawn through the slide number.
3 Select the first slide	To begin the slide show from the first slide.
Click 🔲	Runs the presentation.
Move through the presentation	Notice that the third slide, titled Payment, doesn't appear in the slide show.
4 Select the third slide	
Click 🔲	Unhide the third slide.
5 Switch to Normal View	
6 Update the presentation	

Topic D: Customizing the environment

Explanation

When you create a blank presentation, the toolbars that display are:

- Standard
- Formatting
- Drawing

You can customize these toolbars to suit your preference, or you can create your own toolbar. You can also customize other environmental settings through the Options dialog box.

Customizing toolbars

You can customize toolbars by removing buttons you don't use very often and adding buttons that you do use. For example, you might find that you duplicate objects frequently, so you decide to add the Duplicate button to the Drawing toolbar.

To customize a toolbar:

1. Choose Tools, Customize to open the Customize dialog box, as shown in Exhibit 22-8.
2. In the Toolbars tab, notice the toolbars that are checked. To display a toolbar, you check the toolbar.
3. Click the Commands tab to see options.
4. From the Categories list, select the category to display the associated commands.
5. From the Commands list, drag the command to the toolbar.
6. Close the Customize dialog box.

Exhibit 22-8: The Commands tab of the Customize dialog box

Do it!

D-1: Customizing a toolbar

Here's how	Here's why
1 Choose **Tools**, **Customize...**	Opens the Customize dialog box.
2 Click the **Commands** tab	If necessary.
From the Categories list, select **Edit**	View the commands within the Edit category.
From the Commands list, select **Clear**	Add this button to the toolbar.
Drag the button to the Standard toolbar as shown	
	Notice that the shape of the pointer changes.
Observe the toolbar	Notice that the Clear button is added to the Standard toolbar.
3 Click **Close**	Closes the Customize dialog box.

The Options dialog box

Explanation

You can modify default settings, such as the default file location, by using the Options dialog box. To open the Options dialog box, as shown in Exhibit 22-9, choose Tools, Options. The Options dialog box contains various tabs, to customize features.

Exhibit 22-9: The Save tab of the Options dialog box

The following table describes the functions of each tab:

Tab	Description
View	Modify the view options when building or running presentations. For example, show or hide status bar when building a presentation, or show popup menu button when running a presentation.
General	Specify general options. For example, you can check the Recently used file list to view the recently used files on the File menu.
Edit	Control the way text appears in a presentation. For example, you can check the Use smart cut and paste option under the Text options to remove extra spaces as you cut text from a presentation.
Print	Specify how presentations are to be printed. For example, you can select Background Printing so that presentations print in the background while you continue working on your presentation.
Save	Determines how presentations are saved. For example, you can choose to save your presentation in a preferred file format. You can also set the Default file location.
Spelling and Style	Adjust the settings for spell check. For example, select the Check Spelling as you type option to highlight misspelled words with red underlines.

Do it!

D-2: Using the Options dialog box

Here's how	Here's why
1 Choose **Tools**, **Options...**	Opens the Options dialog box.
2 Click the **General** tab	
Under User information, edit the Name box to read **Susan Gianni**	Sets the user name to Susan Gianni.
Under User information, edit the Initials box to read **SG**	Set initials as SG.
3 Click the **Save** tab	
Check **Save AutoRecover info every**	(If necessary.) Creates a file that can be automatically recovered in case there is a problem with the document you are working on
In the minutes box, enter **2**	Saves your document every two minutes.
Verify that in the Save PowerPoint files as list, PowerPoint Presentation is selected	Saves the file as a PowerPoint presentation.
4 Click **OK**	Closes the Options dialog box.
5 Update the presentation	

Topic E: Adding speaker notes and footers

Explanation

Every slide includes a notes page, which contains the slide image and space for speaker notes. The presenter can use the speaker notes as a reference tool, and can also print them to distribute to the audience.

You can add speaker notes in:

- Normal view
- Outline view
- Notes Page

The *notes master* controls the format of the notes page. Enter any formatting changes in the Master Object Area.

Adding speaker notes

To add speaker notes to a slide:

1 Click the Notes pane for the slide on which you want to add speaker notes.
2 Enter the text.
3 Choose View, Notes Page to view the notes page as shown in Exhibit 22-10.

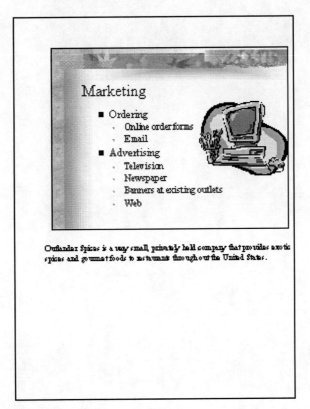

Exhibit 22-10: The notes page

Do it!

E-1: Adding speaker notes

Here's how	Here's why
1 Move to the first slide	If necessary.
2 Place the insertion point in the Notes pane	(It is below the slide.) To enter text in this pane.
Enter the text as shown	Outlander Spices is a very small, privately held company that provides exotic spices and gourmet foods to restaurants throughout the United States.
3 Move to the fourth slide	The slide is titled "Delivery."
Enter text in the Notes pane as shown	The project team is made up of six internal employees and four outside consultants.
4 Choose **View**, **Notes Page**	View the slide with the notes.
5 Click 🔲	Switches back to Normal view.
6 Update the presentation	

Adding headers and footers to speaker notes

Explanation

You might want to include the date and company name on the speaker notes. The *header* in the notes page view is the text that appears at the top of each page, and the *footer* refers to the text that appears at the bottom.

To add headers and footers to speaker notes:

1 Choose View, Header and Footer.

1 Click the Notes and Handouts tab, as shown in Exhibit 22-11.

2 Select the options of your choice.

3 In the Header box, enter the text you want to display in the header.

4 In the Footer text box, enter the text you want to display in the footer.

5 Click Apply to All.

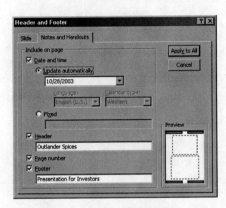

Exhibit 22-11: The Header and Footer dialog box

Do it!

E-2: Adding headers and footers to notes

Here's how	Here's why
1 Open the Header and Footer dialog box	Choose View, Header and Footer.
2 Click the **Notes and Handouts** tab	The various options on the tab appear.
Under Include on page, check **Date and Time**	If necessary.
Select **Update automatically**	Displays the current date.
3 Check **Header**	If necessary.
In the Header box, enter **Outlander Spices**	
4 Check **Page number**	(If necessary.) Inserts page numbers.
5 Check **Footer**	(If necessary.) Displays the footer.
In the box under Footer, enter **Presentation for Investors**	
6 Click **Apply to All**	Applies the new settings to all the notes in the presentation.
7 Choose **View, Notes Page**	
Observe the Notes page	Notice the footer in the lower left corner of the Notes page.
Scroll through the list	Notice that the header and footer have been applied to all pages.
8 Click 🔲	Switches back to Normal view.
9 Update and close the presentation	

Unit summary: Modifying presentations

Topic A   In this topic, you learned how to **create a presentation** based on a design template. You also learned how to **apply a design template** to an existing presentation.

Topic B   In this topic, you learned about the various **elements** of a **slide master**. You learned how to **modify** the slide master. You also learned how to **add** and **remove** a **picture** from the slide master. Finally, you learned how to **add footer** to a slide master.

Topic C   In this topic, you learned how to **add transition effects** and **timings** to an individual slide and to an entire presentation. You learned how to **animate** specific **objects** on a slide and **customize** the **animation** by setting specific **time intervals** and **sound effects** on them. Next, you learned how to **reorder** the **animation effects**. You learned how to **setup** a **slide show** to deliver a presentation. You learned how to **customize** slide shows. Finally, you learned how to **hide** and **unhide** slides.

Topic D   In this topic, you learned how to **customize** the **environment** by **modifying toolbars**. You also learned how to use the **Options dialog box** to modify the default settings.

Topic E   In this topic, you learned how to **add speaker notes** to slides. You also learned how to add **headers** and **footers** to the **notes page**.

Independent practice activity

1 Open Progress To Date.

2 Apply a design template of your choice to the presentation.

3 Switch to the Slide Master view.

4 Change the font of the Master Title Area to **Verdana**.

5 Change the font of the Master Object Area to **Arial Narrow** and change the font size to **32**.

6 Change the **bullet style** of the Master Object Area to the one of your choice.

7 Switch to Normal View.

8 Add Outlander Spices as the **footer** of the presentation.

9 Insert a Title Only slide to the end of the presentation.

10 Insert the image **Spices** from the current unit folder to the newly inserted slide.

11 Move to the second slide.

12 Open the Custom Animation dialog box.

13 Add an animation effect of your choice to the **title** and **text** of the **second slide**.

14 Set the animation timings to be **2 seconds**.

15 Reorder the animation effects such that the animation for the text appears before the animation for the title.

16 Preview the animation.

17 Close the Custom Animation dialog box.

18 Add transition effects of your choice across the presentation.

19 Save the presentation as **My progress to date**.

20 Add speaker notes to slides **2** and **3** containing the following text "Identifying milestones for the next phase."

21 Switch to Slide Sorter view.

22 Hide slides **3** and **5** and run the presentation.

23 Set up the slide show so that it is **looped** continuously.

24 Run the presentation.

25 Create a custom show containing slides **1**, **2**, and **4**.

26 Save the custom show as **My customized show**.

27 Execute **My customized show**.

28 End the custom show.

29 Update and close the presentation.

Unit 23

Charts

Unit time: 30 minutes

Complete this unit, and you'll know how to:

A Create and format a chart.

B Create, add levels, and format an organization chart.

Topic A: Creating and modifying charts

Explanation

Charts are the graphical representations of numeric data. A program called Microsoft Graph includes various chart types and multiple formatting options for creating charts.

Creating a chart

You can use any of the following methods to create a chart:

- Add a slide with Chart AutoLayout.
- Choose Insert, Chart.
- Click the Insert Chart button on the Standard toolbar.

When you use any of these methods, Microsoft Graph opens and displays two windows:

- Datasheet window
- Chart window

The Datasheet window contains sample data, and the chart window displays the data in graphical form.

When you insert a chart into a slide, the menu bar displays additional menu options. One of these options determines the chart type. There are fourteen kinds of chart types available, such as Column, Bar, Pie, and Line. By default, the Column chart type is selected.

The Datasheet and Chart window

The Datasheet window, as shown in Exhibit 23-1, contains the chart data. This window contains the row (legend) and column (series) headings, which are the dark boxes located to the left of the rows and above the columns. The cells of the datasheet contain values that form the basis for the chart.

To modify a chart, select a cell and type data. You can also edit the row headings to change the legend and edit the column headings to change the series label.

As you make changes or add data to the datasheet, the chart is automatically updated in the Chart window.

Column heading

My chart - Datasheet		A	B	C	D	E
		1st Qtr	2nd Qtr	3rd Qtr	4th Qtr	
1	East	20.4	27.4	90	20.4	
2	West	30.6	38.6	34.6	31.6	
3	North	45.9	46.9	45	43.9	
4						

Row heading

Legend

Exhibit 23-1: A sample Datasheet window

Moving and copying a chart

Explanation   Once a chart is created, you can duplicate it by choosing Edit, Duplicate or pressing Ctrl+D.

You can also copy and paste a chart to another slide:

1   Select the chart.

2   Choose Edit, Copy or press Ctrl+C.

3   Move to another slide.

4   Choose Edit, Paste or press Ctrl+V.

This same method applies when moving a chart. The only change is instead of using the copy command, you choose Edit, Cut or press Ctrl+X.

To copy a chart to another presentation:

1   Select the chart.

2   Choose Edit, Copy or press Ctrl+C.

3   Choose Window and the name of an open presentation.

4   Navigate to the appropriate slide.

5   Choose Edit, Paste or press Ctrl+V.

This same method applies when moving a chart from one presentation to another. The only change is instead of using the copy command, you choose Edit, Cut or press Ctrl+X.

Deleting a chart

You can delete a chart that is no longer needed. To delete a chart, select it and press the Delete key.

Do it!

A-1: Using Microsoft Graph

Here's how	Here's why
1 Create a new blank presentation	
2 Select the Chart AutoLayout	
Click **OK**	Adds a chart layout slide to your presentation.
3 In the title placeholder, type **Comparison Chart**	This will be the slide's title.
4 Double-click the chart icon	
Observe the screen	By default, sample data and its corresponding chart are included.
Observe the menu bar	File Edit View Insert Format Tools Data Chart Window Help
	The menu bar shows additional options for working with charts and datasheets.
Observe the pointer	It changes to a plus sign when you move it over the datasheet.
5 In the Datasheet, click **A**	The entire column is selected.
Click **1**	The entire row is selected.
Click **East**	Selects the cell.
Replace East with **Outlander Spices**	Change the row heading.
6 Press ⬇	Move to the next row.
Observe the Chart window	
Replace West with **Competitors**	
7 Click **3**	

		1st Qtr	2nd Qtr	3rd Qtr	4th Qtr
1	Outlander Spices	20.4	27.4	90	20.4
2	Competitors	30.6	38.6	34.6	31.6
3	North	45.9	46.9	45	43.9

	(Selects the entire row.) To delete the data in this row.
Press (DELETE)	Deletes the data in this row.

8   Replace the column headings as
shown

		A	B	C	D
Presentation1 - Datasheet					
		Price	Inventory turnover	Cost	Profit

9   Select cell A1   To change text in this cell under the Price
                                           column heading.

Enter **25**

10 Press ⬇   Move to cell A2.

Enter **30**

11 Select cell B1   To enter text under Inventory turnover.

Enter **60**

12 Replace the values in other cells
as shown

	Price	Inventory turnover	Cost	Profit
Outlander Spices	25	60	35	70
Competitors	30	40	50	30

Observe the chart   The default chart automatically updates to
                                           display the data in graphical form.

13 Save the presentation as   In the current unit folder.
My chart

Formatting charts

Explanation   Modify the default chart by changing the formatting. Within Microsoft Graph, you can format each individual item, or you can format the entire chart area. The chart area consists of four items, as shown in Exhibit 23-2.

- Plot area
- Legend
- Value axis
- Category axis

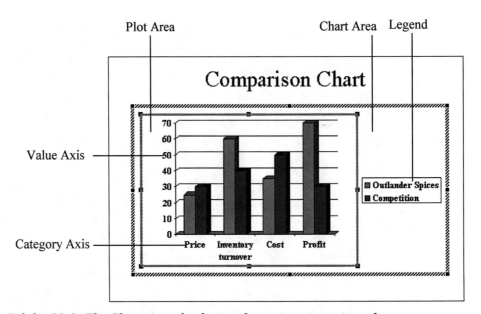

Exhibit 23-2: The Chart Area displaying the various items in a chart

Using the Format menu

When you select a chart item, the selected item becomes the first command in the Format menu. For example, when you select the plot area, the first command in the Format menu becomes the Selected Plot Area. The *plot area* contains the chart along with the two axes. To format any chart item you would:

1   Select the item.
2   Choose the first command from the Format menu. You can also change the color; add borders and a shadow to the area.

Using the Chart menu

Another way to format the chart is by choosing Chart, Chart Options. The Chart Options dialog box contains tabs for formatting, as shown in Exhibit 23-3.

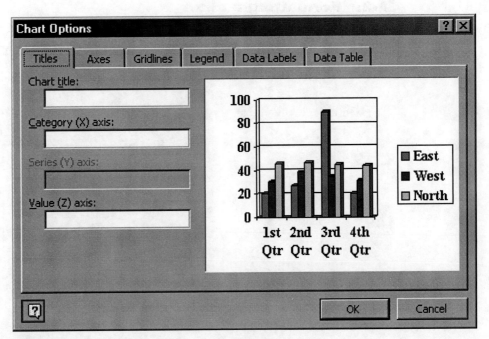

Exhibit 23-3: The Chart Options dialog box

You can also duplicate, move or delete a chart just like you would any object.

Resizing a chart

You may want to resize a chart. To do so you would:

1 Select the entire chart. Selection handles will appear around it.
2 Point to a horizontal or vertical selection handle, if you want to increase the width or height of the object. To keep the same proportions while increasing or decreasing the size, press the Shift key.
3 Drag the selection handle until the object reaches the desired size.
4 Release the mouse button.

Do it!

A-2: Formatting a chart

Here's how	Here's why
1 Click [icon]	(The View Datasheet button is on the Standard toolbar.) Closes the datasheet.
2 Observe the menu bar	The Chart menu is now available.
3 Click the **Plot Area** as shown	
Choose **Chart, Chart Options...**	The Chart Options dialog box opens.
Click the **Gridlines** tab	
Under Value (Z) axis, clear **Major gridlines**	To clear the gridlines from the plot area.
Click **OK**	The gridlines clear.
4 Click any blue bar	
	Selects the Competitors series.
Choose **Format, Selected Data Series...**	The Format Data Series dialog box opens.
Under Area, from the color palette, select yellow	To change the column color to yellow.
Click **OK**	Applies the color.

5 Change the color of Outlander Spices series to red	Select one of the columns for the Outlander Spices series and choose red from the color palette.
Observe the chart	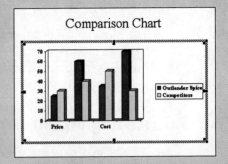
	The colors of both series have changed.
6 Choose **Chart**, **Chart Type...**	The Chart Type dialog box opens.
Observe the dialog box	It displays various Chart types and Chart sub-types.
From the Chart type list, select as shown	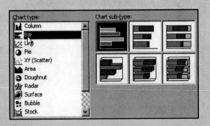
	Change the chart type from Column to Bar.
Click **OK**	Applies the new chart type.
Observe the chart	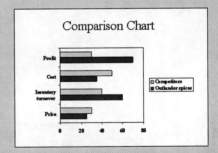
	The chart has changed to a bar chart.
7 Deselect the chart	
Update the presentation	

Topic B: Creating and modifying organization charts

Explanation

The hierarchical details of your company can be displayed by using organization charts. You can modify the default organization charts to accommodate your standard, and in instances of complex organizational changes, you can modify charts to add additional levels.

Adding organization charts

To add an organization chart to a presentation:

1 Insert a new slide.
2 Choose the Organization Chart AutoLayout from the New Slide dialog box.
3 Double-click the organization chart icon to display the Microsoft Organization Chart window, as shown in Exhibit 23-4.

The window has its own menu and toolbar. It displays a chart template containing several boxes, by default; the template shows two levels of boxes. The topmost box is level 1 and the boxes directly below it are level 2.

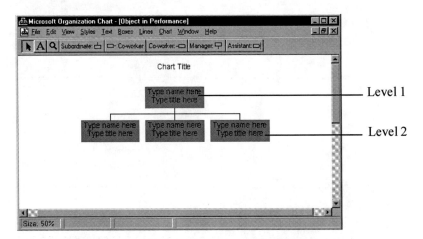

Exhibit 23-4: The Microsoft Organization Chart window

Each box in the chart has its own field labels. *Field labels* are placeholders for names, titles, and comments. Enter text into a box by selecting the box and typing over the field labels.

Do it!

B-1: Adding an organization chart

Here's how	Here's why
1 Insert a new slide with a Organization Chart AutoLayout	
2 In the title placeholder, type **The project team**	This will be the title of the slide.

3 Double-click the organization chart placeholder	Opens the Microsoft Organization Chart window.
Observe the window	By default, first box is selected. Add text to the box.
4 In the Type name here field label, type **Kathy Sinclair**	This will be the name of the project leader.
Press (↵ ENTER)	Notice the next field label is highlighted.
5 In the Type title here field label, type **Project Mgt. Consultant**	This will be the title of the project leader.
Press (↵ ENTER)	
6 In the Comment 1 field label, enter **(External)**	This will be the comment in the box.
Deselect the box	
7 Select the first box at level 2	To add text to it.
Add text as shown	

Add text to other boxes as shown

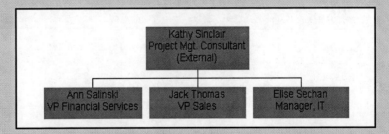

8 Choose **File**, **Update My chart**	Adds the organization chart to the slide in the presentation.
Choose **File**, **Close and Return to My chart**	Return to the slide.
Observe the slide	The text that you added to the chart appears on the slide.
Update the presentation	

Adding levels to organization charts

Explanation

An organization chart, by default, has two levels. If you want to add more levels, just add more boxes. The chart window contains a toolbar with buttons for adding boxes at different levels. Box levels include the following:

- Subordinate
- Left Co-worker
- Right Co-worker
- Manager
- Assistant

To add a box:

1   Click the appropriate button.
2   Click inside the box where you want the new one to attach.

For example, if you want to add a Subordinate box to the second box at level 2, click the Subordinate button, and then click inside the box. This creates the third level of the chart, as shown in Exhibit 23-5.

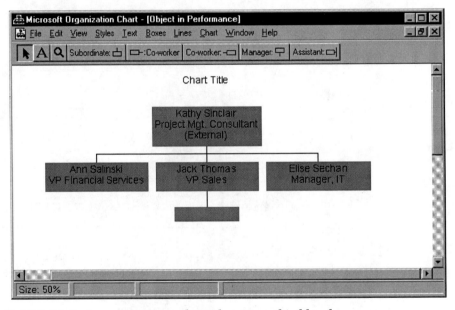

Exhibit 23-5: An organization chart showing a third level

If you need to remove a box, select it and press delete.

Do it!

B-2:   Adding levels to an organization chart

Here's how	Here's why
1 Double-click the chart placeholder	Opens the Microsoft Organization Chart window.
2 Select as shown	Subordinate: 凸
	To add a subordinate box.
Click inside the second box at level 2	Adds a subordinate box to Jack Thomas.
Observe the chart	There is a box at level 3, as shown in Exhibit 23-5.
3 Select as shown	Co-worker: ⊣▢
Add the co-worker to the first box at level 3	Now there are two boxes at the third level.
4 Add levels to the chart as shown	

5 Update the chart	Choose File, Update My chart.
Close the window	Click the Close button.
Update the presentation	

Modifying organization charts

Explanation

You can modify an organization chart by:

- Adding borders
- Adding colors
- Adding shadows
- Changing the font
- Changing font color
- Changing alignment of the text

If you want to apply the same formatting to multiple boxes you would:

1 Select boxes by holding down the Shift key while clicking each one.
2 Select the required formatting options.

Do it!

B-3: Modifying an organization chart

Here's how	Here's why
1 Double-click the chart	
2 Verify that the box in level 1 is selected	To change the color of the box.
Choose **Boxes, Color...**	Opens the Color dialog box.
From the Color palette, select the red color	To apply a red color to the box.
Click **OK**	Applies the color.
3 Select **Kathy Sinclair**	To change the font type of the name.
Choose **Text, Font...**	Opens the Font dialog box.
From the Font list, select **Arial Black**	
Click **OK**	The font type changes.
4 Update the chart and return to the presentation	
Update and close the presentation	

Unit summary: Charts

Topic A
In this topic, you learned how to create a **chart** using the **Microsoft Graph**. You also learned how to **format** the chart using the **Chart Options** dialog box.

Topic B
In this topic, you learned how to create an **organization chart** using the **Microsoft Organization Chart** window. You learned how to **add** and **remove** levels to the organization chart. You also learned how to **modify** the organization chart by applying **formatting**.

Independent practice activity

1 Open Sales from the current unit folder.

2 Add a new slide containing a chart AutoLayout.

3 Replace the row headings with the text in the first column in the datasheet, as shown in Exhibit 23-6.

4 Replace all values in the datasheet, as shown in Exhibit 23-6.

5 Save the presentation as **My Sales**.

6 Add a new slide containing an Organization Chart AutoLayout.

7 Add boxes to the chart, as shown in Exhibit 23-7.

8 Add text to all boxes, as shown in Exhibit 23-8.

9 Observe the chart. Your chart should have all the text that you entered.

10 Update and close the presentation.

		A	B	C	D	E
		1st Qtr	2nd Qtr	3rd Qtr	4th Qtr	
1	Cumin	30	35	45	30	
2	Thyme	50	65	80	60	
3	Oregano	85	55	60	75	
4						

Exhibit 23-6: The Sales datasheet

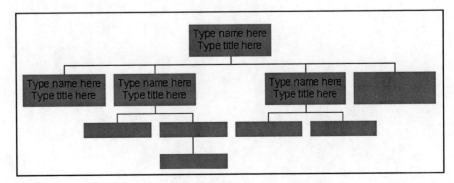

Exhibit 23-7: The organization chart with additional boxes

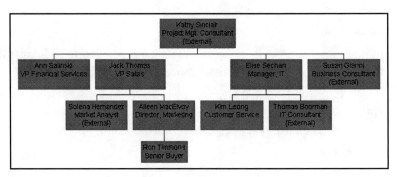

Exhibit 23-8: The complete organization chart

Unit 24

Proofing and delivering presentations

Unit time: 40 minutes

Complete this unit, and you'll know how to:

A Check the spelling and style consistency in a presentation.

B Print an entire presentation, an individual slide, handouts, and notes pages.

Topic A: Proofing presentations

Explanation

You can easily check for spelling errors by using the spelling checker. Along the same line, you can check for inconsistencies in style by using the style checker.

The Spelling dialog box

When you misspell a word, it is underlined, by default, in red. Correct any misspellings by using the Spelling dialog box, as shown in Exhibit 24-1. To open the Spelling dialog box, you can do any of the following:

- Choose Tools, Spelling.
- Press F7.
- Click the Spelling button on the Standard toolbar.

You can check for spelling errors from either Normal, Outline, or Slide view.

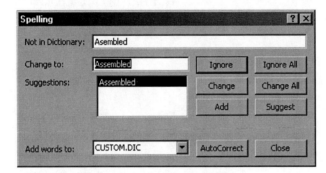

Exhibit 24-1: The Spelling dialog box

Do it!

A-1: Checking the spelling in a presentation

Here's how	Here's why
1 Open Presentation	(From the current unit folder.) To check the spelling in the entire presentation.
2 Choose **Tools, Spelling...**	Opens the Spelling dialog box.
Observe the window	Notice the sixth slide. This is the first slide with incorrect spelling. The incorrectly spelled words are underlined in red as well as highlighted.
Observe the dialog box	Notice the options to correct the spelling, as shown in Exhibit 24-1.
3 Click **Change**	Notice that the misspelled word "asembled" has changed to "assembled." Now, the text "mangement" is selected.
4 Change the spelling	Click Change to enter the correct spelling of "management."
Click **Close**	Closes the dialog box.
5 Press (F7)	The Spelling dialog box opens. Continue checking spelling by using the shortcut key.
Change the spelling	(Notice the word "service" misspelled in the seventh slide.) Click Change in the Spelling dialog box to enter the correct spelling of "service."
Close the dialog box	
6 Click [ABC]	(On the Standard toolbar.) Opens the Spelling dialog box. The word "Developing" has been misspelled in the seventh slide.
Change the spelling	A message box appears, indicating that the spelling check is complete.
Click **OK**	Closes the message box.
7 Save the presentation as **My presentation**	

The style checker

Explanation

A presentation with multiple slides could have minor variations in style. You may not notice these variations, but your audience could.

To check your presentation for style consistency, use the style checker. The style checker scans your presentation and highlights potential style problems using a light bulb icon. You have the choice to ignore or correct these problems. The light bulb is available only if you turn on the Office Assistant.

Do it!

A-2: Using the style checker

Here's how	Here's why
1 Choose **Tools, Options...**	The Options dialog box opens.
Click the **Spelling and Style** tab	If necessary.
Under Style, check **Check style**	If necessary.
2 Click **Style Options**	(The Style Options dialog box opens.) To change the style options.
Under Case, check **Slide title style**	If necessary.
Verify that Title Case appears in the list	
Click **OK**	The Style Options dialog box closes.
3 Click **OK**	The Options dialog box closes.
4 Move to the first slide of the presentation	To check the style of the presentation.
5 Choose **Help, Show the Office Assistant**	Shows the Office Assistant.
Observe the slide	A light bulb appears.
6 Click the light bulb	The Office Assistant displays various style options.
Select **Change the text to title case**	
Observe the title	It has changed from "Outlander spices" to "Outlander Spices."
7 Move to the next slide	Check the style of the rest of the slides.

8	Select **Change the text to title case**	Click the light bulb and select Change the text to title case.
9	Change the title style for the rest of the slides	
10	Right-click the Office Assistant	You'll hide the Office Assistant.
	Choose **Options...**	The Office Assistant dialog box opens.
	Clear **Use the Office Assistant**	Hides the Office Assistant.
	Click **OK**	The Office Assistant dialog box closes.
11	Update the presentation	

Topic B: Printing presentations

Explanation

PowerPoint has multiple options for printing a presentation. When printing, you can choose to print an entire presentation or an individual slide. You can also print handouts or notes pages.

Modifying page setup

You can print slides in a variety of formats. Presentation's page setup determines the size and orientation of the printed output. The *size* refers to the size of the slide on a printed page, and *orientation* refers to whether the pages are set as portrait (8.5" × 11") or landscape (11" × 8.5"). The default settings for any new presentation are for an on-screen slide show with landscape orientation. The slide numbering begins with 1. Handouts, outlines, and notes print in portrait orientation by default. You can change these settings in the Page Setup dialog box, as shown in Exhibit 24-2.

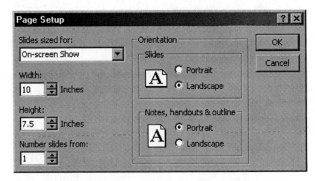

Exhibit 24-2: The Page Setup dialog box

To change the page setup for slides you would:

1. Choose File, Page Setup to open the Page Setup dialog box.
2. From the Slides sized for list, select the format of your choice.
3. Under orientation, select an orientation (Portrait or Landscape) for the slides and the other components of the presentation.
4. Click OK.

Slide size format options

The following table describes the available size options in the Slides sized for list:

Format	Description
On-screen Show	This is the default setting. Use it when designing a presentation you plan to show on-screen. The slides are sized smaller than a standard sheet of paper.
Letter Paper (8.5×11 in)	Prints the presentation on standard U.S. letter stock (8.5" × 11").
A4 Paper (210×297 mm)	Prints the presentation on an international letter stock (210 mm × 297 mm).
35mm Slides	Adapts the presentation to 35mm slides.
Overhead	Prints your slides on overhead transparency stock (8.5" × 11").
Banner	Adjusts the slide size to create an 8" × 1" banner when printed.
Custom	Adjusts the slide size to accommodate special sizing needs.

Do it!

B-1:   Modifying the page setup

Here's how	Here's why
1 Choose **File**, **Page Setup...**	(Opens the Page Setup dialog box.) To change the page setup of the presentation.
From the Slides sized for list, select **A4 Paper (210x297mm)**	Set the paper size.
Under Slides, select **Portrait**	Notice that the Width and Height fields change automatically.
Verify that the Number slides from box reads 1	To apply the page setup from slide 1 onwards.
Click **OK**	(Closes the Page Setup dialog box.) The change in page setup is reflected in the slide on the screen.
2 Press ⌐CTRL⌐ + Z	Undo the last step and restore the default page setup.

Printing entire presentations

Explanation To open the Print dialog box, as shown in Exhibit 24-3, choose File, Print. Use this dialog box to specify:

- Printer
- Range of slides
- Number of copies

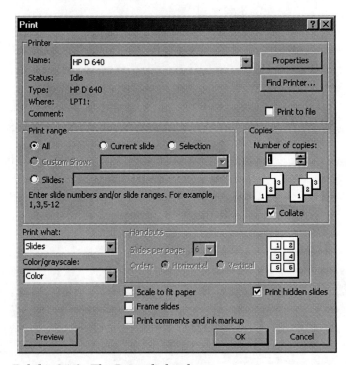

Exhibit 24-3: The Print dialog box

The Print button, located on the Standard toolbar, prints a presentation without using the Print dialog box. The entire active presentation prints to the current printer using the default settings.

Do it!

B-2: Printing a presentation

Here's how	Here's why
1 Choose **File, Print...**	The Print dialog box displays, as shown in Exhibit 24-3.
Observe the Print range options	If you have a multiple slide presentation, you can choose to print a specific range. By default, All is selected.
Observe the Print what options	Notice that Slides is selected.
Observe the Copies options	Print multiple copies, collated or not.
Click **OK**	Print the entire presentation using all the current settings.
2 Update the presentation	

Printing individual slides

Explanation

To print an individual slide:
1 Select the slide you want to print.
2 Open the Print dialog box.
3 Select Current slide (under Print range).
4 Specify the number of copies of that slide that you want to print.

Do it!

B-3: Printing an individual slide

Here's how	Here's why
1 Select the first slide	If necessary.
2 Press (CTRL) +**P**	(This is the shortcut key for the File, Print command.) The Print dialog box appears.
Under Print range, select **Current slide**	Print only the first slide.
Click **OK**	Print the slide using all the current settings.
3 Update the presentation	

Print output options

Explanation

PowerPoint provides several print output options. You can print:

- Slides
- Audience handouts
- Speaker notes
- Presentation outline

Use the Print what list to specify the type of output you want to create.

Audience handouts

Audience handouts print a number of slides on one page. You can choose to print a maximum of nine slides on a handout. When you're deciding how many slides to include, consider the readability of the handout. If you include too many slides with text, the handouts might be difficult for your audience to read.

To print audience handouts:

1   Choose File, Print.

2   Select Handouts, from the Print what list.

- Under Handouts, select how many Slides per page.
- Under Handouts, select the Order of the slides.
- At the bottom of the dialog box, check Grayscale to print the handouts without color. Check Pure black and white to print the handouts in only black and white, no gray. Check Scale to fit paper if you are using a custom sized slide or a paper size other than 8.5" by 11".

3   Select the number of slides you want to include from the Slides per page list.

4   Click OK.

Presentation outlines

The printed outline shows your content as it appears on screen in the Outline tab. For example, if your outline is completely collapsed, only the slide titles will print in the outline. If your outline is fully expanded, everything will print.

To print an outline of a presentation:

1   Choose File, Print.

2   Select Outline View, from the Print what list.

- At the bottom of the dialog box, check Grayscale to print the outline without color.
- Check Pure black and white to print the outline in only black and white, no gray.
- Check Scale to fit paper if you are using a paper size other than 8.5" by 11".

3   Click OK.

Speaker notes

Each page of speaker notes includes a small version of the associated slide. This helps keep track of your progress as you deliver your presentation.

To print speaker notes:

1 Choose File, Print.

2 Select Notes Pages, from the Print what list.

3 Select Slides, under Print range.

- At the bottom of the dialog box, check Grayscale to print the notes pages without color.

- Check Pure black and white to print the notes pages in only black and white, no gray.

- Check Scale to fit paper if you are using a paper size other than 8.5" by 11".

- Check Frame slides to add a frame around each slide.

4 Enter the slide range, in the Slides box. For example, you can print the speaker notes for slides 1, 2, 3, 4, and 7 by entering "1-4, 7."

5 Click OK.

Do it!

B-4: Printing handouts and notes

Here's how	Here's why
1 Open the Print dialog box	(Choose File, Print.) You'll print the handouts of the presentation.
2 From the Print range options, select **All**	If necessary.
3 From the Print what list, select **Handouts**	Print the presentation handouts.
Observe the Handouts options	You can specify how many slides you want to print on a single page.
4 Click **OK**	Print the handouts for the presentation using all the current settings.
5 Open the Print dialog box	(Choose File, Print.) You'll now print the notes pages of the presentation.
6 From the Print what list, select **Notes Pages**	Print the speaker notes for your presentation.
7 Click **OK**	Print the notes pages using all the current settings.
8 Update and close the presentation	

Unit summary: Proofing and delivering presentations

Topic A
In this topic, you learned how to **proof** a **presentation** by using the **spell checker**. You also learned how to use the **style checker** to check the styles used in the presentation.

Topic B
In this topic, you learned how to **modify** the **page setup** so that you can print the presentation in a variety of formats. You learned how to use the **Print dialog box** to **print** the **entire presentation**. You also learned how to print an **individual slide**. Finally, you learned how to print **handouts** and **speaker notes**.

Independent practice activity

1 Open Outstanding issues. (From the current unit folder.)

2 Check the spelling in the entire presentation.

3 Show the Office Assistant.

4 Check the styles in the presentation.

5 Hide the Office Assistant.

6 Save the presentation as **My outstanding issues**.

7 Print the third slide of the presentation in the **Portrait** orientation.

8 Print **handouts** of the presentation.

9 Print **notes pages** of the presentation.

10 Update and close the presentation.

11 Close PowerPoint.

10/23/06

Unit 25

The Internet and Internet Explorer

Unit time: 40 minutes

Complete this unit, and you'll know how to:

A Describe the Internet and the World Wide Web, and discuss Internet addresses.

B Start and navigate in Internet Explorer, and change the browser home page.

C Use Internet Explorer help and Web help.

Topic A: Introducing the Internet

Explanation

The Internet, the World Wide Web, and e-mail have become part of our everyday lives. Many people have computers in their homes for personal research, entertainment, and communication with others. For an increasing number of companies, using the Internet is an important way to conduct business. Internet and e-mail addresses have become commonplace on business cards.

The Internet

The Internet was initially intended to support military research by connecting various computer networks to the U.S. Department of Defense's ARPANET. A *computer network* is a collection of computers connected to each other for the purpose of sharing resources. While the Internet's roots are in government applications, no single organization controls the Internet.

Connecting one network to another network creates an *internetwork.* Connection devices include telephones lines, modems, and cables. Each new network that connects to the Internet can bring thousands of new users. Thus, the Internet is a constantly growing internetwork of global proportions.

The World Wide Web

The *World Wide Web* (*WWW,* or *W3,* or *Web*) is the hypertext storage and retrieval system developed in 1991 by the CERN High-Energy Physics Laboratories in Geneva. CERN's hypertext programming language enabled their physicists to communicate and share research with other scientists.

Often the terms "Internet" and "World Wide Web" are used interchangeably. However, there are differences between the two. The *Internet* refers to the entire network of networks, while the Web provides just one of the ways in which information is exchanged on the Internet. Computer software applications called *Web browsers* (such as Internet Explorer) are used to access Web sites. A *Web site* is a collection of *Web pages,* which can contain text, graphics, animation, sound, and a variety of interactive elements. Web pages are connected by *hyperlinks*. You can move from page to page by clicking these hyperlinks. Links can move you through a large document or take you to another Web site altogether. The act of using links to move from page to page is known as browsing, or "surfing," the Web.

The Web's easy-to-use system has made it the most popular part of the Internet. Because the information on the Web changes constantly, there is always something new to see.

Connecting to the Internet

To connect to the Internet, you'll need the following things:

- A personal computer with a Web browser, such as Internet Explorer. Many Web browsers can be downloaded from the Internet for free.

- Access to a *host computer:* a computer connected to the Internet. The host computer might be maintained by your company or by a commercial Internet service provider (ISP).

- A connection device, such as a modem or a network cable, attached to your computer.

To enhance your Web browsing experience, you might want to have additional equipment such as a color printer, high-quality speakers, media players, and so on.

Internet host computers

You can access the Internet by using an Internet service provider to connect to an Internet host computer. A service provider supplies you with an Internet account that includes a user name and password, which enable you to access the host computer. There are three major types of Internet access:

- **Corporate network** — If your company network is connected to the Internet, you can use the existing network cable to gain access. As a network user, you first log onto your corporate network; then you can connect to the Internet. If you're connecting from a remote location, you need a remote connection to your corporate network.

- **Community network or free net** — As part of the National Public Telecomputing Network (NPTN) organization, local communities provide Internet access at public facilities, such as libraries or community centers. In this situation, you might be given a user account to log on at a walk-up terminal.

- **Commercial Internet service provider (ISP)** — You can purchase an Internet connection, an Internet account, and e-mail service from an ISP, such as EarthLink or AT&T WorldNet. The cost might include a one-time registration fee, a monthly fee, or charges based on how long you're connected. Online service providers, such as America Online, not only give you access to the Internet but also provide proprietary Web browsing software and content.

Communication protocols

When using the Web, you might run across references to these protocols:

- Transmission Control Protocol/Internet Protocol (TCP/IP) was created to standardize data transmission.

- Hypertext Markup Language (HTML) is the standard markup language used to build documents for the Web, and Hypertext Transfer Protocol (HTTP) is the set of rules used to distribute hypertext documents on the Web. For most Web sites, you'll need to use HTTP.

- HTTPS is HTTP with Secure Sockets Layer (SSL) security added. This protocol is typically used for e-commerce Web sites and requires a user name and password to protect credit card information.

- File Transfer Protocol (FTP) was one of the initial Internet protocols used to transfer files between computers. Some FTP sites permit you to access them anonymously, while others require a user name and password.

Do it!

A-1:   Introducing the Internet

Questions and answers

1   What are the three requirements for connecting to the Internet? *Pg 25-2*

2   Describe the difference between the Internet and the World Wide Web.

none - interchangeable -

3   What are the three major types of Internet access?   *Pg 25-3*

Internet addresses

Explanation

1. Each computer on the Internet must have a unique number for identification. This number, known as an *IP address*, is used for communication and connection purposes.

The IP address consists of four sets of numbers separated by periods. Each set can have an integer value between 1 and 255. For example,

```
198.52.104.8
220.98.234.9
```

Host names

2. IP numbers are registered with the Internet Network Information Center (InterNIC) and are given host names that are easier for people to remember. Instead of having to remember a string of numbers, you need to recall only the assigned host name. Host names are usually company names, such as "Microsoft," or easy-to-remember abbreviations. The *Domain Name Service* (DNS) is a method of matching host names with their unique IP addresses and vice versa. At least one computer on each network is designated as the DNS server.

Domain names

Computer networks are divided into organizational units called *domains*. The domain name might be the same as the host name. In large networks, however, the domain name might be different. Domains can be divided into subdomains for organizational purposes. The *fully qualified domain name* combines the host and domain names in the following syntax:

```
Hostname.subdomain.domain
```

Top-level domains

The top-level domain name typically identifies the type of organization to which a Web site belongs. Outside the United States, the top-level domain contains a two-letter country code as well. For example, ".ca" represents Canada, ".de" represents Germany, and ".kr" represents South Korea. You can search for "Internet country codes" on the Web to view a complete listing.

3. The following table lists the top-level domains.

Domain	Description
.com	Commercial businesses
.edu	Educational institutions
.gov	Governmental institutions
.mil	Military institutions
.net	Networks
.org	Organizations (usually nonprofit)

User names and Internet addresses

Each person who accesses the Internet has a unique user name and address. A common user-name format consists of the user's first and last names separated by an underscore or period, as in "Jane_Doe" or "Jane.Doe." Another format might be the first initial followed by the last name, as in "jdoe." If you obtain Internet access from an ISP, you are usually allowed to define your own user name; therefore, your user name might be a nickname or a combination of letters and numbers.

In corporations, user names are determined by company naming standards to guarantee unique names within the company domain. The combination of your user name and the host computer name creates your complete Internet address. Reading from right to left, the Internet address moves from general to specific. The syntax for an Internet address is:

```
Username@Hostname.subdomain.domain
```

For example, Jane Doe in the marketing department of Acme Corporation might have the following address:

```
Jane_Doe@marketing.acme.com
```

When you're reading Internet addresses, the @ symbol is pronounced as "at," and the periods are pronounced as "dot." The example address is read as "Jane Doe at marketing dot Acme dot com."

Uniform Resource Locators (URLs)

To identify a particular page or document on the Internet, you need an Internet address called a *Uniform Resource Locator,* or *URL.* A URL consists of three major components that provide the information necessary to find a specific document. These components are separated by a forward slash (/). For example, the URL for the page that contains downloadable files for Microsoft Internet Explorer might be as follows:

```
http://www.microsoft.com/ie/downloads
```

In this example:

- `http://` is the protocol used.
- `www.microsoft.com/` is the server's host name and domain.
- `ie/downloads` is the directory path specifying where the page is stored. The path might also include file names.

Do it!

A-2:   Discussing Internet addresses

Questions and answers

1   What is an IP address? *pg 25-5*

2   How are IP addresses assigned names? *Pg 25-5*

3   Name three top-level domains. *Pg 25-5*

4   Identify the components of the following Internet address: *Pg 25-6*

GeorgeB@Jungle.com   commerical business (Domain)

username
At
hostname

addresses are set up by host company or bussiness u work 4.

Topic B: Introduction to Internet Explorer

Explanation

Internet Explorer is Microsoft's Web browser. It provides a user-friendly interface for viewing Web pages. Internet Explorer is installed by default when you install Windows 2000.

Internet Explorer components

Internet Explorer is an integral part of your Windows operating system and is one of the most comprehensive Web browsers available today. A typical installation of Internet Explorer includes the following components:

- Internet Explorer for browsing the Internet and corporate intranets.
- Outlook Express for sending and receiving e-mail and participating in newsgroups.
- Windows Media Player for playing multimedia files.
- NetMeeting for conducting online business meetings.
- Chat for participating in online chat rooms.
- Web Publishing Wizard for publishing your own Web pages.
- Internet Connection Wizard for connecting to the Internet.
- Offline Favorites Wizard for accessing Web content while disconnected.
- Wallet for safely storing credit card information for online shopping.

You can download additional components from the Internet Explorer Products Web site at http://www.microsoft.com/windows/ie/download/default.asp.

Starting Internet Explorer

To start Internet Explorer, you can use one of the following methods:

- Choose Start, Programs, Internet Explorer.
- Double-click the Internet Explorer icon on the desktop.
- Click the Internet Explorer icon on the Quick Launch toolbar. The Quick Launch toolbar appears in the Windows taskbar.

Internet Explorer

Exhibit 25-1: The Internet Explorer icon on the Quick Launch toolbar

Closing Internet Explorer

To close Internet Explorer, you can choose File, Close. You can also press Ctrl+W to close the current Internet Explorer window.

Do it!

B-1: Launching Internet Explorer

Here's how	Here's why
1 On the desktop, locate the Internet Explorer icon	Internet Explorer
Point to the icon	This icon is a shortcut to launch the Internet Explorer browser or to access your corporate intranet.
2 Observe the Quick Launch toolbar at the bottom of the screen	As shown in Exhibit 25-1.
Locate the Internet Explorer icon	This is another way to launch Internet Explorer. This method is useful if you're working in a maximized application. Using this method opens a new Internet Explorer window.
3 Choose **Start, Programs, Internet Explorer**	To use the menu commands and launch Internet Explorer. The www.microsoft.com Web site appears.
Maximize the window	If necessary.

The Internet Explorer interface

Explanation

Internet Explorer contains features that are common in other Windows applications, such as:

- Windows title bar
- Control menu
- Control buttons
- Menu bar
- Status bar

These components function in the same manner as they do in other Windows applications. Some of these components, plus components that are specific to Internet Explorer, are shown in Exhibit 25-2.

Exhibit 25-2: The Internet Explorer window, displaying the Microsoft home page

Toolbars

Three toolbars are displayed by default:

- Standard Buttons toolbar
- Address bar
- Links bar

You can show or hide a toolbar by choosing View, Toolbars and selecting the desired toolbar; you can also right-click any toolbar to use the Toolbars shortcut menu. Each toolbar makes it possible for you to perform certain actions:

- **Standard Buttons toolbar** — Contains buttons for navigating, searching, printing, and other common tasks.

- **Address bar** — Displays the Internet address of the current Web page. To go to a different Web page, enter an address in the text box, and press Enter or click the Go button. To display previously visited Web pages, click the down arrow to the right of the Address bar. Select an address to return to that previously viewed URL.
- **Links bar** — Contains buttons for quickly navigating to specific Web sites.

Exhibit 25-3: The Standard Buttons toolbar

Content window

The first page displayed in the content window is the Web browser's *home page*. You can specify the Web page to be used as your browser's home page. This page can contain plain text, graphics, buttons, or underlined text. The underlined text indicates a hypertext link that, when clicked, opens another Web page or document. By clicking links, you can move between pages of related information. While Web page data is being accessed, the logo at the far-right end of the menu bar becomes animated.

Explorer bar

When you click the Search, Favorites, Media, or History buttons, the Explorer bar appears as a separate pane on the left side of the screen. You can also choose View, Explorer Bar. You can hide the Explorer bar by clicking its Close button.

Status bar

Located at the bottom of the screen, the status bar displays context-sensitive messages based on your actions. For example:

- When you access a Web page, the status bar displays the progress.
- When you point to a link, the status bar displays the address of the destination Web page.
- When you access a secure Web site, a padlock icon is displayed at the right end of the status bar.

Hyperlinks   *Blue in color*

Hyperlinks are shortcuts to other Web pages or sites. Hyperlinks are often underlined and might appear in a color different from the other text. When the mouse pointer is over a hyperlink, the pointer shape changes to a hand icon. To use a hyperlink, just click it.

Do it!

B-2: Navigating in Internet Explorer

Here's how	Here's why
1 Observe the title bar	It displays "Microsoft Corporation" as well as the program name, Microsoft Internet Explorer.
Observe the content window	It displays graphics, text, news article links, shortcut menus, and a special search bar for this site.
2 Observe the menu bar	File Edit View Favorites Tools Help
	This is the default menu bar with familiar Windows commands. The animated logo is located at the right end of the menu bar.
3 Observe the Address bar	Address [icon] http://www.microsoft.com/
	It displays the address of the Web page shown in the content window.
In the Address bar, select **microsoft.com**	You will replace this text with a new address.
Type **msn.com**	
Press (↵ ENTER)	Goes to the MSN Web page. MSN.com is an example of a portal site. *Portal sites* contain links to popular sites.
4 Move the mouse pointer around the page	Observe that sometimes when you're pointing to a word, the pointer changes to a pointing hand. This indicates that the word is a link.
Click any hyperlink	To open a different Web page.
5 Click [⇐ Back]	To return to the previous page.
Click [⇒]	To move to the page you just left.
Click [⌂]	To navigate to the home page.
6 In the Address bar, type **www.cnn.com**	Click the Address bar, and type the new Internet address.
Press (↵ ENTER)	CNN's home page appears.

The browser home page

Explanation

The more experience you have with the Internet, the more comfortable you'll become with your browser and the more you'll see how it can best suit your working style. The Internet Options dialog box provides a way for you to modify the browser based on your personal preferences.

The Internet Options dialog box

You can choose Tools, Internet Options to change many of your browser settings. This dialog box has six tabs:

- General
- Security
- Content
- Connections
- Programs
- Advanced

From the General tab, shown in Exhibit 25-4, you can:

- Specify the home page.
- Modify the settings for storing temporary Internet files.
- Define the History period.
- Change the appearance settings, such as colors and fonts; change language settings; and change accessibility settings.

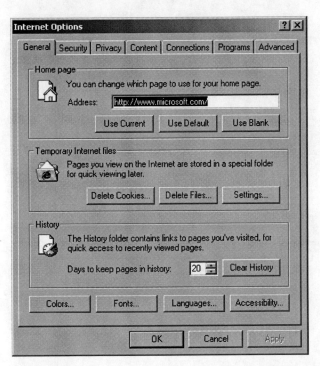

Exhibit 25-4: The General tab in the Internet Options dialog box

Changing the browser home page

The first page that appears when you start Internet Explorer is the home page. This is also the page that appears when you click the Home button. You can change this setting to a Web page that you view frequently or one that is customized to provide you with relevant information. For example, some Web pages permit you to set up links to local news and weather, favorite stock quotes, and other pages of personal interest. By setting one of these pages as your home page, you can let the Web provide you with the information you want without your having to search for it.

To change the home page:

1 Navigate to the Web page that you want to set as your home page.
2 Choose Tools, Internet Options.
3 On the General tab, under Home page, click the Use Current button.
4 Click OK to save your settings.

You can always return to the default home page by clicking the Use Default button. The Use Blank button defines a blank Web page as your default. Opening a blank page would avoid activating your Internet connection. This might be useful if you often want to open your browser and work offline.

Do it!

B-3: Changing the browser home page

Here's how	Here's why
1 Navigate to **www.course.com**	Enter "www.course.com" in the Address bar, and press Enter.
2 Choose **Tools, Internet Options...**	Opens the Internet Options dialog box.
Verify that the General tab is active	
Under Home page, click **Use Current**	To make this Web page your default home page.
Click **OK**	To change your browser home page to the current page.
3 Go to **www.yahoo.com**	To display the Yahoo home page.
4 Click [home icon]	To display your newly designated home page.

Topic C: Getting Help

Explanation

In addition to using the Internet Explorer Help files, you also have the benefit of accessing online support. If you are new to Internet Explorer, you can take an online tour that provides a brief introduction to the Web browser.

Internet Explorer Help

The Standard Help interface is similar to other Windows applications. The Contents, Index, and Search tabs are displayed in the left frame of the Help window. Each tab provides a different way to access Help documents.

Tab	Description
Contents	Provides a list of available Help categories and topics.
Index	Displays an alphabetical list of keywords used in the Help topics, much like an index at the end of a book.
Search	Searches the entire Help system for a keyword or phrase that you specify.

The right frame contains the content window, which displays the Help documents. The toolbar provides buttons for:

- Navigating forward and backward.
- Changing Help window settings.
- Accessing online support.

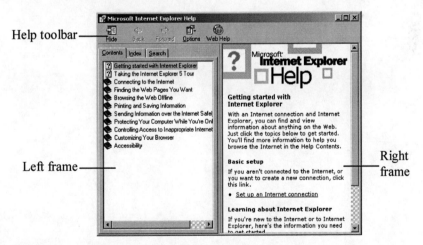

Exhibit 25-5: The Internet Explorer Help window

Do it!

C-1: Navigating in Internet Explorer Help

Here's how	Here's why
1 Choose **Help**, **Contents And Index**	Opens the Microsoft Internet Explorer Help window, as shown in Exhibit 25-5.
Maximize the Help window	
Observe the Getting Started text	In the right frame, Microsoft gives the Help information that first-time users might want.
2 In the right frame, click **Finding the information you want**, as shown	**Learning about Internet Explorer** If you're new to the Internet or to Internet Explorer, he • Introducing the Internet Explorer Web browser • Learning how to browse the Web faster and easier • Finding the information you want
Read the Help window	It tells you that you need to click the Search button to initiate a search. Other search tips are also provided.
3 Click Hide	Hides the left frame. Notice that the Help window is cropped rather than letting the right frame flow into the empty space.
4 Click Show	Displays the Contents, Index, and Search tabs in the left frame.

Using Web Help

Explanation   You can access the Microsoft Help and Support site by clicking the Web Help button and following the links to find support online. You will be prompted to connect to the Internet, if you are not connected already. The Microsoft Help and Support site, shown in Exhibit 25-6, contains a wide variety of links to help you find answers to your questions.

You can use the links to search the Microsoft Knowledge Base, download necessary components, or view the FAQs (frequently asked questions) database to obtain answers on your own. The Contact Microsoft link provides a way for you to ask questions and receive answers, or to obtain phone numbers if you prefer to speak to someone.

Exhibit 25-6: The Microsoft Help and Support Web page

Do it!   ## C-2: Using Web Help to access Support Online

Here's how	Here's why
1 Click **Web Help**	Initiates Support Online.
2 Click **Support Online**	(In the right-hand pane.) The Microsoft Help and Support site appears in a new window.
3 Maximize the new window	From here, you can query the online technicians or use other links to obtain answers on your own.
4 Close the Microsoft Help and Support window	
5 Close the Help window	To return to the Internet Explorer window.
6 Close Internet Explorer	

Unit summary: The Internet and Internet Explorer

Topic A In this topic, you learned about the **history of the Internet** and the **requirements for connecting** to the Internet. You learned that **TCP/IP** is the standard communications protocol, and you identified the components of an **Internet address**.

Topic B In this topic, you learned how to **launch Internet Explorer**. You learned how to browse Web pages by clicking **hyperlinks**, entering an address in the **Address bar**, or clicking buttons on the **Standard Buttons toolbar**. Finally, you learned how to change your browser's home page.

Topic C In this topic, you discussed the basic features of Internet Explorer **Help**. You learned how to access **Web Help**.

Independent practice activity

1 Start Internet Explorer.

2 Verify that the Course Technology home page (www.course.com) appears.

3 Follow a link on the Our Catalog sidebar to see the available Operating Systems titles.

4 Return to the Course Technology home page. (Use the Back button.)

5 Use Help to learn more about searching the Web.

6 Close Help when finished reading.

7 Close Internet Explorer.

10/23/06

Unit 26

Exploring the Web

Unit time: 45 minutes

Complete this unit, and you'll know how to:

A Open multiple Web pages, stop downloading a page, refresh a page, save a Web page, and download files from a Web site.

B Use the Search Assistant, search for a person's address, and use the Autosearch feature.

C Perform a multiple-word search, and use the advanced search options.

D Customize the Autosearch and Search Assistant features.

Topic A: Working with Web pages

Explanation

While viewing a Web page within an Internet browser, you can do several things, such as:

- Display a Web page in a new window.
- Stop downloading a Web page.
- Refresh a Web page.
- Save a Web page.
- Download files.

Displaying a Web page in a new window

There might be times when you'll want to access multiple Web pages simultaneously. For example, suppose that you're viewing an e-learning Web site. You might want to compare that site's courses with the ones offered by a competitor. To do this, you can open the competitor's site in a separate window.

To display a Web page in a new window:

1 Open Internet Explorer.

2 In the Address bar, enter the name of a Web site of your choice.

3 Click Go to access the Web page.

4 Choose File, New, Window to open the Web page in a new window. Alternately, you can press Ctrl+N.

Do it!

A-1: Opening a Web page in a new window

Here's how	Here's why
1 Open Internet Explorer	
2 In the Address bar, enter **www.yahoo.com**	
Click **Go**	To access the Web page.
3 Choose **File**, **New**, **Window**	Opens the Web page in a new window.
In the new window, access **www.google.com**	To access the Google Web site. You are displaying different Web sites in different browser windows.
4 Close the newly opened window	

Stopping and refreshing a Web page

Explanation

When the Web page you're accessing takes a long time to download because of issues such as poor network connectivity, you can use the Stop button to stop downloading the page. On the other hand, if you get an error message while accessing a Web page, you can use the Refresh button to refresh the page.

Do it!

A-2: Stopping and refreshing a Web page

Here's how	Here's why
1 Access **www.amazon.com**	To open the Amazon.com Web site.
Click [×]	To stop downloading the page.
Click [↻]	To refresh the Web page.

Saving a Web page as a file

Explanation

The Save Web Page dialog box saves a Web page to a file. After saving the page, you can open and view it even if you're disconnected from the Internet. The following table lists several options available when saving a page as a file.

Option	Result
Web page, complete	Saves the Web page and all the files necessary to view the Web page (including graphics, sound files, and so on).
Web archive	Saves a snapshot of the Web page.
Web page, HTML only	Saves the Web page without its associated files (graphics, sound files, and so on).
Text only	Saves the Web page as a text file.

To save a Web page as a file:

1　Choose File, Save As to open the Save Web Page dialog box.
2　Open the folder in which you want to save the page.
3　In the File name box, enter a name for the page.
4　From the Save as type list, select the desired file type.
5　Click Save.

Do it!

A-3:　Saving a Web page

Here's how	Here's why
1　Access **www.course.com**	
2　Choose **File, Save As...**	To open the Save Web Page dialog box.
From the Save in list, navigate to the current unit folder	
In the File name box, type **My web page**	
In the Save as type box, verify that Web Page, complete is selected	You'll save the page in its complete form.
Click **Save**	To save the file and close the dialog box.

Downloading files from Web sites

Explanation

Many Web sites provide download buttons or hyperlinks to facilitate the downloading of files. The File Download dialog box (shown in Exhibit 26-1) opens when you initiate a download from a Web site. You can choose to either open the file or save it to disk. It's preferable to choose the save option and check for viruses before opening the file. It's also a good idea to keep the default option to always be prompted before opening a downloaded file.

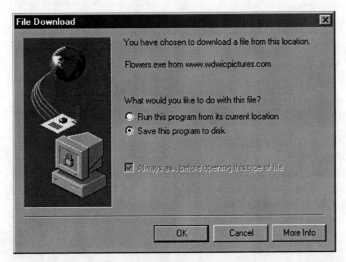

Exhibit 26-1: The File Download dialog box

You can speed the downloading of Web pages by clearing the Show pictures option in Internet Explorer. To clear this option:

1 Choose Tools, Internet Options.
2 Click the Advanced tab in the Internet Options dialog box.
3 Under Multimedia, clear Show pictures.
4 Click OK.

When this check box is cleared, you download Web pages more quickly, but you do not see any images unless you specifically opt for them. The browser uses small placeholders to represent the images. Checking the Show pictures option again will display the images.

Copying from a Web page

You can save only part of a Web page instead of the entire thing by copying and pasting the content you want. You can copy text, images, or hyperlinks. Generally, however, you shouldn't do this unless you have permission from the Web site owner to copy the content; otherwise, you could be violating a copyright.

To copy text, an image, or a hyperlink from a Web page:

1 Select the text, the image, or the hyperlink. Or in the Address bar, select the URL.
2 Choose Edit, Copy or press Ctrl+C.
3 Open the document, worksheet, e-mail, or other application. Place the insertion point in the correct location.
4 Choose Edit, Paste or press Ctrl+V.

Other download options

If you find an image you want to download from a Web site, you don't need a download button or hyperlink to do it. Instead, right-click on the image and choose Save Picture As to open the Save Picture dialog box. Navigate to the folder that you want to save the image in and click Save.

This method will also work with text files, sound files, video file, software and so on. The only difference is you'll need to right-click on the object or the hyperlink and choose Save Target As. When the Save As dialog box opens, complete the process of saving the file to the location of your choice.

Again, downloading a file from a Web site without permission can be in violation of the owner's copyright.

Do it!

A-4:   Downloading files from a Web site

Here's how	Here's why
1 Access **download.cnet.com**	
2 Under Desktop Enhancements, click **Screensavers**	"Screensavers" is a hyperlink.
Click **Animals & Nature**	
Locate a screensaver of your choice	
Click **Download now**	(In the Availability column.) The File Download dialog box opens.
3 Verify that Save this program to disk is selected	This is the best way to safeguard against downloading files with viruses. After downloading, you can check for viruses before opening the file.
Click **OK**	The Save As dialog box opens.
4 Save the file as **My screen saver**	In the current unit folder.
Click **Save**	Begin downloading the screensaver file.
Observe the File Download box	Statistics for your downloaded file are displayed. This dialog box closes automatically when the download is completed.
5 Click **Cancel**	Quits the download.

Topic B: Searching the Internet

Explanation

The Internet is overflowing with information, so it can be difficult to sort through the vast number of pages to find the one you want. To help decrease the amount of time spent reading unwanted pages, you can use the search features of Internet Explorer.

The Search Assistant window

A *search engine* is a tool designed specifically for searching the Internet. Internet Explorer's built-in *Search Assistant window* provides access to a collection of search engines.

When you use the Search Assistant window, several predefined search engines perform the same search. The Search Assistant window dynamically switches between search engines to maximize searching power. By default, results of the MSN Search are displayed first. As you might expect, you can customize the Search Assistant window to suit your search preferences.

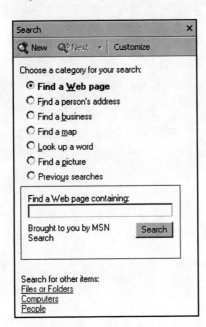

Exhibit 26-2: The Search Assistant window

To find a Web page by using the Search Assistant window:

1   Click the Search button on the Standard Buttons toolbar. The Search Assistant window appears, as shown in Exhibit 26-2.

2   In the Search box, enter a word (also called a "keyword") or a question that describes the type of information you want to find.

3   Click Search or press Enter. The first six matches are displayed as links in the content window. When you point to a link, a screen tip displays the URL for that link.

Do it!

B-1: Using the Search Assistant window

Here's how	Here's why
1 Click **Search**	(On the Standard Buttons toolbar.) The Search Assistant window opens.
Observe the Search Assistant window	Internet Explorer offers various options to categorize the Search criteria. Find a Web page is selected by default.
2 In the Find a Web page containing box, enter **Hawaii vacation**	
Click **Search**	To initiate the Web search.
3 In the content window, observe the search results	By default, the MSN Web Search engine is used. The first six Web sites containing the keywords "Hawaii" and "vacation" are displayed, along with images of their sites. Unvisited links are displayed as blue underlined text. Once you visit the site, the link color changes.
4 Scroll to the bottom of the search results list	In the Search Assistant window.
Click **NEXT**	(In the Search Assistant window.) The additional results are displayed.

Using the Search Assistant window to find people

Explanation

Using the Search Assistant window to find a person's mail or e-mail address is easy. MSN is the default search engine. However, you can also use Bigfoot, InfoSpace, or WorldPages. All of these services use the standard telephone yellow or white pages. So, if you search for someone with an unlisted telephone number, your search might not find the person. You can still search for the person's e-mail address, however.

To use the Search Assistant window to find a person:

1 In the Search Assistant window, click New.

2 From Choose a category for your search, select Find a person's address.

3 Enter as much information about the person as you can. The more specific you are, the better are your chances of finding the right person.

4 Click the Search button (in the Search Assistant window, not on the Standard Buttons toolbar).

Do it!

B-2: Searching for a person's address

Here's how	Here's why
1 Click **New**	(In the Search Assistant window.) To clear the current search and return to the default Search Assistant window.
2 From Choose a category for your search, select **Find a person's address**	You'll search for your address.
3 From the Search For list, select **e-mail address**	The Search Assistant window tries to help you narrow your search. You can click the option that best describes what you're searching for.
4 In the First Name box, enter your first name	
5 In the Last Name box, enter your last name	
6 In the City box, enter your city	To broaden your search within a state, you can leave this box empty.
7 In the State/Province box, enter your state or province	To broaden your search within the country, you can leave this box empty.
8 Click **Search**	To initiate the search.
9 Close the Search Assistant window	Click the Search button on the Standard Buttons toolbar, or click the Close button in the Search Assistant window.

Using Autosearch

Explanation

Autosearch, by default, uses MSN Web Search and displays the results in the content window. To perform an Autosearch:

1   Type keywords directly in the Address bar.
2   Click the Go button or press Enter.

Do it!

B-3:   Using Autosearch

Here's how	Here's why
1 Click in the Address bar	To select its contents.
Enter **chocolate**	
Observe the Address bar	The words "Search for" indicate that Autosearch is activated.
Click **Go**	To start the search.
Observe the address bar	You can see that search.msn.com is used. By default, the Autosearch results appear in the content window.
2 In the Address bar, enter **cars**	A list of Web sites containing the word "cars" appears in the content window.
3 Perform an Autosearch on a word of your choice	

Topic C: Performing advanced searches

Explanation

The number of matching documents resulting from a single keyword search can reach into the thousands. Since you probably don't want to search all of those pages, you can refine your search by adding more keywords or other criteria.

Using search operators

In the keyword box, you type words related to the information you want to find. By default, multiple keywords are treated as if there was a Boolean OR operator between them. For example, a search for "rocket ship" finds pages that contain either the word "rocket" or the word "ship," as well as those pages that contain both words.

To better refine your search, you can use special characters and punctuation that serve as search operators. Some common operators that are used by search engines include the following:

- A plus sign (+) between words specifies that all words must be contained in every result.
- Single or double quotation marks specify an exact phrase.
- A minus sign (-) preceding a word specifies that it should be excluded.
- An asterisk (*) following a partial keyword specifies that anything is acceptable. For example, "roc*" would find words such as "Rochester," "rocks," "rocket," "Rococo," and so on.

Do it!

C-1: Performing a multiple-word search

Here's how	Here's why
1 Click **Search**	(On the Standard Buttons toolbar.) The Search Assistant window opens.
Click **New**	In the Search Assistant window.
2 Select **Find a Web page**	
In the Find a Web page containing box, enter **rocket ship**	To search for Web pages containing the word "rocket" or the word "ship."
Click **Search**	
Observe the search result	By default, the Web pages containing both "rocket" and "ship" appear at the top of the list. However, we might not be interested in all Web pages containing these words.
3 In the Search box, enter **rock***	
Click **Go**	
Observe the search results in the Search Assistant window	Notice that Web pages containing words starting with "rock" appear, such as "rockhounds," "rock'n'roll," and "rocks."

Using advanced search options

Explanation   The Advanced Search button, shown in Exhibit 26-3, displays additional search options. Using this option, you can search on:

- Language
- Domain
- Multimedia types

Home | Advanced Search | My Preferences | Submit a Site | Help

Exhibit 26-3: The Advanced Search option in MSN Web Search

When you use the MSN Web Search engine, you can specify how you want multiple keywords to be handled. You can use the Find list to specify that:

- All words must be included.
- Any of the words can be included.
- Words must appear in the title.
- Words must appear as the exact phrase.

You can also search for Web pages that link to a specified URL.

Finally, you can use *Boolean operators*. The acceptable Boolean operators are AND, OR, AND, or NOT. Boolean operators create complex search criteria and must be typed in uppercase.

The types of Boolean operators available are as follows:

- AND is used to find at least one occurrence of each word.
- OR is used to find at least one occurrence of any word.
- AND NOT is used to exclude pages with an occurrence of the word.

Do it! **C-2: Using the Advanced Search option**

Here's how	Here's why
1 Verify that you are using MSN Search	This search engine provides a large number of advanced search options.
2 Click **Advanced Search**, as shown	Advanced Search
In the Search box, enter **Holiday Package**	You can use this form to define your search criteria based on words, dates, and attachments, such as video, audio, and image files.
From the Find list, select **the exact phrase**	The search criteria are considered to be a phrase, and the resulting documents must contain at least one occurrence of the entire phrase.
Click **Search**	The search is narrowed down to contain pages that have the exact phrase "Holiday Package."

Topic D: Customizing the search features

Explanation   The search feature provides a wide variety of options. You can customize how the search feature works on your computer.

Changing the Autosearch settings

You can customize the Autosearch settings to select a search engine and specify how the search results are displayed. To access the Customize Autosearch Settings dialog box, as shown in Exhibit 26-4:

1   Display the Search Assistant window.

2   Click Customize.

3   Click the Autosearch settings button.

4   Choose a search provider from the search provider list.

5   Choose one of the display options listed below. Only MSN Search offers all four options. The other search providers offer only two of the options:

- **Display results, and go to the most likely site** — This option displays the search results in the Search Assistant window and displays a list of Web sites in the content window.

- **Do not search from the Address bar**— This option disables the Autosearch feature.

- **Just display results in the main window** — This option displays the search results in a full content window and not in the Search Assistant window.

- **Just go to the most likely site** — This default setting displays a particular Web site in a full content window and does not display the search results.

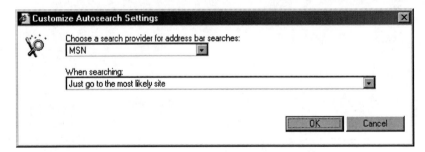

Exhibit 26-4: The Customize Autosearch Settings dialog box

Do it!

D-1: Customizing the Autosearch feature

Here's how	Here's why
1 Perform an Autosearch on **weather**	In the Address bar, type "weather"; click Go.
2 Observe the screen	MSN Search is the default search engine. Results appear in the content window.
3 Click **Customize**	(In the Search Assistant window.) The Customize Search Settings dialog box opens.
Click **Autosearch settings**	The Customize Autosearch Settings dialog box opens, as shown in Exhibit 26-4.
4 From the Choose a search provider for address bar searches list, select **Yahoo!**	To make Yahoo! the default search engine.
Click **OK**	To close the Customize Autosearch Settings dialog box.
Click **OK**	To close the Customize Search Settings dialog box.
5 Perform an Autosearch on **furniture**	In the Address bar, type "furniture"; click Go.
Observe the screen	Yahoo! is the default search engine.
6 Make MSN the default search engine	Click Customize. Then click Autosearch settings. Select MSN from the search providers list.
7 Verify that the Customize Autosearch Settings dialog box is still open	
From the When searching list, select **Display results, and go to the most likely site**	To display the search results in the Search Assistant window and preview pages in the content window.
Click **OK**	To close the Customize Autosearch Settings dialog box.
8 Click **OK**	To close the Customize Search Settings dialog box.
9 Perform an Autosearch on **literature**	View the results in the Search Assistant window as well as in the content window.

Search Assistant window options

Explanation

You can customize the Search Assistant window so it uses your favorite search engine. To do this:

1 Click the Search button on the Standard Buttons toolbar to display the Search Assistant window.
2 Click Customize to open the Customize Search Settings dialog box.
3 From Find a Web page, check a search engine of your choice.
5 Click OK.

Do it!

D-2: Customizing the Search Assistant window

Here's how	Here's why
1 Open the Customize Search Settings dialog box	Click Customize in the Search Assistant window.
Select **Use Search Assistant – allows you to customize your search settings**	If necessary.
Observe the Find a Web page category	Use the check box next to the blue category header to show or hide this category in the Search Assistant window. You can determine which search providers to include as well as their order of appearance.
Scroll down to observe all categories	You can set the default settings of every category of search criteria in the Search Assistant window.
Clear **Find a map**	Remove this category from the Choose a category for your search list.
2 Click **OK**	To close the dialog box and save your changes.
Click New	In the Search Assistant Window.
Observe the Search Assistant window	The Find a map category is no longer available.
3 Close the Search Assistant window	

Unit summary: Exploring the Web

Topic A
In this topic, you learned how to **display** a Web page in a **new window**. You learned how to **stop downloading** and **refresh** a Web page. You also learned how to **save** a Web page. Finally, you learned how to **download files** from Web sites.

Topic B
In this topic, you learned how to use the **Search Assistant window** to search for Web pages. You learned how to use Search Assistant window to find a person's **address** or **e-mail address**. Finally, you learned how to use **Autosearch** to perform a search based on **keywords**.

Topic C
In this topic, you learned how to perform a **multiple-word search**. You learned how to perform a search using **advanced search options**.

Topic D
In this topic, you learned how to **customize** the **Autosearch feature**. You learned how to customize the **Search Assistant window options**.

Independent practice activity

1 Access www.course.com.

2 Save the document as **My information** (save it as a Web page).

3 Visit http://download.cnet.com, and download a screensaver of your choice from the Download section.

4 Click Search on the Standard Buttons toolbar.

5 In the Search Assistant window, click New.

6 Using the Search Assistant window, search on the keyword **browsers**.

7 Change the default Autosearch engine to **Yahoo**.

8 Perform an Autosearch on **Christmas**.

9 Change the default Autosearch engine back to **MSN**.

10 Show the Find a Map category in the Search Assistant window.

11 Perform an Autosearch on words starting with **pre**. (*Hint:* Search by using the * wildcard, as in "pre*".)

12 Using MSN Advanced Search, search for the exact phrase **antivirus software**.

13 Close Internet Explorer.

10/25/06

Unit 27

Working with Web pages

Unit time: 70 minutes

Complete this unit, and you'll know how to:

A Navigate by using the Favorites list, add to Favorites, create a Favorites subfolder, and organize the Favorites list.

B Use, add, rearrange, and delete buttons on the Links bar.

C View and add a link to the History list, examine and delete temporary Internet files, modify History and AutoComplete settings, and examine the Content Advisor.

D Print Web pages, and modify print options.

Topic A: Working with Favorites

Explanation

While some Internet addresses, or URLs, are relatively simple and easy to remember, others can be quite cryptic and hard to remember. For example, you might access some Web sites by using the server's IP address, such as 209.34.128.9. To make these Web sites easier to access, you can use the Favorites menu to store links to frequently visited Web sites.

Viewing Favorites

To display the Favorites menu, do either of the following:

- Choose Favorites from the menu bar.
- Click the Favorites button on the Standard Buttons toolbar to display the Favorites list in the Explorer bar.

By default, Microsoft has included a few folders and Web sites that you might want to have in your Favorites folder. You can delete them if you wish.

Enabling Full Screen view

The Full Screen view option provides a way to maximize the amount of data that appears on the screen. Choose View, Full Screen to hide all of the window components except for the Standard Buttons toolbar. This menu command switches between Full Screen and Regular views. You can also toggle between views by pressing the F11 key.

Do it!

A-1: Navigating in the Favorites folder

Here's how	Here's why
1 Start Internet Explorer	There are two ways to open the Favorites folder.
2 Choose **Favorites**	
	The Favorites menu appears.
Observe the menu	The top portion of the menu contains two choices for managing your Favorites folder. The rest lists your frequently visited Web sites and folders.

3 Choose **Media**

🌐 Bloomberg
🌐 Capitol Records
🌐 CBS
🌐 CNBC Dow Jones Business Video
🌐 CNET Today - Technology News
🌐 CNN Videoselect
🌐 Disney
🌐 ESPN Sports
🌐 Fox News
🌐 Fox Sports
🌐 Hollywood Online
🌐 Internet Radio Guide
🌐 MSNBC
🌐 MUSICVIDEOS.COM
🌐 NBC VideoSeeker
🌐 TV Guide Entertainment Network
🌐 Universal Studios Online
🌐 Warner Bros. Hip Clips
🌐 What's On Now
🌐 Windows Media Showcase

The Media submenu appears. By default, Internet Explorer includes links to a variety of Web sites.

Choose any site

To open the selected site's home page in the content window.

4 Choose **View**, **Full Screen**

To hide all components except for the Standard toolbar. In Full Screen view, the labels aren't displayed with the toolbar icons. This feature displays a larger portion of the page on your screen.

Press (F11)

To return to Regular view.

5 Click [🔅 Favorites]

To display the contents of the Favorites folder in the Explorer bar. The same organizational commands and shortcut links are available.

6 In the Favorites list, click the **Media** folder

To expand the Media folder and view its contents. These are the same links as those in the Favorites menu.

Click **Media** again

To collapse the folder.

Adding links to the Favorites folder

Explanation

You can easily add links to Web sites you visit frequently. To do so, open the Web page, and then use one of the following methods to add it to your Favorites folder:

- Choose Favorites, Add to Favorites.
- Click the Favorites button on the Standard Buttons toolbar. Then, in the Favorites list, click Add.
- Right-click the Web page, and choose Add to Favorites from the shortcut menu.

Naming conventions for links

The Add Favorite dialog box, shown in Exhibit 27-1, contains several options. By default, Internet Explorer copies the title bar text and places it in the Name box. However, you can change this default name to better reflect the content of the page or to change its place in the alphabetical listing.

When naming favorites, keep the names short and descriptive.

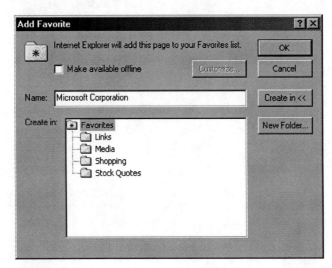

Exhibit 27-1: The Add Favorite dialog box

Do it!   **A-2: Adding a new Favorite**

Here's how	Here's why
1 Use the Favorites list to navigate to **www.msn.com**	To display the MSN home page. As you move your mouse pointer around the page, the target address for each link appears in the status bar.
2 Follow your instructor's directions to locate the MSN Business link	The link appears under the title "News & Sports" on the left side of the Web page.
Click the **Business** link	
3 Locate the empty text box to the right of the page	Get quote: [ ] [Go]
Enter the stock symbol for a stock of your choice	Get quote: [MSFT] [Go] Or use "MSFT" for Microsoft Corporation.
Click **Go**	To view the Quick Quote for Microsoft Corporation.
4 Choose **Favorites, Add to Favorites...**	(The Add Favorite dialog box opens.) Because the URL for this particular page is slightly cryptic, it's easier to use your Favorites menu.
Observe the Name box	You can use the default name of this Web page, or you can change it to something more meaningful to you. Use the Create in button to select a folder or to create a new folder for organizing your links.
Click **OK**	To close the Add Favorite dialog box.
5 Choose **Favorites**	To display the Favorites menu.
Observe the newly added item	The shortcut has been added to the Favorites menu in the menu bar.

Using the Add Favorite dialog box

Explanation

By default, new links are added at the first level of Favorites. This might be convenient if you have only a few links. However, frequent Web surfers might soon find that their Favorites list is too large and cumbersome.

To organize your Favorites, use a folder structure that resembles the Windows Explorer structure and functions in a similar manner. To organize your Favorites links, choose Favorites, Organize Favorites, or click Organize in the Favorites list.

To organize and place each new Favorite in a folder, do the following:

1 In the Add Favorite dialog box, click the Create in button to display the hierarchical folder structure, as shown in Exhibit 27-2.

2 Select the folder that you want to use.

3 If no appropriate folder exists, you can click the New Folder button to create one. Enter a folder name and click OK.

4 Click OK to add the new item to the selected folder.

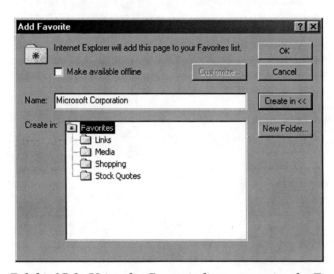

Exhibit 27-2: Using the Create in list to organize the Favorites menu

Do it!   ## A-3:   Creating a new subfolder while adding Favorites

Here's how	Here's why
1 Navigate to an online shopping site	Examples are Amazon.com, Ebay.com, and Toysrus.com.
2 In a blank area of the content window, right-click and choose **Add to Favorites...**	To open the Add Favorite dialog box.
Click **Create in**	You will create a new folder.
3 Click **New Folder**	To open the Create New Folder dialog box.
In the Folder name box, enter **Shopping**	
Click **OK**	To add the folder name.
4 Verify that the Shopping folder is selected	Name: Amazon.com Welcome Create in: Favorites Links Media Shopping
Click **OK**	To add the shopping site to the Favorites list and place it in the Shopping folder.

Using the Organize Favorites dialog box

Explanation   In addition to organizing Favorites, you can do any of the following activities by using the Organize Favorites dialog box, as shown in Exhibit 27-3:

- Create a new folder.
- Move a folder.
- Rename a folder.
- Delete folders and links.

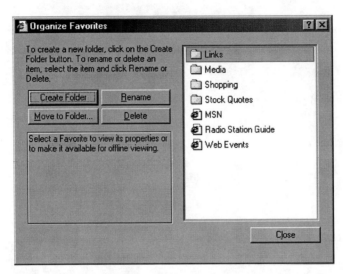

Exhibit 27-3: The Organize Favorites dialog box

To display a folder's contents:

1 Select it.
2 A description of the selected folder or favorite item appears in the lower-left corner of the dialog box.

To create a new folder:

1 Choose Favorites, Organize Favorites, or click Organize in the Favorites list, to open the Organize Favorites dialog box.
2 Click the Create Folder button.
3 Type a name for the new folder, and press Enter (or deselect the folder).
4 Click Close.

To move a shortcut between folders:

1 Open the Organize Favorites dialog box.
2 In the list of Favorites, select the shortcut or folder you want to move. A description of the item appears in the lower-left section of the dialog box.
3 Click the Move to Folder button to open the Browse For Folder dialog box.
4 In the Browse for Folder dialog box, expand the Favorites folder structure, and select the destination folder.
5 Click OK to close the Browse for Folder dialog box.
6 Click Close to close the Organize Favorites dialog box.

Do it!   **A-4:   Organizing Favorites**

Here's how	Here's why
1 Choose **Favorites**, **Organize Favorites...**	To open the Organize Favorites dialog box.
2 Click **Create Folder**	A new folder is added to the list.
Type **Stock Quotes**	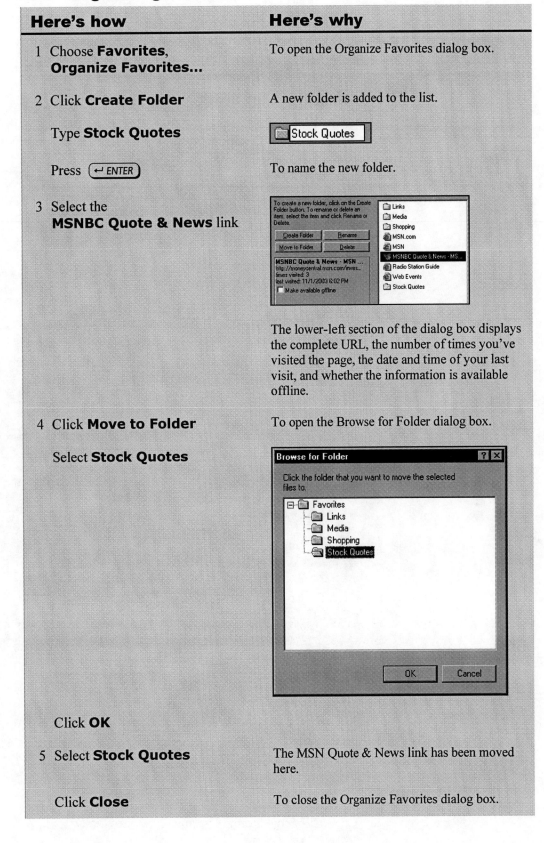
Press (← ENTER)	To name the new folder.
3 Select the **MSNBC Quote & News** link	
	The lower-left section of the dialog box displays the complete URL, the number of times you've visited the page, the date and time of your last visit, and whether the information is available offline.
4 Click **Move to Folder**	To open the Browse for Folder dialog box.
Select **Stock Quotes**	
Click **OK**	
5 Select **Stock Quotes**	The MSN Quote & News link has been moved here.
Click **Close**	To close the Organize Favorites dialog box.

Topic B: Using links

Explanation

The Links folder is a folder within Favorites that contains hyperlinks to a variety of Microsoft Web sites. The Links button appears at the right end of the Address bar.

Displaying the Links bar

To display the Links bar, shown in Exhibit 27-4, choose View, Toolbars, Links. If your company has customized Internet Explorer, then your Links buttons might be different from the default buttons.

Exhibit 27-4: The Links bar

Do it!

B-1:   Using the Links bar

Here's how	Here's why
1 Observe the right end of the Address bar	By default, the Links bar appears here. It appears as a button with the word "Links" and a double chevron. You can either click the double chevron to display a Links list, or move the Links bar to a different location.
2 Choose **View, Toolbars**	By default, Internet Explorer locks the toolbars so that they can't be accidentally moved.
Clear **Lock the Toolbars**	(If necessary.) To unlock the toolbars so that you can move them.
3 In an empty space on the Links bar, point to the Links bar and press the mouse button	⊕

The mouse pointer changes to a four-headed arrow, indicating that you can move the toolbar. |
Drag the Links bar beneath the Address bar	To display all of the Links buttons.
4 Click **Windows**	(On the Links bar.) This link takes you to the Windows Family Home Page.
5 Select a topic and browse	Continue to click hyperlinks to surf the Web.
6 Click **Customize Links**	(On the Links bar.) To display some tips on how to modify the Links bar.

Customizing the Links bar

Explanation

The Links bar can be customized to match your working style. You can add, delete, and rearrange toolbar buttons. To add a link, simply drag its URL shortcut to a location on the Links bar. Adding your favorite Web sites to the Links bar lets you view them with a single mouse click. You can rearrange the toolbar by dragging icons to a new position. You can also modify the target URLs. However, the Links bar must be displayed for you to use the buttons.

Adding a button

You can add buttons to the Links bar by dragging the URLs from the Address bar, from Favorites, or from within a document. To add a link button:

1 Select the link that you want to add.

2 Drag the item to the desired location on the Links bar. A bold insertion point appears to indicate the button's location.

3 Release the mouse button to place the button in the selected location.

Do it!

B-2: Adding a button to the Links bar

Here's how	Here's why
1 Display your favorite stock quote	(Use the Favorites menu.) You will add a button for this page to the Links bar.
2 In the Address bar, point to the icon	
Press and hold the mouse button	
Observe the mouse pointer as you drag the icon	
Drag the icon to the leftmost position on the Links bar	(The icon briefly changes to a hollow black circle with a line.) A bold insertion point appears to indicate the button's new location.
Observe the Links bar	
	The stock quote link has become a new button on the Links bar.
3 Choose **Favorites, Links**	(To display the Links submenu.) The Quote & News shortcut has also been added to the Links folder in the Favorites menu.
Close the menu	

Changing the order of Links bar buttons

Explanation

You can change the order of buttons on the Links bar by dragging them to new locations. When the bold insertion point appears in the new location, release the mouse button.

Do it!

B-3:   Rearranging buttons on the Links bar

Here's how	Here's why
1 Point to the **Quote & News** button	You'll move this button to the right end of the toolbar.
2 Drag the button to the right end of the toolbar	
3 When the bold insertion point appears, release the mouse button	The Quote & News link is now located at the right end of the Links bar.

Deleting a button

Explanation

To keep the Links bar uncluttered, you might want to remove buttons that you no longer need.

Simply right-click the button you want to remove; then choose Delete. When asked to confirm the deletion, click Yes.

Do it!

B-4:   Deleting a button from the Links bar

Here's how	Here's why
1 Right-click the **Quote & News** button	Open Print Make available offline Send To ▶ Cut Copy Create Shortcut Delete Rename Properties The shortcut menu is displayed.
Choose **Delete**	A Confirm File Delete message box appears.
Click **Yes**	To remove the button from the Links bar.
2 Verify that the button has been removed	It's no longer displayed on the Links bar or in the Favorites, Links menu.

Topic C: Using the History list

Explanation

The History list, as the name implies, tracks all the Web sites you visit each day. You can specify the number of days to keep the history records.

The History list

When you click the History button, a History list appears, as shown in Exhibit 27-5. By default, the History list is sorted by date. To display a list of the Web sites you visited on a specific day, simply select the desired date.

Exhibit 27-5: An example History list in the Explorer bar

AutoComplete

Similar to the History feature, AutoComplete keeps track of Web addresses and information you've entered on Web forms. As you type a URL in the Address bar, AutoComplete attempts to finish your entry. If one of the AutoComplete suggestions is correct, simply click it; you don't have to finish typing. This feature can be useful when you're entering long URLs.

Do it!

C-1:   Viewing the History list

Here's how	Here's why
1 Click	The History list appears in the Explorer bar.
Observe the History list	The Web sites that you have visited are listed. You can click a link to return to a specific site.
2 Click **View**	A menu appears. By default, the History list is sorted by date. You can also view the list sorted alphabetically, sorted by the most frequently visited sites, or sorted by the order in which sites were visited today.
Choose **By Site**	Sorts the History list alphabetically by site name.
View history by date	(Click View, choose By Date.) To sort the history by date.
3 Observe the Search button	If a particular site is not readily visible, you can search through the History list to find it.
4 Click one of today's sites	To expand the site folder and display the individual pages that you visited today.
5 In the Address bar, type the first few letters of a favorite site	AutoComplete displays a list of URL suggestions that begin with the same letters you typed.
Click any of the suggestions	The corresponding Web page is displayed without your having to type the entire URL.

Using History to add to Favorites

Explanation

You can add a link to your Favorites list from within the History list.

To do this, just right-click the History link, and choose Add To Favorites from the shortcut menu. From this menu, you can also:

- Open the Web page in a new window.
- Copy the link.
- Delete a link from the History list.

Do it!

C-2: Adding a History link to Favorites

Here's how	Here's why
1 In the History list, click the Microsoft site folder	To display a list of all the Microsoft Web pages you have visited today.
2 Click any page link	To display the Web page in the content window.
Right-click the page link	To display the shortcut menu for a History link.
Choose **Add To Favorites**	
Click **OK**	To add the selected Microsoft Web page to your Favorites.
3 Close the History list	

Temporary Internet files

Explanation

By using the files stored in the C:\Windows\Temporary Internet Files folder, the browser can load previously visited pages faster.

Frequency of checking for updates

You can use the Settings button to change how Web-related files are stored on your hard drive. The option you select at the top of the Settings dialog box defines the frequency with which the browser checks for updates to Web pages. These options include the following:

Option	Result
Every visit to the page	The browser checks for updates to stored files every time you go to a previously visited page. This is the slowest way to browse the Internet.
Every time you start Internet Explorer	The browser checks for updates of only those pages that were viewed in the previous session of Internet Explorer or on another day. This option allows faster Web browsing than does the previous option.
Automatically	Like the previous option, the browser checks for updates of only those pages that were viewed in another session or on different day. However, if the browser determines that a page changes infrequently, then it automatically decreases the checking frequency. This default setting is the most efficient way to work.
Never	The browser never checks for updates to cached files. While this is the fastest way to browse the Web, you might not be viewing the most up-to-date information.

You can manually bypass the frequency setting by clicking the Refresh button to check for newer versions of cached files on demand.

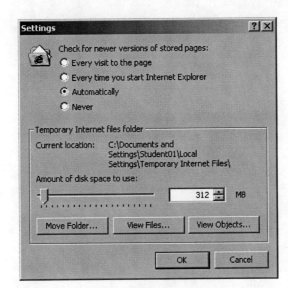

Exhibit 27-6: The Settings dialog box

Other options

In the Settings dialog box, under the Temporary Internet files folder, you can do the following:

- Use the slider bar or the spinner controls to set the amount of disk space reserved for storing Web files.

- Click the Move Folder button to change the location of temporary Internet files.

- Click the View Files button to view the current files in a new browser window. You might want to view the files before clearing them.

- Click the View Objects button to display the contents of the C:\Windows\Downloaded Program Files folder. These small files are used to help display animation on Web pages.

Deleting temporary Internet files

If you are a frequent Internet user, the number of files in the Temporary Internet Files folder can become quite large. It's a good idea to periodically clear the contents of this folder.

You can delete the files in the temporary folder by clicking the Delete Files button on the General tab in the Internet Options dialog box. A Delete Files dialog box appears, which gives you the option to delete all offline content stored on your hard drive.

Do it!

C-3: Examining and deleting temporary Internet files

Here's how	Here's why
1 Choose **Tools**, **Internet Options...**	To open the Internet Options dialog box.
Under Temporary Internet files, click **Settings...**	To open the Settings dialog box, as shown in Exhibit 27-6.
2 Click **View Files**	The contents of the Temporary Internet Files folder appear in a new window. Another name for this folder is a *cache*. Files are copied to this folder to help the browser load previously visited pages faster.
Close the window	
3 Click **View Objects**	The contents of the object files stored in a different location appear in a new window. These files are used to run animations on previously visited Web pages.
Close the window	
4 Click **Cancel**	To close the Settings dialog box without making any changes.
5 Under Temporary Internet files, click **Delete Files...**	Delete Files ☒ ⚠ Delete all files in the Temporary Internet Files folder? You can also delete all your offline content stored locally. ☐ Delete all offline content [OK] [Cancel] To clear the cache. A Delete Files dialog box appears.
Click **OK**	If you wish, you can check the option to delete all offline content as well.

History settings

Explanation

By default, the History list displays the Web pages that you have visited in the past 20 days. You can increase or decrease the number of days that the History is stored.

In the Internet Options dialog box, under History, you can use the spinner controls to change the history period, or you can just type a new number in the box. To start fresh and delete all past links, you can click the Clear History button.

Do it!

C-4:   Changing History settings

Here's how	Here's why
1 Under History, use the spinner controls to specify **14** days	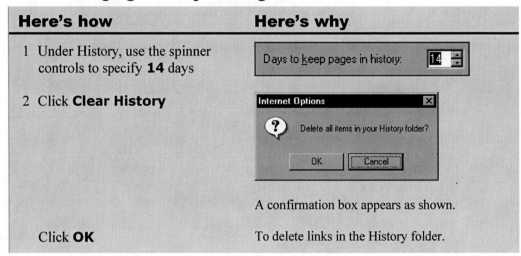
2 Click **Clear History**	
	A confirmation box appears as shown.
Click **OK**	To delete links in the History folder.

AutoComplete settings

Explanation

Earlier you used the AutoComplete feature to navigate to a previously visited site. In addition to Internet addresses, AutoComplete can try to match what you type in Web page forms. For example, when you're filling out an online shopping order, AutoComplete can recognize your name, address, and phone number so that you can select that information from a list rather than typing it. Another convenient option is to save your user names and the associated passwords for various sites by using Internet Explorer. Passwords aren't saved by default, but you can indicate that you want to be prompted.

To open the AutoComplete Settings dialog box:

1 In the Internet Options dialog box, click the Content tab.

2 Under Personal information, click AutoComplete.

Exhibit 27-7: The AutoComplete Settings dialog box

Clearing the AutoComplete history

You can clear the AutoComplete history by clicking the Clear Forms and Clear Passwords buttons in the AutoComplete Settings dialog box.

Do it!

C-5: Changing AutoComplete settings

Here's how	Here's why
1 Click the **Content** tab	In the Internet Options dialog box.
2 Under Personal information, click **AutoComplete**	To open the AutoComplete Settings dialog box, shown in Exhibit 27-7.
Observe the Use AutoComplete for section	By default, the options Web addresses and User names and passwords on forms are checked.
Clear **User names and passwords on forms**	It's not always advisable to allow this feature to complete names because it sometimes does so incorrectly.
Click **OK**	To close the AutoComplete Settings dialog box.

Content Advisor

Explanation

Although the Internet is a valuable source of information, it also contains information that you might find inappropriate or offensive. The *Content Advisor* provides a way for you to filter out undesirable information. The Recreational Software Advisory Council on the Internet (RSACi) has developed a ratings system based on content. To view information on the rating system:

1   In the Internet Options dialog box, click the Content tab to open the Content Advisor dialog box.

2   On the Ratings tab, click the More Info button to view the RSACi Web page and learn more about the rating system.

RSACi has four categories of potentially offensive Web content: Language, Nudity, Sex, and Violence. You can define the allowable level for each of these categories. You can further control the content by identifying specific sites as approved or not approved.

Once the Content Advisor is enabled, you need to create a Supervisor password. This password is required to change the Content Advisor settings. If someone attempts to open an unapproved site, a warning box appears.

Do it!

C-6:   Examining the Content Advisor

Here's how	Here's why
1 Under Content Advisor, click **Enable**	The Content Advisor dialog box opens.
Verify that the Language category is selected	
2 Use the slider bar to examine the levels	Each category has four rating levels that range from mild to offensive. The Description box provides additional details.
3 Click **More Info**	The RSACi home page opens in a new browser window.
Close the new browser window	
4 Click **Cancel**	To close the Content Advisor dialog box.
Click **OK**	To close the Internet Options dialog box.

Topic D: Printing Web content

Explanation

If you print Web pages instead of e-mailing them, you can save valuable mailbox space. Printing documents also helps you share them with people who might not have access to the Internet. You can print:

- An entire Web page
- Selected items on a page
- An entire page along with all linked documents

Printing

The quickest way to print the current Web page is to click the Print button on the toolbar. Using the Print button sends the Web page to the printer, using the default settings. You can also right-click a Web page item and choose Print.

The Print dialog box

The File, Print command opens the Print dialog box, shown in Exhibit 27-8. The Print dialog box contains multiple tabs with printing options, which can vary according to the model of printer you have installed. If the selected Web page contains frames, the Print frames section on the Options tab specifies how frames should be printed. By default, each frame is printed as a separate document.

In addition to printing just the current Web page, you can choose to print all of the linked documents or print only a listing of the links by using the check boxes at the bottom of the Options tab. Keep in mind that printing all of the links as documents can take a long time and require a lot of paper.

On the General tab, you will find the usual print options. From this tab, you can select the printer you want to use, what page range, and how many copies you want to print.

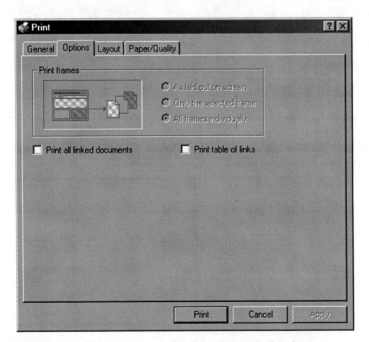

Exhibit 27-8: The Options tab of the Print dialog box

Print Preview

To view a Web page before printing it, choose File, Print Preview. A Print Preview window is displayed. There are number of tools and options for you to use in this window. For example, you can:

- Click the Print button to open the Print dialog box. In this dialog box, you can set the printing options and actually print the Web site.
- Click the Page Setup button to display the Page Setup dialog box. Here you can change the paper size, headers and footers, orientation, and margins before printing the Web site.
- Use the zoom options to increase and decrease the magnification.
- Navigate to different pages
- Click the Close button to close the Print Preview window.

Do it!

D-1: Printing the current Web page

Here's how	Here's why
1 Choose **File, Print...**	To open the Print dialog box.
2 Click the **Options** tab	
Observe the Print frames section	You can choose to print all frames as they appear on screen, or print the frames as separate documents. If the current page has no frames, this section won't be available.
3 Observe the check box options	You can print each linked document separately or print a list of the links. The latter option saves time and paper.
4 Click **Print**	To close the Print dialog box and print the page.

Print options

Explanation

You can configure print options by using the Page Setup dialog box, shown in Exhibit 27-9. To configure page setup options:

1   Choose File, Page Setup to open the Page Setup dialog box.
2   Choose settings from the Paper, Header, Footer, Orientation, and Margins options.
3   Click OK.

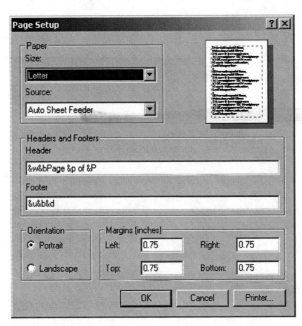

Exhibit 27-9: The Page Setup dialog box

Do it!

D-2:   Working with print options

Here's how	Here's why
1 Choose **File, Page Setup...**	The Page Setup dialog box opens.
Under Paper, from the Size list, select **Letter**	If necessary.
Under Orientation, select **Landscape**	Prints the page horizontally.
2 Observe the Margins area	The units are set to inches by default.
Click **OK**	To close the dialog box.

Unit summary: Working with Web pages

Topic A

In this topic, you learned how to **navigate** to a Web site by using the **Favorites** feature. You learned how to **add links** to the Favorites folder. You also learned how to create a **new subfolder** to save a link. Finally, you learned how to **delete, rename, move,** and **create folders** to **organize** your Favorites folder.

Topic B

In this topic, you used the **Links bar** to find a Web site. You learned how to **add a link button** to the Links bar. You learned how to **rearrange buttons** on the Links bar. Finally, you learned how to **delete** a link button that you no longer need.

Topic C

In this topic, you learned how to view **recently visited** Web sites by using the **History list.** You learned how to **add** a History link to the **Favorites** list. You learned how to **examine** and delete **temporary Internet files.** You learned how to **modify** the **History settings.** You also learned how to **modify** the **AutoComplete settings.** Finally, you learned how to view and modify the **Content Advisor** settings.

Topic D

In this topic, you learned how to **print a Web page.** You also learned how to work with **print options** in the Print dialog box.

Independent practice activity

1 Switch to Full Screen view to maximize the Internet Explorer window.

2 Return to Regular view.

3 Add a movie Web page to your Favorites list, and put it in a new folder called **Entertainment**.

4 Add the movie favorite to the Links bar.

5 Close the Favorites list.

6 Move the Links bar to its original location at the end of the Address bar.

7 Display a list of the Web sites you visited today. (Click the History button.)

8 Close the History list.

9 Activate AutoComplete only for forms. (*Hint:* Open the AutoComplete Settings dialog box. Under Use AutoComplete for, check forms.)

10 Verify that the Orientation is set to Portrait. (*Hint:* Use the Page Setup dialog box.)

11 Close Internet Explorer.

10/25/06

Unit 28

Internet transactions and security

Unit time: 40 minutes

Complete this unit, and you'll know how to:

A Purchase goods online by using credit cards and Web-based forms.

B Describe the concepts of Web security, cookies, caches, Web site protection, digital certificates, encryption, and firewalls.

Topic A: Internet transactions

Explanation

The availability and use of the Internet have increased tremendously over the past couple of decades. High-speed access and low-cost availability have provided businesses with new opportunities to reach potential customers. Online business transactions—referred to as *e-commerce*—have emerged as an efficient and popular way of conducting business. E-commerce offers several advantages over the traditional ways. Some of the advantages are:

- Adapting more rapidly to market changes
- Responding faster to customer needs
- Operating at the lowest cost

The e-commerce business models include the following:

- Business-to-business (B2B)
- Business-to-consumer (B2C)
- Business-to-employee (B2E)
- Business-to-government (B2G)
- Government-to-consumer (G2C)
- Consumer-to-consumer (C2C)

Online buying with Web-based forms

The most common of these business models is the business-to-consumer model. In this model, consumers have the flexibility of purchasing goods over the Internet from the comfort of their homes or offices, and then paying by using a credit card or electronic cash transfer.

Many companies host Web sites that serve as online stores, where you can purchase products ranging from books to real estate. Browse through these online stores to view pictures of products and their prices before ordering. When you decide to buy a product, place it in a list called a *shopping cart*.

After you complete your shopping, you enter personal information, such as your name, mailing address, e-mail address, telephone number, and credit card details, into a Web-based order form. This information is sent to the store's server for order processing. The credit card information is sent to the credit card company's server, and authorization is obtained.

Do it! **A-1: Discussing Web-based order forms**

Questions and answers
1 What is e-commerce?
2 What is a shopping cart?
3 What kind of information do you have to enter while buying online?

Credit cards and security

Explanation

To ensure security and confidentiality, and to prevent misuse when you enter credit card information, you should check the following:

- Check the credentials of the store. The store should be respected and have a good track record.

- Ensure that the store has a registered Web site and does not use free Web space available on any server.

- Ensure that the store's contact information, such as the postal address and phone number, is listed on the Web site.

- Check the store's refund and return policy on the Web site. This will help you understand how you can return items, such as when you receive goods that are damaged.

- Read the privacy policy on the Web site. Understand the type of customer information that the Web site collects, and determine whether the site has a secure ordering system, or a *secure server*. If the site is hosted on a secure server, it provides a *secure Web page* that automatically encodes a customer's information before sending it to the store's server.

Most browsers indicate the Web site's level of security. Some browsers display a message, and other browsers display a key icon or a locked-padlock icon in the status bar. If the site is not secure, the icon changes to a broken key or an unlocked padlock.

Some online stores that cannot afford a secure Web site accept payments through a secure third-party service, such as PayPal. The third-party server provides a secure payment gateway or connection to ensure that credit card payments are securely transacted.

Do it!   **A-2:   Discussing the use of credit cards on the Internet**

Questions and answers

1   How can you prevent the misuse of credit card information that a customer enters on a Web site?

2   How do you ensure that the Web site you're using to purchase goods is secure?

3   What information should you look for on a site before purchasing a product online?

Topic B: Web security considerations

Explanation   To make browsing faster and more efficient, some Web servers collect information about their users and the type of computers they use. Unauthorized users can install *spyware* or software to use this information and record surfing habits and other vital information, such as credit card details. Hackers might also access Web sites to copy the contents of a site. Several Internet security measures can help prevent these problems.

Understanding cookies and caches

A *cookie* is a small piece of information stored in a text file. A Web server stores cookies on the hard disk of your computer after you access the server's Web site. By default, cookies are stored in the following folder:

```
C:/Documents and Settings/<username>/Cookies
```

A cookie records information about your visit to the Web site. Cookies can record identification details, but this is considered poor practice so most Web developers do not use cookies in this manner. Web sites use cookies when you revisit the sites so that the Web pages open faster. Cookies also determine how many new visitors accessed a Web site or how many times each visitor accessed a site.

Unless you block them, cookies can be stored on your computer without your knowledge or consent, and they can be transmitted to Web sites. Advertisers and marketers on the Internet can misuse cookies to record browsing habits and preferences and then sell the information for commercial interests. To prevent these problems, some browsers permit you to turn off cookies. For example, you can use the Internet Explorer privacy settings to turn off cookies. Other security tools, such as firewalls, can also warn users or turn off cookies.

Caching

To increase the speed of accessing the Web, browsers use a technique called *caching*. The browser stores a local copy of the Web pages you access. When you access the same page again, the browser displays the local copy of the page instead of accessing the page from the Internet.

The local copy is called the *cached page*. Sometimes you might need to use the Refresh command to display the updated version of the page.

Do it!   **B-1:** **Discussing cookies and caching**

Questions and answers
1 What is spyware?
2 How can cookies increase the speed of browsing?
3 How does caching increase the speed of browsing?

Protecting a Web site

Explanation

Developing a Web site requires a substantial amount of effort and time. Therefore, it's important to spend time protecting your investment by taking the necessary security precautions.

Hackers can copy the text, images, and HTML code of the Web site and misuse this content. Hackers can also download an entire Web site to their hard disks by using an automated downloader. Servers that host Web sites store users' personal information. Hackers can view this information and send *spam* (unwanted commercial e-mail) and viruses to the stored e-mail addresses.

To protect your Web site against such attacks:

- Encrypt the HTML code of the site. Translation of the code into an unreadable format is called *encryption*.
- Disable page caching and offline viewing. You can also disable the right-click action of the mouse on your site and disable Web page printing.
- Password-protect the site so that only authorized users can view the content.
- Insert a copyright notice.
- Install firewalls, which can block unauthorized access and sometimes protect your site from spam and viruses.

Do it!

B-2: Discussing Web site protection

Questions and answers

1 List the problems that make the implementation of Web site security imperative.

2 List the measures you can take to protect a Web site.

Digital certificates

Explanation

Many of the standard protocols for electronic communication use digital certificates. *Digital certificates* are electronic files that authenticate the identity of the holder. A trusted third party such as VeriSign, called a *certificate authority*, issues these certificates after verifying the holder's identity. Digital certificates cannot be tampered with.

There are two types of certificates: server and personal. Server certificates authenticate servers so that users can securely access the site. Clients, customers, and vendors can exchange confidential information without the fear of tampering or interception by unauthorized users.

Personal certificates authenticate a user's identity and allow user-specific content to be displayed. For example, a personal certificate can restrict vendor access and ensure that vendors will update only their information, such as product availability, delivery dates, and inventory management.

Secure Sockets Layer

Digital certificates are included in a security protocol called *Secure Sockets Layer* (SSL). To encrypt data, SSL uses a private key. SSL security creates a secure connection between a server and a client's browser so that any information can be transmitted securely over this connection. SSL security enables:

- Data encryption
- Server and client authentication
- Message integrity

To turn on a browser's SSL capabilities, you can simply install the digital certificate.

Do it!

B-3: Discussing digital certificates

Questions and answers
1 What is a digital certificate?
2 What types of certificates are available?
3 What are the advantages of SSL?

Encryption

Explanation

Encryption translates information into an unreadable format to protect its integrity. It enables information to be transmitted across unsecured networks without the risk of interception or tampering.

In cryptography, information is *encrypted* or translated before transmission and then decrypted or deciphered after it reaches the destination. Encryption can be used to protect code, e-mail messages, Internet transactions, and any type of communication between a server and a client.

The type of encryption you can use to protect messages is public key encryption. In this kind of encryption, there are two keys, called the *public* and *private* keys. The key used for encryption, the public key, is published and is known to many users.

The private key, used for decryption, is unpublished, and only the recipient of a message knows this key. A message sender uses the public key to encrypt messages. After receiving the message, the recipient uses the private key to decrypt the message. Any intermediary intercepting the messages cannot decrypt them. Public key encryption is also known as *asymmetric key encryption* because it uses two keys. Public key encryption systems, such as Pretty Good Privacy (PGP), are popular, secure, and easy to use.

Do it!

B-4: Discussing encryption

Questions and answers
1 How does cryptography address concerns about the privacy and integrity of data?
2 What is PGP?
3 Explain the purpose of the public and private keys in public key encryption systems.

Firewalls

Explanation

A *firewall* is an electronic blocking mechanism that prevents unauthorized intruders from accessing a computer system or network. A firewall can be a software program, a hardware device, or a combination of both. In addition to locking out hackers, some firewalls can help block viruses and spam from entering your computer or network.

Firewalls are placed between an internal network or an intranet and an external network, such as the Internet. They inspect and filter all incoming traffic and restrict access to specific URLs.

It's always a good idea to protect a server with a firewall. Any computer connected to the Internet for a long time, such as by a DSL or cable modem, requires a firewall. Many firewall packages are available. Installing a firewall package requires careful consideration and planning.

Do it!

B-5: Discussing firewalls

Questions and answers
1 What is a firewall?
2 When do you need a firewall?

Pg 28-11

Pg 28-11

Unit summary: Internet transactions and security

Topic A In this topic, you learned how to use the Internet to make shopping easier and how to order online by filling out **Web-based forms**. You also learned how to use **credit cards** to pay for online purchases.

Topic B In this topic, you learned about the importance of **Web security**. You also learned how **cookies** and **caches** can increase the speed of browsing the Web. You learned about various measures to **protect** a Web site. Next, you learned about **digital certificates** and **encryption**. Finally, you learned that **firewalls** can protect computers and networks from hackers and sometimes from spam and viruses.

Independent practice activity

1 What is a cookie, and what does it contain?

2 What is a cached page?

3 Explain server and personal digital certificates.

4 What is encryption?

5 How do firewalls protect a network?

Unit 29

Outlook basics

Unit time: 45 minutes

Complete this unit, and you'll know how to:

A Discuss e-mail, and keep e-mail messages secure.

B Explore the Outlook 2000 window, use shortcuts or the Folder List to access folders, change the size of an icon, and customize toolbars.

C Use the Help window.

Topic A: E-mail basics

Explanation   E-mail is one of the fastest and most widely used information exchange methods. Electronic mail, or *e-mail*, is a method of sending and receiving messages over a network or over the Internet. To send and receive e-mail, all you need to have is an e-mail address and Internet access.

Understanding e-mail

You can use e-mail to exchange official and personal messages. Many Web sites, such as www.hotmail.com, offer facilities for sending and receiving e-mail messages. These Web sites have *mail servers* that use the following protocols that make e-mail possible:

- Post Office Protocol 3 (POP3)
- Internet Message Access Protocol (IMAP)
- Hypertext Transfer Protocol (HTTP)

A *protocol* is a set of rules or standards that govern the communication between two computers on a network.

Using a site that offers Web-based e-mail, you can create an e-mail account and an associated mailbox, used for sending and receiving e-mail messages. To register an e-mail account, you enter the following into an online registration form:

- User name
- Password
- Other personal information

A *user name* identifies the user, and a *password* is a identification string required for security purposes. The combination of your unique user name and password ensure restricted access to your e-mail account.

After registering your e-mail account, you can send, receive, and read messages. Information too large to fit into an e-mail message—such as data files, pictures, and video and sound files—can be sent as an e-mail attachment.

E-mail addresses

An *e-mail address* is a combination of the user name you choose when creating an e-mail account and the name of associated Web site (for Web-based e-mail) or Internet service provider. For example, in the e-mail address john_wayne@hotmail.com, john_wayne is the user name, and hotmail.com is the name of the Web site.

Benefits of e-mail

Following are some advantages of e-mail over other types of communication:

- E-mail is faster than postal communication.
- E-mail is efficient because you can send messages to recipients across the world in a few seconds. You can also send the same message to several (or many) recipients simultaneously.
- E-mail is inexpensive because you don't have to buy postage stamps for e-mail messages.
- E-mail provides flexibility because users can view their messages by accessing the Internet from any location around the world.
- E-mail software enables you to save messages for future reference, and storing messages electronically takes up just a little disk space.

E-mail etiquette

E-mail etiquette refers to the set of rules you should follow when communicating online. Some of the rules include the following:

- Be careful with your word choices. Because e-mail is not accompanied by facial expressions and body language, it's easy for readers to misinterpret. Tone of voice is harder to convey in e-mail than in person.
- Choose an appropriate font and the correct case for the text so that messages are easy to read.
- Limit the use of uppercase letters to sentence beginnings or to headings. (Using all capital letters for a message is considered to be the e-mail equivalent of shouting.)
- Use double-spacing only between paragraphs.
- Avoid using jargon unless the recipient is familiar with it.
- Write the subject of your message, stating the purpose of the e-mail.
- Be concise and to the point.
- Check your messages for spelling errors before sending.

Do it!

A-1: Discussing e-mail

Questions and answers
1 E-mail is a method of exchanging messages over a network or over the Internet. True or false?
2 What is an e-mail address?
3 What can be sent as attachments with an e-mail message?

E-mail security considerations

Explanation

You can use various methods, such as *encryption* and *digital signatures*, to secure your e-mail. Also, it's important to ensure that the messages you send and receive are virus-free because e-mail messages are susceptible to viruses.

Encryption

Messages that you exchange over the Internet are usually in the plain text format. Unauthorized users who intercept messages during transmission can gain access to confidential information. To secure your e-mail and data, you can use encryption.

Encryption encodes a message on the sender's computer so that only the recipient of the message can read it. The sender encrypts the message by using an encryption key, and the recipient decrypts it by using a decryption key. A *key* is a long multi-digit number, which is similar to a password. If your system provides the encryption feature, you need to obtain a certificate from your administrator or a certified security authority to use this feature.

Digital signatures

Digital signatures are encrypted signatures that ensure that no one can alter your messages. A digital signature attaches a *digital authentication certificate* or a *digital ID* to the message, with information about the sender's identity. Digital certificates authenticate the sender and assure the recipients of the sender's identity. To use the digital signature option, you need to obtain a certificate from your administrator or a certified security authority, such as VeriSign.

Viruses and unsolicited e-mail

An e-mail message might be transmitted over various networks before it reaches your mailbox. This makes messages prone to virus attacks. An e-mail message infected by a virus can corrupt the data on your computer.

Viruses might corrupt your e-mail attachments or be sent within attachments. It's essential to use antivirus software to scan messages for viruses before opening the messages or attachments. Do not open attachments you're not expecting or attachments from people you don't know.

Unsolicited e-mail, or *spam*, can also carry viruses. Even if spam does not carry a virus, it can cause problem by flooding your Inbox with commercial advertising that you are not interested in.

Do it!

Test

A-2:   Discussing e-mail security

Questions and answers

1 What are the two ways to secure your e-mail messages?

2 What are digital signatures?

3   *A code that ids who u r*

3 How does encryption work?

9   *Writing n code*

4 Name a certified security authority that can authorize you to use digital signatures.

Topic B: Introduction to Outlook 2000

Explanation

Outlook is a Microsoft application used to send and receive e-mail. You can configure multiple e-mail accounts in Outlook. You can also use Outlook as a personal organizer to schedule meetings, appointments, and tasks. Any e-mail message, contact, or task created in Outlook is called an *item*. Items are stored in folders, such as Inbox, Calendar, Contacts, and Tasks. You can access the items within each folder by using the buttons in the Outlook window.

Starting the application

Start Outlook by choosing Start, Programs, Microsoft Outlook. You can also start Outlook by double-clicking the Outlook icon on the desktop.

The Outlook window elements

The Outlook 2000 window contains elements that are common to other Windows-based applications. These elements, shown in Exhibit 29-1, include the following:

- Control menu icon
- Title bar
- Menu bar
- Toolbar
- Status bar

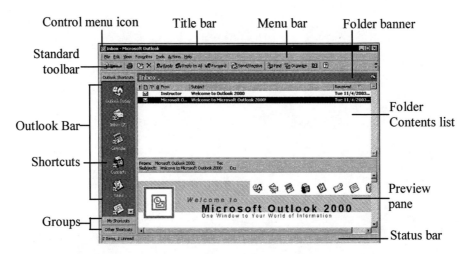

Exhibit 29-1: The elements of the Outlook 2000 window

The following table describes the elements of the Outlook 2000 window.

Element	Description
Control menu icon	Changes the size and position of the window.
Title bar	Displays the name of the active folder (by default, Inbox), followed by the name of the program (Microsoft Outlook).
Menu bar	Provides menus, such as File, Edit, and View.
Standard toolbar	Contains buttons for performing common tasks. The buttons available on the Standard toolbar depend on the active folder.
Outlook Bar	Contains shortcuts to commonly used folders. The Outlook Bar consists of three groups: Outlook Shortcuts, My Shortcuts, and Other Shortcuts.
Shortcuts	Provide access to Outlook folders (such as Inbox and Tasks) with one click.
Groups	Divides shortcut buttons into logical categories. By default, Outlook contains three groups: Outlook Shortcuts, My Shortcuts, and Other Shortcuts.
Folder banner	Displays the name of the active folder.
Scrollbar	Displays the areas of the active folder that are not currently visible on screen.
Folder Contents list	Displays the contents of the active folder. This list is the top pane on the right side of the window. By default, Inbox is the active folder.
Preview pane	Displays the contents of the item selected in the Folder Contents list.
Status bar	Displays the number of items in the active folder.

Closing Outlook

You can close Outlook by choosing File, Exit or by clicking the program window's Close button.

Do it!

B-1: Exploring the Outlook 2000 window

Here's how	Here's why
1 Choose **Start**, **Programs**, **Microsoft Outlook**	To start Microsoft Outlook.
Observe the window	The Outlook window contains several elements, such as a title bar, menu bar, folder banner, and Outlook Bar (shown in Exhibit 29-1).
2 Observe the title bar	It contains the Control menu icon, used to change the size and position of the window. The title bar also shows the title as "Inbox - Microsoft Outlook."
Observe the menu bar	The menu bar provides the names of the available menus, such as File, Edit, and View.
Observe the Standard toolbar	It contains buttons that you use to perform common tasks.
3 Observe the Outlook Bar	It contains shortcuts to Outlook folders, including Inbox, Contacts, and Tasks.
Observe the Folder Contents list	It displays items stored in the Inbox folder. Currently, it contains four messages: three sent to you by your instructor, and the Microsoft welcome message.
Observe the Preview pane	It shows you the contents of the Microsoft welcome message. Notice that this welcome message is selected in the Folder Contents list.
4 Point to the right border of the Outlook Bar	◄╟►
	The pointer changes to a double-headed arrow.
Drag the border to the right	To increase the size of the Outlook Bar.
5 Increase the size of the Preview pane	(Point to the upper border of the Preview pane, and drag upward.) Notice that the size of the Folder Contents list is reduced.
6 Decrease the size of the Outlook Bar and Preview pane	Bring the Outlook Bar and the Preview pane back to their original sizes.
7 Choose **File**, **Exit**	To close Outlook.

The Outlook 2000 folders

Explanation Outlook contains folders where you can store items. You can use the default folders or create your own folders. You access the folders by using the shortcuts in the Outlook Bar. The following table describes the default folders.

Folder	Description
Outlook Today	Displays a snapshot view of the activities you've planned for the day.
Inbox	Used to create, send, receive, delete, and move e-mail messages.
Calendar	Provides a place for you to plan and schedule work-related and personal activities, including appointments, meetings, and events.
Contacts	Stores information about people with whom you frequently communicate.
Tasks	Provides a place for you to manage your to-do list.
Notes	Stores your reminders about important activities to complete and meetings to attend.
Deleted Items	Stores items that have been deleted from other folders.

Shortcut groups on the Outlook Bar

Default shortcuts on the Outlook Bar provide access to commonly used folders. You can add or remove shortcuts to meet your needs. The shortcuts are divided into three groups on the Outlook Bar:

- Outlook Shortcuts
- My Shortcuts
- Other Shortcuts

Display the shortcut buttons for a group by clicking on the group name. The Outlook Shortcuts is displayed by default and has shortcuts to the following folders:

- Outlook Today
- Inbox
- Calendar
- Contacts
- Tasks
- Notes
- Deleted Items

The My Shortcuts group has shortcuts to these folders:

- Drafts
- Outbox
- Sent Items
- Journal
- Outlook update

The Other Shortcuts group has shortcuts to these folders:

- My Computer
- My Documents
- Favorites

Do it!

B-2: Using shortcuts to access folders

Here's how	Here's why
1 Start Outlook	Choose Start, Programs, Microsoft Outlook.
Observe the Folder Contents list	It displays the contents of the Inbox folder. You use Inbox to store, compose, receive, and read e-mail messages.
Observe the Standard toolbar	It contains buttons to compose, format, and send e-mail.
2 Click **Calendar**	 (On the Outlook Bar.) To activate the Calendar.
Observe the Folder Contents list	A planner appears. Use this to schedule your activities, appointments, and events.
Observe the Standard toolbar	The buttons on the Standard toolbar change according to the active folder. Currently, the toolbar contains buttons for tasks that can be done using the Calendar.
3 Click **Contacts**	To display the contents of the Contacts folder. Use this folder to store information about your business and personal contacts. By default, the Contacts folder is empty.
4 Click **Tasks**	To display the contents of the Tasks folder. Schedule your tasks by using this shortcut.
5 Click **Notes**	To display the contents of the Notes folder. Create notes to remind yourself of important activities.
6 Click **Outlook Today**	(On the Outlook Bar.) To display Outlook Today in the Folder Contents list.
Observe the Folder Contents list	Outlook Today provides a summary of the day's plan. It displays the summary of the day's scheduled activities in three sections: Calendar, Tasks, and Messages.

The Folder List

Explanation

In addition to the Outlook Bar, you can also access folders by clicking the appropriate folder in the Folder List. To display the Folder List, click the Folder List button on the Advanced toolbar. You can also display the Folder List by choosing View, Folder List.

Do it!

B-3:   Using the Folder List

Here's how	Here's why
1 Activate **Inbox**	
2 Choose **View**, **Folder List**	The Folder Contents list splits, and the Folder List appears.
Observe the Folder List	
	You can see folders, such as Inbox, Contacts, Calendar, and Notes. These folders contain the items that you create in Outlook.
3 Click **Calendar**	(In the Folder List.) The planner appears in the Folder Contents list.
4 Click **Tasks**	In the Folder List.
5 Click **Outlook Today**	To activate Outlook Today.
6 Choose **View**, **Folder List**	To close the Folder List. Because the Folder List occupies space in the Folder Contents list, it's advisable not to keep it open.
7 Choose **View**, **Toolbars**, **Advanced**	To display the Advanced toolbar. It contains buttons for moving to the next or previous item, displaying the Folder List, and showing or hiding the Preview pane.
Click [icon]	(On the Advanced toolbar.) To display the Folder List.
Click [icon]	To close the Folder List.

Folder List box contents:

```
Folder List                              ×
⊟ Outlook Today - [Mailbox - Student]
     Calendar
     Contacts
     Deleted Items
     Drafts
     Inbox (2)
     Journal
     Notes
     Outbox
     Sent Items
     Tasks
⊞ Public Folders
```

Changing the icon size on the Outlook Bar

Explanation

You can reduce the size of the icons on the Outlook Bar to avoid scrolling to view the shortcuts.

To change the icon size on the Outlook Bar to small icons, right-click the Outlook Bar and choose Small Icons.

Do it!

B-4: Changing the display to small icons

Here's how	Here's why
1 In the Outlook Bar, verify that Outlook Shortcuts is active	You'll reduce the size of icons in this group.
Right-click a blank area of the Outlook Bar	
	A shortcut menu appears.
Choose **Small Icons**	The icons in the group are smaller.
2 Change the size of the icons back to large icons	Right-click the Outlook Bar, and choose Large Icons.

Customizing toolbars

Explanation
Outlook provides four built-in toolbars that you can display or hide at any time. The toolbars are:

- Standard
- Advanced
- Remote
- Web

By default, only the Standard toolbar appears in the Outlook window. You can add and remove icons or commands on the toolbars. You can also create a custom toolbar that contains frequently used commands.

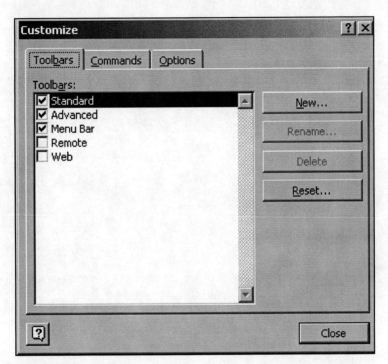

Exhibit 29-2:The Toolbars tab of the Customize dialog box

To display or hide a toolbar:

1 Choose Tools, Customize to open the Customize dialog box.
2 Click the Toolbars tab.
3 Check the toolbar you want to display, or clear it to hide it.

To add commands to a toolbar:

1 Open the Customize dialog box.
2 Click the Commands tab. From the Categories list, select the icon you want.
3 Drag the required command from the Commands list to the toolbar.

Do it!

B-5: Customizing toolbars

Here's how	Here's why
1 Choose **Tools, Customize...**	To open the Customize dialog box.
2 Click the **Toolbars** tab	(If necessary.) To view the names of the toolbars. The toolbars that are already displayed are selected, as shown in Exhibit 29-2.
Check **Web**	Observe that an additional toolbar is visible below the Standard toolbar.
3 Click the **Commands** tab	You'll customize the Web toolbar.
From the Categories list, select **View**	You'll move some of the commands on this toolbar to the Web toolbar.
From the Commands list, select **Filter**	You will need to scroll down the list of commands to find the Filter command.
Drag Filter from the Commands list to the Web toolbar, as shown	
	The Filter button is added to the Web toolbar.
4 Activate the Toolbars tab	You'll hide the Web toolbar.
Clear **Web**	Observe that the Web toolbar no longer appears.
5 Click **Close**	To close the Customize dialog box.

Topic C: Using Help

Explanation
The Help system provides assistance while you're working. You can access Help by choosing Help, Microsoft Outlook Help, by pressing F1, or by using the Office Assistant.

The Help window

To open the Help window, choose Help, Microsoft Outlook Help. The Outlook Help window has three tabs you can use to find the desired help topic:

- Contents
- Index
- Answer Wizard

The Help database

The Help database is a collection of topics. It contains answers to frequently asked questions about Microsoft Outlook and its interactions with other Office programs.

Index

The Help database is divided into three tabs: Contents, Answer Wizard, and Index. By default, when you access help, the Index tab is displayed. You'll see two panes. The left pane allows you to search for a help topic and select the related topics by typing or selecting a keyword and clicking Search. A list of topics appears in the lower portion of the left pane. The right pane then displays the information on the topic you've selected.

Answer Wizard

The Answer Wizard uses plain language to find an answer to your question. Like the Index, you'll see a left and right pane. You type a question in the text box of the left pane and click Search. A list of topics appears in the lower portion of the pane. You can then select a topic and the contents will appear in the right pane. The Answer Wizard is really the Office Assistant without the animated character.

Contents

The Help Contents tab also has two panes. The left pane lists the various topics available by category. Double-clicking on a category displays the information documents related to that category. You may then select a document. The information and a list of any related topics appear in the right pane.

Do it!

C-1: Using the Help window

Here's how	Here's why
1 Choose **Help, Microsoft Outlook Help**	To open the Microsoft Outlook Help window.
2 Observe the window	It's divided into two panes. The left pane contains three tabs: Contents, Answer Wizard, and Index. The right pane contains the information for the selected Help topic.
3 Verify that the Contents tab is active	
Double-click **Getting Started**	

Click **Take the Microsoft Outlook Tour**	
In the right pane, click the graphic	To begin the tour.
Follow the screen prompts to view the tour	
4 Close the Microsoft Outlook Help window	To close the tour.
Close the Help window	Click the Close button.
5 Close Outlook	

Unit summary: Outlook basics

Topic A In this topic, you learned how **e-mail** works, and you learned about the **advantages** of e-mail over other types of communication. You learned how to **secure** your e-mail messages by using **encryption** or **digital signatures**.

Topic B In this topic, you learned how to **start** and **close** Outlook 2000. You learned how to use **shortcuts** to access folders. You also learned how to access folders by using the **Folder List**. You learned how to change the **size** of the **icons** on the Outlook Bar. Finally, you learned how to **customize** toolbars.

Topic C In this topic, you learned how to use the **Help** window.

Independent practice activity

1 Start Outlook.

2 Activate Calendar.

3 Activate Outlook Today.

4 Activate the Office Assistant.

5 Get help on Notes.

6 Close the Help window.

7 Turn off the Office Assistant.

8 Open the Help window directly, and search for Tasks.

9 Close the Help window.

10 Close Outlook.

10/27/06

Unit 30

Working with e-mail messages

Unit time: 60 minutes

Complete this unit, and you'll know how to:

A Explore the Inbox, and read, create, send, reply to, format, and check the spelling of messages.

B Attach files to a message, save an attachment, and forward, recall, set a priority for, and apply a flag to a message.

Topic A: E-mail messages

Explanation

One of the most frequently used folders in Outlook is the Inbox. By default, all messages that you receive are stored in the Inbox folder. Using the Inbox, you can read, create, reply to, and forward messages.

The Inbox

By default, the Inbox is divided into two panes:

- Folder Contents list
- Preview pane

The Folder Contents list displays a list of messages with their header information. The Preview pane displays the message text. An e-mail header contains the following information:

- **From** — Identifies the sender of the message.
- **Subject** — Identifies the content of the message.
- **Received** — Contains the date and time that the message was received.

The header information also contains an icon. The following table describes the icons that you might see in the message list as a part of the header information.

Icon	Description
	New and unread message.
	Message that's been read.
	Message that's been read and replied to.
	Message that's been read and forwarded.
!	High-priority message.
	Message with a file attachment.
	Flagged message.

Modifying header information

To modify the header information and choose what should be included in the headings:

1 Choose View, Current View, Customize Current View to open the View Summary dialog box.

2 Click the Fields button.

3 From the Available fields list, select the fields you want to display in the header.

4 Click the Add button. The fields are moved to the Show these fields in this order list. This list shows the order of the fields in the header.

5 Select each field, and use the Move Up and Move Down buttons to adjust the order in which fields appear in the header.

6 To remove a field from the header, you select the field in the Show these fields in this order list, and click the Remove button.

Do it!

A-1: Exploring the Inbox

Here's how	Here's why
1 Start Outlook	
2 Activate **Inbox**	To display the Inbox.
Observe the Folder banner	It indicates that Inbox is the active folder.
3 In the Folder banner, click **Inbox**	To display the Folder list.
Examine the toolbars	Notice the mail-specific buttons.
Observe the status bar	It shows the total number of messages and the number of unread messages.
4 In the Folder banner, click **Inbox** again	To close the Folder list.
5 Observe the header information of the first message	It shows the name of the sender (instructor), the subject ("Welcome to Outlook 2000"), and the date of receipt. It also shows an icon of a closed envelope to the left of the sender's name.
Observe the Preview pane	It shows the content of the message that is selected in the Folder Contents list. However, this pane does not permit you to edit the message.

Reading messages

Explanation

All new messages are delivered to the Inbox. Messages that have not been read appear in bold, and messages that have been read appear in regular text.

To read a message:

1   In the Folder Contents list, select the message you want to read.
2   Read the message in the Preview pane, or open it in a message window by double-clicking it. You can open several messages simultaneously.

When you read a message, Outlook marks the message as read. The header information in the Folder Contents list does not appear in bold. You can mark an unread message as read by right-clicking it in the Folder Contents list and selecting Mark as read. If you right-click a message that you've read, the shortcut menu will contain the option Mark as unread.

It is not uncommon to have several messages open at one time. This happens when you've double-clicked on multiple messages and each is open in a message window. To navigate between these open messages, you can just click on the appropriate message window to read the desired e-mail or you can click on the message icon located in the Taskbar at the bottom of the screen (under the application window).

Do it!

A-2:   Reading a message

Here's how	Here's why
1 Double-click the Welcome message from Microsoft Outlook	(In the Folder Contents list.) Opens the message in the message window.
Read the message	
Observe the toolbar	In addition to buttons for replying to and forwarding messages, the toolbar contains buttons to set the flag and to move to the next and previous messages.
2 Close the message window	Click the Close button.
3 Observe the Folder Contents list	The icons for both messages change to an open envelope, and the header information no longer appears in bold. You might need to deselect the text to see that it's no longer bold.

Creating and sending messages

To open a new Message window, as shown in Exhibit 30-1, and create a message:

1   Choose File, New, or click the New button on the Standard toolbar.
2   Address and compose your message.
3   Send the message by clicking the Send button on the Standard toolbar or by pressing Ctrl+Enter.

Whenever you're online and you receive a new message, a message box appears, indicating that you have received a new message.

By default, Word is the e-mail editor for new messages if Word is installed on your computer. New messages are composed in HTML format, by default. HTML formatting allows you to apply character and paragraph formats to your message text.

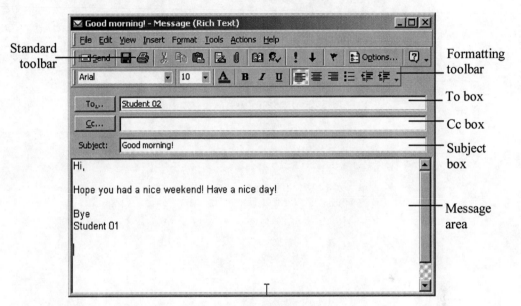

Exhibit 30-1: The message window with a sample message

The following table describes the elements of the message window.

Element	Description
To box	Contains the e-mail address of the person to whom the message will be sent.
Cc box	Contains the e-mail addresses of all the people to whom you want to send a copy of the message.
Bcc box	Contains the e-mail addresses of all the people to whom you want to send a blind copy of the message. The addresses of other recipients in the Bcc box are not displayed in the message received by a recipient.
Subject box	Contains a word or phrase that describes the message.
Message area	Contains the contents of the message.
Standard toolbar	Contains buttons for frequently used actions, such as sending messages, attaching files, setting priority, and flagging messages.
Formatting toolbar	Contains buttons that apply styles, fonts, and other formats to your message text.

Do it!

A-3: Creating and sending a message

Here's how	Here's why
1 Verify that the Inbox is activated	
2 Choose **File, New, Mail Message**	To open the message window.
3 In the To box, enter **Student ##**	(## represents the student number one higher than your number.) The student with the highest number should use "Student 01."
Press `TAB` twice	To move to the Subject box.
4 In the Subject box, type **Hello**	
Press `TAB`	To move to the message area.
5 In the Message area, enter a brief message of your choice	
Click **Send**	To send the message.

Replying to a message

Explanation There are two instant-reply buttons: Reply and Reply to All. The Reply button creates a return message addressed only to the sender. The Reply to All button creates a return message addressed to the sender and to everyone else who received the original message.

Reply messages, by default, contain the body of the original message. This is useful when you need to refer to the original message. However, you can also choose not to include the original message.

To send a reply:

1 Open the message that you want to answer.
2 Click the Reply button in the message window. This opens another message window with the name of the recipient in the To address field. (The sender of the original message now appears as a recipient.) The Reply message inherits the subject of the original message with "RE:" prefixed (it means that the message is a reply).
3 Type the message in the message area of the message window. The text appears in blue.
4 Click Send to send the message.

Reply without original message

To reply to a message that automatically does not include the original message, you'll need to change the default option. Here's how:

1 Choose Tools, Options to open the Options dialog box.
2 On the Preferences tab, click the E-mail Options button to open the E-mail Options dialog box.
3 Under On replies and forwards, display the When replying to a message list and select Do not include original message.
4 Click OK twice.

Once this default has been changed, every time you reply to a message the original message will not be included.

Moving, copying and deleting text in messages

To move text in a message, select the appropriate text. Point to the selected text and drag to the new location. When you release the mouse button, the move is complete. You can also select the text and choose Edit, Cut. Place the insertion point in the desired location, and choose Edit, Paste.

To move text from one message to another, open both messages and arrange them so they are side by side. Select the appropriate text, point to the selected text and drag to the new location. When you release the mouse button, the move is complete. You can also select the text and choose Edit, Cut. Activate an open message. Place the insertion point in the desired location, and choose Edit, Paste.

To copy text from one message to another, select the appropriate text and choose Edit, Copy. Activate an open message, place the insertion point in the desired location, and choose Edit, Paste.

To copy text from another source, like a Word document, into a message, select the appropriate text and choose Edit, Copy. Activate an open message, place the insertion point in the desired location, and choose Edit, Paste.

To remove text from a message, select the text and press the Delete key.

Do it!

A-4: Replying to a message

Here's how	Here's why
1 Open the message with the subject "Hello"	You will reply to this message.
2 Click **Reply**	To open a message window where you can compose a reply.
Observe the message window	The To field contains the name of the sender of the original message. The Subject field displays the same subject with "RE:" in front of it.
3 Verify that the insertion point is in the first line of the message area	You'll type your reply here.
Type the message as shown	

```
To,...   | Student 02                    |
Cc...    |                               |
Subject: | RE: Hello                     |

Hi,
Thanks for the mail.
Regards

        -----Original Message-----
        From:     Instructor
        Sent:     Friday, November 07, 2003 4:09 AM
        To:       Student 01
        Subject:  Hello
```

	The text in the message area appears blue. By default, reply text appears as blue.
4 Click **Send**	To send the message to the recipient and return to the message window.
Open the same message window again	If necessary.
5 Observe the message below the Standard toolbar	**ⓘ You replied on 11/6/2003 5:50 AM. Click here to find all related message**
	This is called the InfoBar. It indicates the action taken on the message, with the date and time. In this case, the action was replying to a message.
Close the message window	

6 Observe the Folder Contents list	The original message has an icon showing that you have replied to the message.
7 Click the Folder banner	To display the Folder List.
Click **Sent Items**	(In the Folder list.) The reply message that you sent appears as an item. Any message that you send will be stored in this folder.

Saving a message as a file

Explanation You might want to store an important message as a separate file for future reference.

To save a message:

1 Open the message.
2 Choose File, Save As to open the Save As dialog box.
3 Specify a name and location for the file.
4 Specify the file type in the Save as type box.
5 Click Save.

Do it! ### A-5: Saving a message as a file

Here's how	Here's why
1 Activate **Inbox**	
2 Open the message you have just received	
3 Choose **File, Save As...**	To open the Save As dialog box.
From the Save in list, navigate to the current unit folder	To specify where the file should be saved.
In the File name box, type **My first message**	To name the file.
In the Save as type list, verify that Rich Text Format is selected	To specify that the message should be saved as an RTF file.
Click **Save**	To save the file.
4 Close the message window	

Formatting messages

Explanation

You can highlight important text by changing its color, size, or font. You can also underline or italicize text to emphasize it.

Use the Formatting toolbar or the Font dialog box to format the text in a message. To open the Font dialog box, choose Format, Font. Most of the options in the Font dialog box, shown in Exhibit 30-2, are available on the Formatting toolbar.

You can cut and copy formatted text and place it elsewhere within the same message or in a different message. You can also open application files, such as Word, and cut or copy text and then place it in a message.

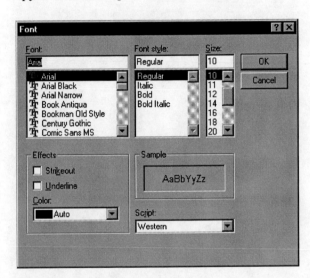

Exhibit 30-2: The Font dialog box

Do it!

A-6: Formatting messages

Here's how	Here's why
1 Create a message, and address it to your e-mail partner	Enter the subject "Sales Analysis."
In the message area, type as shown	

> Hi,
>
> We have done very well in the West Coast operations.
> Hpoe we will be able to maintain the same this year too.
> Solena will send you more details.
> Bye,
> For Outlander Spices

2 Select the message in the message area	
3 Choose **Format, Font...**	To open the Font dialog box, shown in Exhibit 30-2.
In the Font list, verify that Arial is selected	
From the Size list, select **12**	To change the size of the font to 12pt.
From the color list, select **Blue**	To change the color of the message text to blue.
Click **OK**	To close the Font dialog box.
4 Deselect the text	
Observe the message	The size and color of the message text have changed.
5 Place the pointer between the Standard and Formatting toolbars as shown	

	The pointer shape changes to a four-headed arrow. The next step will drag the Formatting toolbar below the Standard toolbar to show it completely.
Drag the Formatting toolbar below the Standard toolbar	Keep the left mouse button pressed.
Release the mouse button	

6 Select **For Outlander Spices**

(It's the last line of the message.) You'll change the formatting for this text.

From the Font list, select **Arial Black**

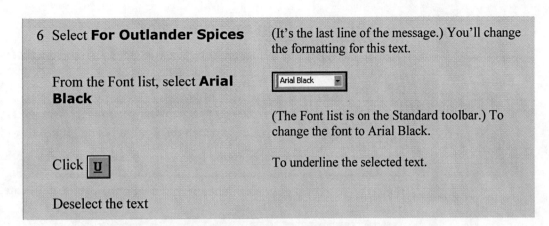

(The Font list is on the Standard toolbar.) To change the font to Arial Black.

Click [U]

To underline the selected text.

Deselect the text

Checking spelling and grammar in messages

Explanation

Outlook has a built-in selling checker that you can use to be sure that you haven't misspelled any words in your messages. To start checking the spelling, do either of the following:

- Press F7.
- Choose Tools, Spelling to open the Spelling dialog box, shown in Exhibit 30-3.

After you open the Spelling dialog box, you can use the available options to correct spelling, ignore spelling, and even add a word to the dictionary. If the Spelling feature finds a repeated word, you can choose to ignore or delete the duplicate.

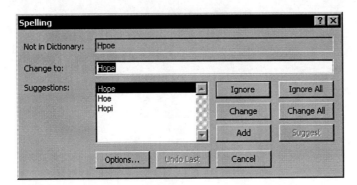

Exhibit 30-3: The Spelling dialog box

The Not in Dictionary box displays words that are not in the dictionary. You can take any of the following actions:

- Choose a suggested spelling from the Suggestions list, and click Change to change a single occurrence of the misspelled word.
- Click Change All to change all occurrences of that word.
- Ignore one instance or all instances of a specific word. Click the Ignore Once button to ignore a single instance, and click the Ignore All button to ignore all instances of a specific word.

Using Word to edit mail messages

If you have Microsoft Word installed on your computer, you can choose to use it, rather than Outlook, to edit your mail message. To use Word as your message editor, choose Tools, Options; activate the Mail Format tab; and check "Use Microsoft Word to edit e-mail messages."

One advantage of this is that Microsoft Word automatically checks spelling as your type. Another advantage is that Word allows you to check grammar as well as spelling.

Do it!

A-7:   Checking the spelling in a message

Here's how	Here's why
1 Choose **Tools, Spelling...**	To open the Spelling dialog box. This dialog box opens only if the message contains a misspelled word.
Observe the Spelling dialog box	It displays the incorrect word ("Hpoe") in the Not in Dictionary box and prompts you to change it to "Hope." It also displays other words in the Suggestions list.
2 In the Suggestions list, verify that "Hope" is selected	
Click **Change**	To change "Hpoe" to "Hope."
3 Observe the dialog box	It now shows "Solena" as a word not found in the dictionary. For frequently used proper names, you can add them to the dictionary by clicking the Add button.
Click **Ignore**	You want to retain the word.
Observe the message box	Microsoft Outlook ⊠ The spelling check is complete. OK
4 Click **OK**	To close the message box.
5 Click Send	To send the message.

Topic B: Handling messages

Explanation

You can attach any type of file (such as a text file, a Word document, or an Excel workbook) to a message. When you receive a message with an attachment, you can open the attached file or save it for future reference. When you want to send the same message along with the attachment to someone else, you can forward the message.

Attaching files

Attachments make it possible to send any type of data, in the original format, through e-mail. For example, you can send Word, Excel, PowerPoint, sound, and movie files as attachments. You can attach a single file or multiple files to a message.

To attach a file:

1   Choose Insert, File to open the Insert File dialog box.
2   Select the file that you want to attach.
3   Click Insert to attach the file to the message.

Alternatively, you can click the attachment icon on the Standard toolbar to display the Insert File dialog box.

Deleting a file attachment

After attaching a file to a message, you might decide that you no longer want to send the attachment. To remove the attachment, click the attachment icon in the open message window, and press Delete.

Do it!

B-1: Attaching a file to a message

Here's how	Here's why
1 Open the message window	
2 Create a message of your choice	
3 Choose **Insert**, **File...**	To open the Insert File dialog box.
From the Look in list, navigate to the current unit folder	If necessary.
Verify that Analysis is selected	Analysis is an Excel Workbook that contains yearly sales data.
Click **Insert**	To attach the Analysis file to the message. Notice that the icon for the attachment appears at the bottom of the window.
4 Send the message	

Saving attachments

Explanation

When you receive a message containing file attachments, a paper clip icon will appear in the Folder Contents list. The icon appears to the left of the sender's name (as a part of the header information). You can view the name and size of the attachment in the header of the Preview pane.

There are several ways to save an attachment:

- Double-click the option to save an attachment from the Preview pane.
- Open the message in a separate window, and double-click the file attachment icon in the message area.
- Right-click the attachment icon, and choose Save As from the shortcut menu.
- Choose File, Save Attachments from the Preview pane.

After you save an attachment, you can start the application and open the file in the associated program (such as Word or Excel).

Do it!

B-2: Saving an attachment

Here's how	Here's why
1 Open the message you have just received	
2 Choose **File, Save Attachments...**	To open the Save Attachment dialog box.
Navigate to the current unit folder	If necessary.
In the File name box, type **My sales 2003.xls**	To rename the attachment.
Click **Save**	To save the file and return to the message window.
3 Close the message window	

Forwarding messages

Explanation

You can forward a message to colleagues. To forward a message:

1 Open the message.

2 Click Forward.

3 In the To box, enter the e-mail addresses of the people you want to send the message to.

4 Click Send to send the message.

Alternatively, you can select the message and choose Actions, Forward to open the message for forwarding.

Do it!

B-3:   Forwarding a message

Here's how	Here's why
1 Select the message with subject "Sales Analysis"	
2 Click **Forward**	The message window opens.
Observe the message window	The message window contains the original message. The subject of the message appears automatically with "FW" prefixed.
In the To box, enter the name of someone in your class	
In the message area, type **I thought you might find this useful in your work.**	
Click **Send**	

Recalling messages

Explanation

You might send a message with incorrect or incomplete information. If this happens, you can *recall* the message after sending it. However, you can recall only those messages that have not been read by the recipients.

To recall a message:

1 On the Outlook Bar, click My Shortcuts.
2 From the list of shortcuts, click Sent Items.
3 Open the message you need to recall.
4 Choose Actions, Recall This Message to open the Recall This Message dialog box.
5 Select the appropriate options. You can choose to either delete the message and replace it with a new message, or just delete the message without replacing it.
6 Click OK to close the Recall This Message dialog box.
7 Close the message window.

Do it!

B-4: Recalling a message

Here's how	Here's why
1 Activate **My Shortcuts**	You will recall the message you have just sent and replace it with a new message.
Click **Sent Items**	
2 Open the message you have just forwarded	(Double-click it to open it.) The message opens in the message window.
3 Choose **Actions, Recall This Message...**	

	You can recall a message only if the recipient has not read it yet.
Select **Delete unread copies and replace with a new message**	
Verify that "Tell me if recall succeeds or fails for each recipient" is checked	To be notified about the status of the recalled message.
Click **OK**	To return to the message window.

4	Observe the InfoBar	It informs you that the message has not been sent.
5	Change the subject to **Important information**	
	Send the message	You can see the window containing your original message.
6	Observe the InfoBar	It shows the date and time you tried to recall the message.
	Close the message	
7	Activate **Inbox**	If necessary.
	Observe the message with the subject "Message Recall Success: Sales Analysis"	This is the notification message sent to you by Outlook.
8	Double-click the message	A message window appears, stating that the message was successfully recalled.
	Close the message window	

Setting the priority for a message

Explanation

The urgency with which you send a message to a recipient defines the *importance* of a message. By setting the Importance level to High, you can ensure faster delivery of a message. This also communicates to the recipient that the message requires an immediate response. The default Importance level for a message is Normal. You can also set the Importance to Low for routine messages.

You might send messages that are confidential or personal. This is referred to as the *sensitivity* of a message. In addition to setting the Importance level of a message, you can set the Sensitivity level. There are four Sensitivity levels:

- Confidential
- Private
- Personal
- Normal (the default level)

By setting the Sensitivity to Private, you prevent other people from editing your original message when they reply to it or forward it to others. If a message is not work-related, you can assign the Personal level of Sensitivity to it.

To change the Importance and Sensitivity settings for a message, do the following:

1 Type the message in the message window.
2 Choose View, Options to open the Message Options dialog box.
3 Under Message settings, change the Importance and Sensitivity levels as you wish.
4 Close the Message Options dialog box, and send the message.

Do it!   ## B-5:   Setting a message's priority

Here's how	Here's why
1 Create a message of your choice	Do not send the message yet.
2 Click **Options**	To open the Message Options dialog box.
Under Message settings, from the Importance list, select **Low**	Importance: Low
Under Message settings, from the Sensitivity list, select **Personal**	
Click **Close**	To close the Message Options dialog box.
3 Send the message	
Observe the blue arrow to the left of the message	This shows that the message was sent with low Importance.
4 Open the message from your partner	
Observe the InfoBar	⚠ Please treat this as Personal. This message was sent with Low importance.
	It informs you that the message is Personal and was sent with Low importance.
Close the message	

Flagging messages

Explanation

When you receive an e-mail message that needs follow-up action, but you can't respond immediately, you can *flag* the message for action at a later date. A flagged message can be sent to others, alerting the recipients that action is needed.

A flagged message is indicated by a flag symbol to the left of the message in the Folder Contents list. You need to specify the action to be taken as well as the due date. You can use the Flag for Follow Up dialog box, shown in Exhibit 30-4, to select one of the following actions:

- Follow up
- FYI
- Forward
- No response
- Read
- Reply or reply to all
- Review

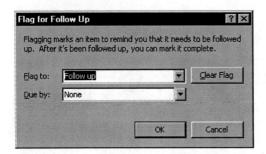

Exhibit 30-4: The Flag for Follow Up dialog box

To flag a message for follow-up:

1 Open the message.
2 Choose Actions, Flag for Follow Up to open the Flag for Follow Up dialog box.
3 From the Flag to list, select the action needed.
4 From the Due by list, select the date by which the action should be completed.
5 Click OK to apply the flag settings.

To remove a flag from a message, open the Flag for Follow Up dialog box and click the Clear Flag button.

Marking a flagged message as completed

When you have completed the desired action for a flagged message, you can mark the flag as completed by following these steps:

1 Open the flagged message.
2 Open the Flag for Follow up dialog box, and check Completed.

You can also right-click the flagged message and choose Flag Complete from the shortcut menu.

Do it!

B-6: Flagging e-mail messages

Here's how	Here's why
1 Send a message to your partner about the new marketing policy	Enter "Marketing policy" in the Subject box.
2 Open the message sent to you by your partner	You can also flag a message within the Folder Contents list. Just right-click the message, and choose Flag for Follow Up from the shortcut menu.
3 Choose **Actions, Flag for Follow Up...**	To open the Flag for Follow Up dialog box.
From the Flag to list, select **Reply**	To specify the action to be taken.
From the Due by list, select today's date	To specify the date by which you need to take the action. By default, the due date's time is 5:00 P.M. You can change the time.
Click **OK**	To assign the Reply flag.
4 Observe the message	! ⬜ ⚑ 🖇 From Subject ✉ ⚑ Student... Marketing policy
	(In the Folder Contents list.) A flag appears before the name of the sender. This mark identifies the messages for which you need to take action.
Observe the InfoBar	ⓘ Reply by Friday, November 07, 2003 5:00 PM.
	It shows that a Reply action is required and shows the due date and time.
5 Send a reply to the message	
Observe the InfoBar	ⓘ Reply by Friday, November 07, 2003 5:00 PM. You replied on 11/6/2003 9:16 PM. Click here to find
	It displays the date and time of your reply.
6 Click ⚑	To open the Flag for Follow Up dialog box.
Check **Completed**	
Click **OK**	To close the Flag for Follow Up dialog box.
Close the message window	
7 Observe the flag	The flag has changed to gray, indicating that follow-up is completed.

Unit summary: Working with e-mail messages

Topic A   In this topic, you learned about the **Inbox** and its interface. You learned how to **read** a message. You learned how to **create** and **send** a message. You learned how to **reply** to a message. You learned how to **save** a message as a **file**. You learned how to **format** a message and change the **font, font size,** or **color.** Finally, you learned how to **check the spelling** of messages.

Topic B   In this topic, you learned how to **attach** a file to a message. You also learned how to **save an attachment** for later reference. You also learned how to **forward** a message to another recipient. You learned how to **recall** a message that has been sent. You learned how to **set the priority** of a message. Finally, you learned how to **flag** a message.

Independent practice activity

1   Compose a message, as shown in Exhibit 30-5.

2   Send the message to your e-mail partner.

3   Read the message you received from your e-mail partner.

4   Reply to the e-mail with the message, **Thanks for the mail. I've forwarded a copy to my colleague.**

5   Recall the message you sent so that you can replace it with a new message.

6   Edit the message, and add the line **Please refer to the attached file.**

7   Attach the Charts file to the message.

8   Set the message's priority to High.

9   Send the message.

10   Read the new message and save the attached file with the name **My charts.xls.**

11   Forward the message you received to your e-mail partner.

12   Save the message that you received with the name **My mail.**

Exhibit 30-5: The message window with a sample message

Unit 31

Managing e-mail

Unit time: 70 minutes

Complete this unit, and you'll know how to:

A Create a personal folder, and move, delete, and restore messages.

B Search and sort e-mail messages.

C Customize page setup, and print messages.

D Create and use distribution lists, and update an address book.

Topic A: Personal folders

Explanation

You can use Outlook to manage personal or business information, such as messages, contacts, and tasks. This information is stored in a data file on your local hard disk. To organize and store this information, you can do all of the following:

- Create a personal folder for storing this data file.
- Create subfolders within a personal folder to organize the information.
- Move, copy, and rename subfolders within a personal folder.

Creating personal folders

By default, all Outlook items are stored on the Exchange server unless you intentionally save them on your hard disk. When you're disconnected from the server, you won't be able to use any of the items in your Outlook folders. For this reason, you might want to create a personal folder on your local hard disk. Because this folder is stored on your local hard disk, it reduces network traffic.

A *Personal Folders file* stores important information that can be viewed even when the e-mail service is not working. The extension for a Personal Folders file is .pst. For every personal folder you create, Outlook automatically creates a Deleted Items folder.

To create a personal folder:

1 Choose File, New, Personal Folders File (.pst) to open the Create Microsoft Personal Folders dialog box.
2 In the File name box, enter the name of the personal folder.
3 Select the folder where you want to keep the personal folder.
4 Click Create to create the personal folder.
5 In the Create Microsoft Personal Folders dialog box, specify the folder name and the password.
6 Click OK to open the Personal Folders Password dialog box.
7 Enter a password, and click OK.

Do it!

A-1:   Creating a personal folder

Here's how	Here's why
1 Choose **File, New, Personal Folders File (.pst)...**	To open the Create Microsoft Personal Folders dialog box.
From the Save in list, select the current unit folder	You'll save the personal folder in the current unit folder.
Edit the File name box, to read **My personal folder**	
Click **Create**	

(dialog box:)
Create Microsoft Personal Folders
File : C:\Student Data\Unit_31\My personal folder.p
Name : Personal Folders
Encryption Setting
○ No Encryption
● Compressible Encryption
○ Best Encryption
Password
Password:
Verify Password:
☐ Save this password in your password list
OK   Cancel   Help

	To open the Create Microsoft Personal Folders dialog box.
2 In the Name box, type **My personal folder**	To name the personal folder.
Observe the Encryption Setting	By default, personal folders are secured by compressible encryption. Though the .pst file is secured from other programs, it can be compressed if necessary.
3 Under Password, in the Password box, type **password**	To specify the password.
In the Verify Password box, type **password**	To confirm "password" as the password.
Click **OK**	(To create the personal folder.) The Personal Folders Password dialog box opens. You are immediately prompted for the password.
4 In the Password box, type **password**	
Click **OK**	The folder My personal folder opens, and it's empty.

Moving messages between folders

Explanation   You can move messages to a personal folder to organize messages and clear out your Inbox.

To move a message:

1   Select the message(s) to be moved. To select multiple consecutive messages, click the first message, hold Shift, and click the last message. To select non-consecutive messages, hold Ctrl and click each message.

2   Right-click the selected message(s), and choose Move to Folder from the shortcut menu.

3   Select the destination folder.

4   Click OK.

Do it!   ### A-2:   Moving messages between folders

Here's how	Here's why
1 Activate **Inbox**	
2 Select a message of your choice	You will move this message to the folder you created.
Right-click the message	To display the shortcut menu.
Choose **Move to Folder...**	To open the Move Items dialog box.
Select **My personal folder** as the destination folder	
Click **OK**	To move the message to My personal folder.
3 From the Folder List, select **My personal folder**	
Observe the Folder Contents list	The message has been moved to My personal folder.

Deleting and restoring messages

Explanation

To organize and save space in the Inbox, delete messages you no longer need. To delete a message:

1   Select the folder from which you want to delete a message.
2   Select the message you want to delete.
3   Click the Delete button on the Standard toolbar. You can also choose Edit, Delete.

The deleted message is stored in the Deleted Items folder. Deleted messages remain there until you empty the folder. The Deleted Items folder can be set to be emptied when you exit Outlook. To empty the Deleted Items folder manually, choose Tools, Empty "Deleted Items" Folder. If you have deleted a message by mistake, you can restore it by dragging it from the Deleted Items folder to the Inbox or another folder.

Do it!

A-3:   Deleting and restoring messages

Here's how	Here's why
1 Activate **Inbox**	
2 Select the message with the subject "Sales Analysis"	
Click ✖	(The Delete button is on the Standard toolbar.) To delete the message.
Observe the Folder Contents list	The message you deleted does not appear in the list.
3 Click **Deleted Items**	(On the Outlook bar.) To open the Deleted Items folder. This folder stores all deleted messages until the folder is emptied. The message you deleted appears here.
Drag the message to the Inbox	(To restore the deleted message.) Select the message and, without releasing the mouse, bring the pointer to the Inbox in the Folder List.
4 Activate **Inbox**	
Observe the Folder Contents list	The deleted message appears again.

Topic B: Searching and sorting messages

Explanation

The Find and Advanced Find features search for items, such as messages and contacts, based on criteria you specify. You can also sort messages in a specific order so that messages are easier to find.

The Find feature

When you have several messages in your Inbox, it might be difficult to locate a specific message. The Find feature locates messages and other items, such as appointments, meeting requests, and tasks. This feature searches for items based on a word or phrase you specify.

To use the Find feature:

1   Click Find on the Standard toolbar to display the Find bar, shown in Exhibit 31-1. The Find bar has a text box that you can use to specify your search criteria.

2   In the Look for box, enter the keyword or phrase you want to search for.

3   Click Find Now to begin the search. Only items containing the specified keyword or phrase appear in the Folder Contents list.

4   After the search is completed, click Clear to clear the search and to display all the folder items in the Folder Contents list.

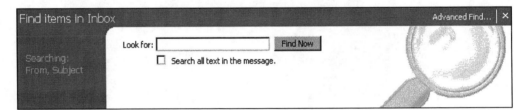

Exhibit 31-1: The Find bar

Do it!

B-1: Using the Find feature

Here's how	Here's why
1 Activate **Inbox**	If necessary.
2 Click **Find**	(On the Standard toolbar.) To display the Find bar.
In the Look for box, type **welcome**	To search for messages containing the word "welcome."
Check **Search all text in the message**	If necessary.
Click **Find Now**	There are two messages in the Folder Contents list.
3 On the Find bar, click **Clear Search**, as shown	Look for: welcome Find Now ☑ Search all text in the message. Did you find it? If not, try: ● Go to Advanced Find... ● Clear Search
	To clear the search and display all messages in the Folder Contents list.

The Advanced Find feature

Explanation   The Advanced Find feature provides several additional options you can use to search for Outlook items. You can search for items by:

- Specifying keywords.
- Specifying certain criteria for the search. For example, while searching for messages, you can specify whether to search the Subject field or the message body.
- Searching items based on message categories.

To search for an item by using the Advanced Find feature:

1 Choose Tools, Advanced Find to open the Advanced Find dialog box, shown in Exhibit 31-2.
2 From the Look for list, select the item you want to search for.
3 Specify the search criteria.
4 Click Find Now to start the search.

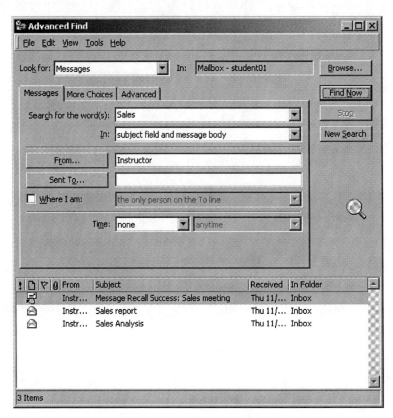

Exhibit 31-2: The Advanced Find dialog box

Do it!

B-2: Finding messages by using Advanced Find

Here's how	Here's why
1 Activate **Inbox**	(If necessary.) You'll search for messages in the Inbox.
2 Click **Advanced Find**	(On the Find bar.) To open the Advanced Find dialog box.
Observe the default settings	By default, messages in the mailbox are searched. You can use the Look for list to change the items to be searched. To change the folder, click Browse and select the folder you want.
3 Verify that the Messages tab is active	
In the Search for the word(s) box, type **Sales**	To find messages containing the word "Sales." By default, only the Subject field is searched. You can change this setting.
From the In list, select **subject field and message body**	To search the subject as well as the text of messages.
In the From box, type **Instructor**	To search for messages sent by the instructor.
Click **Find Now**	To start the search.
4 Observe the Advanced Find dialog box	The search results appear in the window, as shown in Exhibit 31-2.
Close the Advanced Find dialog box	
5 Hide the Find bar	On the Find bar, click Close.

Sorting messages

Explanation

You can sort messages in either ascending or descending order based on one or more fields. For example, you can sort messages based on the date you received them so that the most recent message appears first in the Folder Contents list.

To sort messages:

1 Activate the folder you want to sort.
2 Open the View Summary dialog box.
3 Click Sort to open the Sort dialog box, shown in Exhibit 31-3.
4 Under Sort items by, select a field to sort by, and select Ascending or Descending sort order. To sort the messages on additional fields, you select the fields and sort order under Then by groups.
5 Click OK to close the Sort dialog box.
6 Click OK to close the View Summary dialog box.

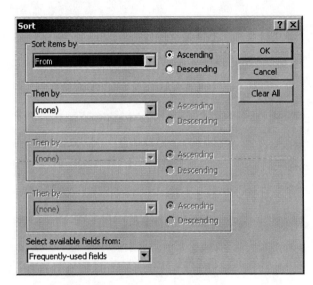

Exhibit 31-3: The Sort dialog box

You can also sort messages by clicking the column heading in the Folder Contents list.

Do it!

B-3: Sorting messages

Here's how	Here's why
1 Choose **View, Current View, Customize Current View...**	To open the View Summary dialog box.
2 Click **Sort**	To open the Sort dialog box.
Under Sort items by, select **From**	(If necessary.) To sort the messages by sender name.
Under Sort items by, select **Ascending**	(If necessary.) The messages will be sorted in ascending alphabetical order (A-Z).
Click **OK**	To close the Sort dialog box.
3 Click **OK**	To close the View Summary dialog box.
Observe the Folder Contents list	The messages are sorted in ascending order based on the column From.

Topic C: Printing messages

Explanation

You can print messages, and you can modify page settings, which include margins, headers and footers, and page orientation.

Page setup

You can configure the way a message prints by modifying the page setup. By default, a message prints in the Memo style. To configure the page setup for the Memo style, as shown in Exhibit 31-4:

1   Choose File, Page Setup, Memo Style.
2   Specify the paper type.
3   Specify the paper source.
4   Specify the margins.
5   Specify the page orientation.
6   Specify the header and footer that should appear in the printed message.

A preview appears in the upper-right corner of the dialog box. You can customize print styles by choosing File, Page Setup, Define Print Styles.

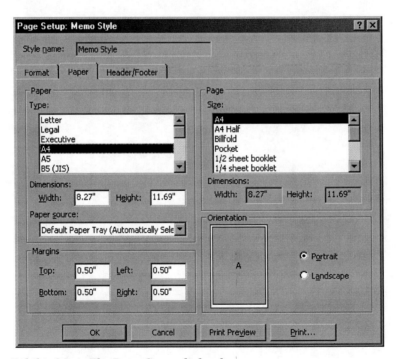

Exhibit 31-4: The Page Setup dialog box

Do it!

C-1: Customizing page setup

Here's how	Here's why
1 Open the message with the subject "Sales Analysis"	
2 Choose **File**, **Page Setup**, **Memo Style**	To open the Page Setup: Memo Style dialog box.
3 Activate the Paper tab	
Verify that under Orientation, Portrait is selected	
4 Click the **Header/Footer** tab	
Under Header, enter **Confidential**	
Click **OK**	To close the dialog box.
5 Close the message window	

Printing

Explanation

You can print a message from the Folder Contents list or from the message window. To send the selected message to the printer without opening the Print dialog box, click the Print button.

Use the File, Print command when you want to change the print style. The Print dialog box differs depending on whether you opened it from the Folder Contents list or from the message window. In the Print dialog box, you can specify details such as:

- Page range
- Number of copies
- Paper size
- Paper source
- Orientation

To print a message from the message window:

1   Open the message you want to print.

2   Choose File, Print to open the Print dialog box.

3   Under Print style, specify the style in which you want to print. The default Print style is Memo style.

4   Under Copies, specify the number of copies you want to print.

5   Under Print options, check Print attached files with item(s) to print the attached files along with the message.

6   Click the Properties button to open the Document Properties dialog box for your printer. In this dialog box, specify properties such as paper size and orientation.

7   Click OK to close the Document Properties dialog box.

8   Click Preview to see how the document will look when it's printed.

9   Click OK to print the document.

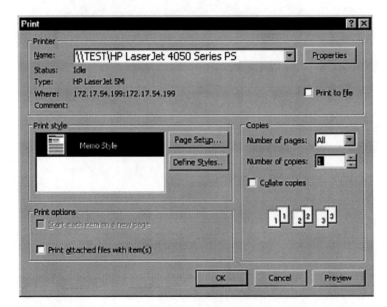

Exhibit 31-5: The Print dialog box

Do it!

C-2: Printing a message

Here's how	Here's why
1 Select the message with subject "Sales Analysis"	
2 Choose **File, Print...**	To open the Print dialog box. The Name list shows the name of the printer. Notice that under Print style, Memo Style is selected. By default, one copy will be printed.
Verify that Number of copies is 1	Use this field to specify the number of copies to be printed.
3 Click **Preview**	The Print Preview window opens to show you how your printed message will look. Your name will appear at the top of the page to show that you are the recipient.
Click **Close**	To close the Print Preview window without printing. If you want to print the memo, clicking Print closes the print preview and returns to the Print dialog box. Then, you can click OK to send the memo to the printer.
4 Close the message window	

Topic D: Address books

Explanation   An address book stores the names, e-mail addresses, and phone numbers of your business and personal contacts. You can add a contact to an address book directly from an e-mail message, and you can delete contacts you no longer need. You can also use the address book to create a distribution list. Use a *distribution list* when you communicate frequently with a specific group of individuals.

The distribution list

When you work with a team, you might find yourself frequently addressing messages to the same group of people. For instance, you regularly send an updated price list to all managers. To make this task quick and easy, you can create a distribution list with the e-mail addresses for this group of people.

To create a distribution list:

1   Choose Tools, Address Book, or click the Address Book icon, to open the Address Book window.
2   Choose File, New Entry to open the New Entry dialog box.
3   Under Put this entry, from the list, select Contacts to store the distribution list as a personal list.
4   From the Select the entry type list, select New Distribution List.
5   Click OK to open a dialog box.
6   In the Name box, enter the name you want to use for the group.
7   Click Select Members to open the Select Members dialog box.
8   Select the members for the distribution list.
9   Click Save and Close.

If you want to send a message to the members of a distribution list:

1   Click the To button in the message to open the Select Names dialog box.
2   From the Show Names list, select Contacts. The distribution list will appear in the Type Name or Select from list.
3   Double-click the distribution list and click OK to include it in the To field of the message.
4   Click Send.

Do it!

D-1:   Creating and using a distribution list

Here's how	Here's why
1 Choose **Tools, Address Book...**	To open the address book.
2 Choose **File, New Entry...**	To open the New Entry dialog box.
Under Put this entry, from the list, select **Contacts**	If necessary.
Under Select the entry type, select **New Distribution List**	To create a new distribution list.
Click **OK**	The Untitled - Distribution List dialog box opens.
3 In the Name box, type **Sales team**	This will be the name of your distribution group.
4 Click **Select Members**	To open the Select Members dialog box.
5 Select the student one higher than you	For example, if you are Student 01, you would select Student 02. If you have the highest number, select the lowest-numbered student.
Click **Add**	To add this student as a member of the Sales team distribution list.
6 Add the next student to the list	Select the student and click Add. If you have the second-highest number, select the lowest; if you have the highest, select the second lowest.
Click **OK**	To add the members to the group.
7 Observe the dialog box	The name of the dialog box has changed to "Sales team - Distribution List."
Click **Save and Close**	To close the Sales team - Distribution List dialog box.
8 Close the Address Book window	
9 Create a message, as shown	

```
To...    [                                  ]
Cc...    [                                  ]
Subject: [                                  ]

Hi,
Please send your individual report to the Sales
Manager today.
Bye.
```

10	Open the Select Names dialog box	Click To.
	From Show Names from the list, select **Contacts**	Under Outlook Address Book.
	Select **Sales team**	To send the message to all the members of the Sales team.
	Click **To**	To add Sales team to the Message Recipient's list.
	Click **OK**	To close the Select Names dialog box.
11	Send the message	

Updating an address list from an incoming message

Explanation

You might often get e-mail messages from people who are not in your address book. You can easily add them to your Contacts list.

To add an e-mail address to your Contacts list:

1 Open the message.
2 Right-click the e-mail ID.
3 Choose Add to Contacts.
4 Click Save and Close to add the e-mail address to the Contacts list.

Do it!

D-2: Updating an address book

Here's how	Here's why
1 Open any message sent by the instructor	To add the instructor's e-mail address to your address book.
2 In the From field, right-click **Instructor**	To display the shortcut menu.
Click **Add to Contacts**	To add the instructor's e-mail address to the Contacts list.
Click **Save and Close**	To update the address book.
3 Close the message window	
4 Send a blank message to the members of the contact list	Notice that the instructor's e-mail address has been included in the address book.

Deleting an entry from your address book

Explanation
You can delete an address from an address book if it's no longer required. To do so:

1 Choose Tools, Address Book, or click the Address Book icon, to open the Address Book window.

2 Double-click the distribution list from which you want to delete an entry.

3 Select the entry you want to delete.

4 Press Delete.

Do it!
D-3: Deleting an e-mail address

Here's how	Here's why
1 Choose **Tools**, **Address Book**	To open the Address Book dialog box.
2 From Show Names from the list, select **Contacts**	
3 Select **Instructor (E-mail)**	In the address book.
Press (DELETE)	A message box appears prompting you to confirm the deletion.
Click **Yes**	To delete the entry from the address book.
4 Close the address book	

Unit summary: Managing e-mail

Topic A   In this topic, you learned how to **create** a **personal folder** to store Outlook items on your local hard drive. You learned how to **move messages** between **folders**. You also learned how to **delete** and **restore messages**.

Topic B   In this topic, you learned how to use the **Find** features to locate messages in your Inbox. You learned how to use the **Advanced Find** features to find items by specifying search criteria. You also learned how to **sort messages**.

Topic C   In this topic, you learned how to **set printing options** by using the **Page Setup** dialog box. You also learned how to **print messages** by using the Print dialog box.

Topic D   In this topic, you learned how to **create** and **use** a **distribution list**. You learned how to **update** an **address book** with an **e-mail address** from an incoming message. Finally, you learned how to **delete e-mail addresses** from your address book.

Independent practice activity

1 Using Advanced Find, search the Inbox for messages you have received from your partner. (*Hint:* In the Advanced Find dialog box, click From to select the name of your partner.)

2 Close the Advanced Find dialog box.

3 Hide the Find bar.

4 Create a personal folder file called **My Customer Service**.

5 Move a message of your choice to My Customer Service.

6 Sort the messages in the Inbox on the Subject field in descending order.

7 Sort the messages in the Inbox on the Received field in descending order.

8 Delete a message of your choice.

9 Restore the deleted message.

10 Print a message of your choice.

11 Create a distribution list for the **Purchase Team** with two other students as members.

12 Close the address book.

13 Send a blank message to the Purchase Team with the subject **Test mail**.

14 Close Outlook.

Appendix A

Exam objectives map

This appendix covers these additional topics:

A The ICDL/ECDL Syllabus 4, Office 2000 exam objectives and where they are covered in this course.

Topic A: ICDL/ECDL exam objectives

Explanation   The following table lists the ICDL/ECDL Syllabus 4, Office 2000 exam objectives and provides a reference to the location of the content that covers each objective.

Location	Knowledge item
Unit 1, Topic A, Page 1-2	Understand the terms hardware, software, Information Technology (IT).
Unit 1, Topic A, Page 4-5	Understand and distinguish between mainframe computer, network computer, personal computer, laptop, personal digital assistant (PDA) in terms of capacity, speed, cost, and typical users.
Unit 1, Topic B, Page 7-15, Page17-18	Know the main parts of a personal computer such as: central processing unit (CPU), hard disk, common input and output devices, types of memory. Understand the term peripheral device.
Unit 1, Topic B Page 27-28	Know some of the factors that impact on a computer's performance such as: CPU speed, RAM size, the number of applications running.
Unit 1, Topic B Page 7-8	Understand some of the functions of the CPU in terms of calculations, logic control, immediate access memory. Know that the speed of the CPU is measured in megahertz (MHz) or gigahertz (GHz).
Unit 1, Topic B, Page 17-18	Understand different types of computer memory such as: RAM (random-access memory), ROM (read-only memory) and distinguish between them.
Unit 1, Topic B, Page 24	Know how computer memory is measured: bit, byte, KB, MB, GB, TB. Relate computer memory measurements to characters, files and directories/folders.
Unit 1, Topic B, Page 9-12	Identify some of the main devices for inputting data into a computer such as: mouse, keyboard, trackball, scanner, touchpad, lightpen, joystick, digital camera, microphone.
Unit 1, Topic B, Page 13-15	Identify common output devices for displaying the results of processing carried out by a computer, such as: monitors, screens, printers, plotters, speakers. Know where these devices are used.
Unit 1, Topic B, Page 15	Understand some devices are both input/output devices such as: touchscreens.
Unit 1, Topic B, Page 17-22	Compare the main types of memory storage devices in terms of speed, cost and capacity such as: diskette, Zip disk, data cartridges, CD-ROM, internal, external hard disk.
Unit 3, Topic A, Page 9	Understand the purpose of formatting a disk.

Location	Knowledge item
Unit 2, Topic B, Page 11	Understand that using electronic documents can help reduce the need for printed materials.
Unit 1, Topic C, Page 29-32	Distinguish between operating systems software and applications software. Understand the reasons for software versions.
Unit 1, Topic C, Page 29-30	Describe the main functions of an operating system and name some common operating systems.
Unit 1, Topic C, Page 31-32	List some common software applications such as: word processing, spreadsheet, database, Web browsing, desktop publishing, accounting, together with their uses
Unit 1, Topic C, Page 29	Understand the term Graphical User Interface (GUI).
Unit 1, Topic C, Page 34	Understand how computer-based systems are developed. Know about the process of analysis, design, programming and testing often used in developing computer-based systems.
Unit 1, Topic D, Page 36-37	Understand the terms, local area network (LAN), wide area network (WAN). Understand the term client/server.
Unit 1, Topic D, Page 36-41	List some of the advantages associated with group working such as: sharing printers, applications, and files across a network.
Unit 1, Topic D, Page 41	Understand what an intranet is and understand the distinction between the Internet and an intranet.
Unit 1, Topic D, Page 41	Understand what an extranet is and understand the distinction between an intranet and an extranet.
Unit 1, Topic D, Page 41	Understand what the Internet is and know some of its main uses.
Unit 1, Topic D, Page 43	Understand what the World Wide Web (WWW) is and distinguish it from the Internet.
Unit 1, Topic D, Page 38-40	Understand the use of the telephone network in computing. Understand the terms Public Switched Telephone Network (PSTN), Integrated Services Digital Network (ISDN), Asymetric Digital Subscriber Line (ADSL).
Unit 1, Topic D, Page 38-40	Understand the terms analogue, digital, modem, transfer rate, (measured in bps – bits per second).

Location	Knowledge item
Unit 2, Topic A, Page 5	Identify some situations where a computer might be more appropriate than a person for carrying out a task and where not.
Unit 2, Topic A, Page 2-4	Know some of the uses of large-scale computer applications in business such as: business administration systems, airline booking systems, insurance claims processing, online banking.
Unit 2, Topic A, Page 5	Know some of the uses of large-scale computer applications in government such as: public records systems (census, vehicle registration), revenue collection, electronic voting.
Unit 2, Topic A, Page 2-3	Know some of the uses of large-scale computer applications in hospitals/healthcare such as: patient records systems, ambulance control systems, diagnostic tools and instruments, specialist surgical equipment.
Unit 2, Topic A, Page 4	Know some of the uses of computer applications in education such as: student registration and timetabling systems, computer-based training (CBT), distance learning, homework using the Internet.
Unit 2, Topic A, Page 3	Understand the term teleworking. List some of the advantages of teleworking such as: reduced or no commuting time, greater ability to focus on one task, flexible schedules, reduced company space requirements. List some disadvantages of teleworking such as: lack of human contact, less emphasis on teamwork.
Unit 2, Topic A, Page 7	Understand the term electronic mail (e-mail) and know its main uses.
Unit 2, Topic A, Page 2	Understand the term e-Commerce. Understand the concept of purchasing goods and services online, including giving personal details before a transaction can be carried out, payment methods, consumer's basic right to return unsatisfactory goods.
Unit 2, Topic B, Page 9	List some of the advantages of purchasing goods and services online, such as: services available 24 hours a day, opportunity to view a wide range of products. List some of the disadvantages of purchasing goods and services online such as: choosing from a virtual store, no human contact, risk of insecure payment methods.
Unit 2, Topic B, Page 10	Understand what elements and practices can help create a good working environment such as: appropriate positioning of monitors, keyboards and adjustable chairs, use of a mouse mat, use of a monitor filter, provision of adequate lighting and ventilation, frequent breaks away from the computer.
Unit 2, Topic B, Page 10	List some common health problems which can be associated with using a computer such as: injuries to wrists caused by prolonged typing, eye strain caused by screen glare, back problems associated with poor seating or bad posture.
Unit 2, Topic B, Page 11	List some safety precautions when using a computer such as: ensuring power cables are safely secured, power points are not overloaded.

Location	Knowledge item
Unit 2, Topic B, Page 11	Be aware that recycling printed outputs, recycling printer toner cartridges, using a monitor that consumes less power while the computer is inactive can help the environment.
Unit 2, Topic C, Page 12	Understand the term information security and the benefits to an organisation of being proactive in dealing with security risks such as: adopting an information security policy with respect to handling sensitive data, having procedures for reporting security incidents, making staff members aware of their responsibilities with respect to information security.
Unit 2, Topic C, Pg 12	Know about privacy issues associated with computers, such as adopting good password policies. Understand what is meant by user ID and differentiate between user ID and password. Understand the term access rights and know why access rights are important.
Unit 2, Topic C, Pg 13	Know about the purpose and value of backing up data, software to a removable storage device.
Unit 2, Topic C, Pg 13	Be aware of possible implications of theft of a laptop computer, PDA, mobile phone such as: possible misuse of confidential files, loss of files, loss of important contact details if not available on a separate source, possible misuse of telephone numbers.
Unit 2, Topic C, Pg 14	Understand the term virus when used in computing and understand that there are different types of virus. Be aware when and how viruses can enter a computer system.
Unit 2, Topic C, Pg 14	Know about anti-virus measures and what to do when a virus infects a computer. Be aware of the limitations of anti-virus software. Understand what 'disinfecting' files means.
Unit 2, Topic C, Pg 14	Understand good practice when downloading files, accessing file attachments, such as: use of virus scanning software, not opening unrecognised e-mail messages, not opening attachments contained within unrecognised e-mail messages.
Unit 2, Topic C, Pg 16-17	Understand the concept of copyright when applied to software, and also to files such as: graphics, text, audio, video. Understand copyright issues involved in downloading information from the Internet.
Unit 2, Topic C, Pg 16-17	Understand copyright issues associated with using and distributing materials stored on removable media such as CD's, Zip disks, diskettes.
Unit 2, Topic C, Pg 16-17	Know how to check the Product ID number for a software product. Understand the terms shareware, freeware, end-user license agreement.
Unit 2, Topic C, Pg 16-17	Know about data protection legislation or conventions in your country. Understand the implications of data protection legislation for data subjects and data holders. Describe some of the uses of personal data.

Location	Knowledge item
Unit 3, Topic A, Pg 2	Start the computer.
Unit 3, Topic A, Pg 2	Shut down the computer using an appropriate routine.
Unit 3, Topic A, Pg 2	Restart the computer using an appropriate routine.
Unit 3, Topic A, Pg 12-13	Shut down a non-responding application.
Unit 3, Topic A, Pg 6-7	View the computer's basic system information: operating system and version number, installed RAM (random access memory).
Unit 3, Topic E, Pg 33-37	Change the computer's desktop configuration: date & time, volume settings, desktop display options (colour settings, screen pixel resolution, screen saver options).
Unit 3, Topic E, Pg 40	Set, change keyboard language.
Unit 3, Topic A, Pg 9	Format removable disk media: diskette, Zip disk.
Unit 3, Topic A, Pg 11	Install, uninstall a software application.
Unit 3, Topic E, Pg 42	Use keyboard print screen facility and paste contents into a document.
Unit 3, Topic B, Pg 14-20	Use available Help functions.
Unit 3, Topic C, Pg 21	Recognize common desktop icons such as those representing: files, directories/folders, applications, printers, recycle bin/wastebasket.
Unit 3, Topic C, Pg 22	Select and move desktop icons.
Unit 3, Topic C, Pg 22	Open a file, directory/folder, application from the desktop.
Unit 3, Topic C, Pg 24	Create a desktop shortcut icon, desktop menu alias.

Location	Knowledge item
Unit 3, Topic B, Pg 17, Topic D, Pg 27-28	Identify the different parts of a window: title bar, menu bar, toolbar, status bar, scroll bar.
Unit 3, Topic D, Pg 30-32	Collapse, expand, resize, move, and close a window.
Unit 3, Topic C, Pg 22	Switch between open windows.
Unit 4, Topic E, Pg 32	Launch a text editing application. Open, create a file.
Unit 4, Topic E, Pg 34	Save the file to a location on a drive.
Unit 4, Topic E, Pg 32	Close the text editing application.
Unit 4, Topic A, Pg 2	Understand how an operating system shows drives, folders, files in a hierarchical structure.
Unit 4, Topic A, Pg 2-3	Know that the devices used by an operating system to store files and folders are the hard disk, diskette, CD-ROM, network drives.
Unit 4, Topic A, Pg 6	Navigate to a file, folder on a drive.
Unit 4, Topic B, Pg 15	Create a directory/folder and a further sub-directory/sub-folder.
Unit 4, Topic A, Pg 8	Open a window to display directory/folder name, size, location on drive.
Unit 4, Topic A, Pg 10-11	Recognize common file types: word processing files, spreadsheet files, database files, presentation files, image files, audio files, video files, compressed files, temporary files.
Unit 4, Topic A, Pg 12	Count the number of files, files of a particular type, in a folder (including any files in sub-folders).
Unit 4, Topic A, Pg 13-14	Change file status: read-only/locked, read-write.
Unit 4, Topic C, Pg 24	Sort files by name, size, type, date modified.
Unit 4, Topic A, Pg 11	Understand the importance of maintaining correct file extensions when re-naming files.
Unit 4, Topic B, Pg 16	Re-name files, directories/folders.

Location	Knowledge item
Unit 4, Topic B, Pg 20	Select a file, directory/folder individually or as a group of adjacent, non-adjacent files, directories/folders.
Unit 4, Topic B, Pg 18	Duplicate files, directories/folders between directories/folders and between drives.
Unit 4, Topic B, Pg 17	Move files, directories/folders between directories/folders and drives.
Unit 4, Topic B, Pg 19	Understand why making a 'backup' copy of files to a removable storage device is important.
Unit 4, Topic D, Pg 28-29	Delete files, directories/folders to the recycle bin/wastebasket.
Unit 4, Topic D, Pg 30	Restore files, directories/folders from the recycle bin/wastebasket
Unit 4, Topic D, Pg 31	Empty the recycle bin/wastebasket
Unit 4, Topic C, Pg 21	Use the Find tool to locate a file, directory/folder
Unit 4, Topic C, Pg 21-23	Search for files by content, date modified, date created, size, wildcards.
Unit 4, Topic C, Pg 21	View list of recently used files.
Unit 4, Topic C, Pg 25	Understand what file compression means.
Unit 4, Topic C, Pg 25	Compress files in a folder on a drive.
Unit 4, Topic C, Pg 25	Extract compressed files from a location on a drive.
Unit 5, Topic B, Pg 11	Know what a virus is and what the effects of a virus might be.
Unit 5, Topic B, Pg 11	Understand some of the ways a virus can be transmitted onto a computer.
Unit 5, Topic B, Pg 11, 12	Understand the advantages of a virus-scanning application.
Unit 5, Topic B, Pg 12	Understand what 'disinfecting' files means.

Location	Knowledge item
Unit 5, Topic B, Pg 12	Use a virus scanning application to scan specific drives, folders, files.
Unit 5, Topic B, Pg 14	Understand why virus-scanning software needs to be updated regularly.
Unit 5, Topic A, Pg 4	Change the default printer from an installed printer list.
Unit 5, Topic A, Pg 2	Install a new printer on the computer.
Unit 5, Topic A, Pg 4	Print a document from a text editing application.
Unit 5, Topic A, Pg 6	View a print job's progress using a desktop print manager.
Unit 5, Topic A, Pg 6	Pause, re-start, delete a print job using a desktop print manager.
Unit 6, Topic A, Pg 2, 10	Open (and close) a word processing application.
Unit 6, Topic A, Pg 5	Open one, several documents. Move between multiple documents.
Unit 6, Topic A, Pg 7, 11	Create a new document (based on default, other available template).
Unit 6, Topic A, Pg 7	Save a document to a location on a drive.
Unit 6, Topic A, Pg 8	Save a document under another name.
Unit 6, Topic A, Pg 10	Save a document in another file type such as: text file, Rich Text Format, HTML, template, software specific file extension, version number.
Unit 6, Topic D, Pg 25-27	Use available Help functions.
Unit 6, Topic A, Pg 11	Close a document.
Unit 6, Topic C, Pg 18	Change between page view modes.
Unit 6, Topic C, Pg 20	Use magnification/zoom tools.

Location	Knowledge item
Unit 6, Topic C, Pg 23	Display, hide built-in toolbars.
Unit 6, Topic C, Pg 21	Modify basic options/preferences in the application: user name, default directory/folder to open, save documents.
Unit 7, Topic A, Pg 2	Display, hide non-printing characters.
Unit 7, Topic A, Pg 2, 6	Insert text.
Unit 7, Topic A, Pg 2, 6	Insert special characters, symbols
Unit 7, Topic B, Pg 8-9	Select character, word, line, sentence, paragraph, entire body text
Unit 7, Topic B, Pg 8-10	Edit content by inserting new characters, words within existing text, over-typing to replace existing text.
Unit 7, Topic A, Pg 4	Use the undo, redo command.
Unit 7, Topic B, Pg 11, 14	Duplicate text within a document, between open documents
Unit 7, Topic B, Pg 12, 14	Move text within a document, between open documents
Unit 7, Topic B, Pg 15	Delete text.
Unit 7, Topic C, Pg 16	Use the search command for a specific word, phrase.
Unit 7, Topic C, Pg 18-19	Use a simple replace command for a specific word, phrase.
Unit 7, Topic D, Pg 21-23	Change text appearance: font sizes, font types.
Unit 7, Topic D, Pg 22-23	Apply text formatting such as: bold, italic, underline.
Unit 7, Topic D, Pg 22	Apply subscript, superscript to text.
Unit 7, Topic D, Pg 28	Apply case changes to text.

Location	Knowledge item
Unit 7, Topic D, Pg 23	Apply different colours to text.
Unit 7, Topic D, Pg 27	Copy formatting from a piece of text to another piece of text.
Unit 7, Topic D, Pg 25	Apply an existing style to a word, a line, a paragraph.
Unit 7, Topic D, Pg 29	Use automatic hyphenation.
Unit 7, Topic A, Pg 2	Insert, remove paragraph marks.
Unit 7, Topic A, Pg 2	Insert, remove soft carriage return (line break) marks.
Unit 8, Topic A, Pg 2	Align text left, centre, right, justified.
Unit 8, Topic A, Pg 4	Indent paragraphs: left, right, first line, hanging.
Unit 8, Topic A, Pg 5	Apply single, double line spacing within paragraphs.
Unit 8, Topic A, Pg 5	Apply spacing above, below paragraphs.
Unit 8, Topic A, Pg 8	Set, remove and use tabs: left, centre, right, decimal.
Unit 8, Topic A, Pg 12	Apply bullets, numbers to a single level list. Remove bullets, numbers from a single level list.
Unit 8, Topic A, Pg 12	Change between the style of bullets, numbers in a single level list from built-in standard options.
Unit 8, Topic A, Pg 13	Add a top and bottom border, box border and shading to a paragraph.
Unit 8, Topic B, Pg 16	Change document orientation, portrait, landscape. Change paper size.
Unit 8, Topic B, Pg 21	Change margins of entire document, top, bottom, left, right.
Unit 8, Topic B, Pg 18	Insert, delete a page break in a document.

Location	Knowledge item
Unit 8, Topic B, Pg 22	Add, modify text in Headers, Footers.
Unit 8, Topic B, Pg 22	Add fields in Headers, Footers: date, page number information, file location.
Unit 8, Topic B, Pg 25	Apply automatic page numbering to a document.
Unit 8, Topic C, Pg 26	Create a table ready for text insertion.
Unit 8, Topic C, Pg 26	Insert, edit data in a table.
Unit 8, Topic C, Pg 27, 30	Select rows, columns, cells, entire table.
Unit 8, Topic C, Pg 29, 34, 39	Insert, delete, rows and columns.
Unit 8, Topic C, Pg 30	Modify column width, row height.
Unit 8, Topic C, Pg 36	Modify cell border width, style, colour.
Unit 8, Topic A, Pg 13-15, Topic C, Pg 34	Add shading to cells.
Unit 9, Topic A, Pg 2-7	Insert a picture, an image, a chart into a document.
Unit 9, Topic A, Pg 2, 3	Select a picture, image, chart in a document.
Unit 9, Topic A, Pg 6	Duplicate a picture, image, chart within a document, between open documents.
Unit 9, Topic A, Pg 6	Move a picture, image, chart within a document, to another document.
Unit 9, Topic A, Pg 6, 7	Resize a picture, image, chart.
Unit 9, Topic A, Pg 11	Delete a picture, image, chart.
Unit 9, Topic B, Pg 12	Understand the term mail merge and the concept of merging a data source with a main document such as a letter or a label document.

Location	Knowledge item
Unit 9, Topic B, Pg 12	Open, prepare a main document for a mail merge by inserting data fields.
Unit 9, Topic B, Pg 14	Open, prepare a mailing list, other data file, for use in a mail merge.
Unit 9, Topic B, Pg 18-23	Merge a mailing list with a letter, label document.
Unit 10, Topic A, Pg 2	Understand the importance of proofing your document such as: checking the layout, presentation (margins, appropriate font sizes and formats) and spelling.
Unit 10, Topic A, Pg 2	Spell-check a document and make changes such as correcting spelling errors, deleting repeated words.
Unit 10, Topic A, Pg 3	Add words to a built-in custom dictionary.
Unit 10, Topic B, Pg 8	Preview a document.
Unit 10, Topic B, Pg 10, 11	Choose print output options such as: entire document, specific pages, number of copies.
Unit 10, Topic B, Pg 10	Print a document from an installed printer using defined options, default settings.
Unit 11, Topic A, Pg 2	Open (and close) a spreadsheet application.
Unit 11, Topic A, Pg 2, 3	Open one, several spreadsheets.
Unit 11, Topic A, Pg 6	Create a new spreadsheet (default template).
Unit 11, Topic A, Pg 8	Save a spreadsheet to a location on a drive.
Unit 11, Topic A, Pg 8	Save a spreadsheet under another name.
Unit 11, Topic A, Pg 10	Save a spreadsheet in another file type such as: text file, HTML, template, software specific file extension, version number.
Unit 11, Topic A, Pg 4	Switch between worksheets, open spreadsheets.
Unit 11, Topic A, Pg 12	Use available Help functions.

Location	Knowledge item
Unit 11, Topic A, Pg 14	Close a spreadsheet.
Unit 11, Topic B, Pg 20	Use magnification/zoom tools.
Unit 11, Topic B, Pg 22	Display, hide built-in toolbars.
Unit 11, Topic B, Pg 24	Freeze, unfreeze row and/or column titles.
Unit 11, Topic B, Pg 18	Modify basic options/preferences in the application: user name, default directory/folder to open, save spreadsheets.
Unit 12, Topic A, Pg 2	Enter a number, date, text in a cell.
Unit 12, Topic A, Pg 4	Select a cell, range of adjacent cells, range of non-adjacent cells, entire worksheet.
Unit 12, Topic A, Pg 4	Select a row, range of adjacent rows, range of non-adjacent rows.
Unit 12, Topic A, Pg 4	Select a column, range of adjacent columns, range of non-adjacent columns.
Unit 12, Topic C, Pg 17	Insert rows, columns in a worksheet.
Unit 12, Topic C, Pg 17	Delete rows, columns in a worksheet.
Unit 12, Topic C, Pg 19	Modify column widths, row heights.
Unit 12, Topic A, Pg 6	Insert additional cell content, replace existing cell content.
Unit 12, Topic A, Pg 7	Use the undo, redo command.
Unit 12, Topic A, Pg 8	Duplicate the content of a cell, cell range within a worksheet, between worksheets, between open spreadsheets.
Unit 12, Topic A, Pg 10	Use the autofill tool/copy handle tool to copy, increment data entries.
Unit 12, Topic A, Pg 11	Move the contents of a cell, cell range within a worksheet, between worksheets, between open spreadsheets.

Location	Knowledge item
Unit 12, Topic A, Pg 13	Delete cell contents.
Unit 12, Topic B, Pg 14	Use the search command for specific content in a worksheet.
Unit 12, Topic B, Pg 14	Use the replace command for specific content in a worksheet.
Unit 12, Topic B, Pg 15	Sort a cell range by one criterion in ascending, descending numeric order, ascending, descending alphabetic order.
Unit 12, Topic C, Pg 21	Insert a new worksheet.
Unit 12, Topic C, Pg 24	Rename a worksheet.
Unit 12, Topic C, Pg 22	Delete a worksheet.
Unit 12, Topic C, Pg 23	Duplicate a worksheet within a spreadsheet, between open spreadsheets.
Unit 12, Topic C, Pg 23	Move a worksheet within a spreadsheet, between open spreadsheets.
Unit 13, Topic A, Pg 2, 3	Generate formulas using cell references and arithmetic operators
Unit 13, Topic A, Pg 5	Recognize and understand standard error values associated with using formulas.
Unit 13, Topic A, Pg 7, 8	Understand and use relative, mixed, absolute cell referencing in formulas.
Unit 13, Topic A, Pg 10-12	Generate formulas using sum, average, minimum, maximum, count functions.
Unit 13, Topic A, Pg 13	Generate formulas using the logical function if (yielding one of two specific values).
Unit 13, Topic B, Pg 14-15	Format cells to display numbers to a specific number of decimal places, to display numbers with, without commas to indicate thousands.
Unit 13, Topic B, Pg 20	Format cells to display a date style.
Unit 13, Topic B, Pg 14	Format cells to display a currency symbol.

Location	Knowledge item
Unit 13, Topic B, Pg 14-15	Format cells to display numbers as percentages.
Unit 13, Topic B, Pg 20	Change cell content appearance: font sizes, font types.
Unit 13, Topic B, Pg 22	Apply formatting to cell contents such as: bold, italic, underline, double underline.
Unit 13, Topic B, Pg 22	Apply different colours to cell content, cell background.
Unit 13, Topic B, Pg 23	Copy the formatting from a cell, cell range to another cell, cell range.
Unit 13, Topic B, Pg 25	Apply text wrapping to contents within a cell.
Unit 13, Topic B, Pg 24	Align contents in a cell, cell range: left, centre, right, top, bottom.
Unit 13, Topic B, Pg 24	Centre a title over a cell range.
Unit 13, Topic B, Pg 24-25	Adjust cell content orientation.
Unit 13, Topic B, Pg 27	Add border effects to a cell, cell range.
Unit 14, Topic A, Pg 2-8	Create different types of charts/graphs from spreadsheet data: column chart, bar chart, line chart, pie chart.
Unit 14, Topic A, Pg 9	Add a title, label to the chart/graph. Remove a title, label from the chart/graph.
Unit 14, Topic A, Pg 9	Change the background colour in a chart/ graph.
Unit 14, Topic A, Pg 9	Change the column, bar, line, pie slice colours in the chart/graph.
Unit 14, Topic A, Pg 8	Change the chart/graph type.
Unit 14, Topic A, Pg 11	Duplicate, move charts/graphs within a worksheet, between open spreadsheets.
Unit 14, Topic A, Pg 11	Resize, delete charts/graphs.

Location	Knowledge item
Unit 14, Topic B, Pg 13	Change worksheet margins: top, bottom, left, right.
Unit 14, Topic B, Pg 13	Change worksheet orientation: portrait, landscape. Change paper size.
Unit 14, Topic B, Pg 24	Adjust page setup to fit worksheet contents on one page, on a specific number of pages.
Unit 14, Topic B, Pg 16	Add, modify text in Headers, Footers in a worksheet.
Unit 14, Topic B, Pg 16	Insert fields: page numbering information, date, time, file name, worksheet name into Headers, Footers.
Unit 14, Topic B, Pg 20	Understand the importance of checking spreadsheet calculations and text before distribution.
Unit 14, Topic B, Pg 22	Preview a worksheet.
Unit 14, Topic B, Pg 24	Turn on, off display of gridlines, display of row and column headings for printing purposes.
Unit 14, Topic B, Pg 24	Apply automatic title row(s) printing on every page of a printed worksheet.
Unit 14, Topic B, Pg 26	Print a cell range from a worksheet, an entire worksheet, number of copies of a worksheet, the entire spreadsheet, a selected chart.
Unit 15, Topic A, Pg 2	Understand what a database is.
Unit 15, Topic C, Pg 2	Understand how a database is organised in terms of tables, records, fields, and with field data types, field properties.
Unit 15, Topic C, Pg 16, Unit 16, Topic A, Pg 11	Understand what a primary key is.
Unit 15, Topic C, Pg 16, Unit 16, Topic A, Pg 12	Understand what an index is.
Unit 15, Topic C, Pg 15	Understand the purpose of relating tables in a database.
Unit 15, Topic C, Pg 16	Understand the importance of setting rules to ensure relationships between tables are valid.
Unit 15, Topic B, Pg 5	Open (and close) a database application.

Location	Knowledge item
Unit 15, Topic B, Pg 6	Open, log onto an existing database.
Unit 15, Topic B, Pg 7	Create a new database.
Unit 15, Topic B, Pg 7	Save a database to a location on a drive.
Unit 15, Topic D, Pg 24	Use available Help functions.
Unit 15, Topic B Pg 14	Close a database.
Unit 15, Topic B Pg 10	Change between view modes in a table, form, report.
Unit 15, Topic B Pg 13	Display, hide built-in toolbars.
Unit 15, Topic C Pg 15, 17	Create and save a table and specify fields with their data types.
Unit 16, Topic A, Pg 2	Add a field to an existing table.
Unit 16, Topic B, Pg 14	Add, modify data in a record.
Unit 16, Topic B, Pg 14, 18	Delete data in a record.
Unit 15, Topic C, Pg 23	Delete a table.
Unit 15, Topic C, Pg 22	Save and close a table.
Unit 16, Topic A, Pg 11	Define a primary key.
Unit 16, Topic B, Pg 14	Add, delete records in a table.
Unit 16, Topic B, Pg 19	Use the undo command.
Unit 16, Topic C, Pg 23	Navigate within a table to next record, previous record, first record, last record, specific record.

Location	Knowledge item
Unit 16, Topic A, Pg, 12	Index a field with, without duplicates allowed.
Unit 16, Topic A, Pg 6-10	Change field format attributes such as: field size, number format, date format.
Unit 16, Topic A, Pg 6-10	Understand consequences of changing field size attributes in a table.
Unit 16, Topic A, Pg 6-10	Create a simple validation rule for number, text, date/time, currency.
Unit 16, Topic C, Pg 25	Change width of columns in a table.
Unit 16, Topic C, Pg 25	Move a column within a table.
Unit 16, Topic D, Pg 28, 29	Create a one-to-one, one-to-many relationship between tables.
Unit 16, Topic D, Pg 32	Delete relationships between tables.
Unit 16, Topic D, Pg 32	Apply rule(s) to relationships such that fields that join tables are not deleted as long as links to another table exist.
Unit 17, Topic A, Pg 8	Open a form.
Unit 17, Topic A, Pg 2-4, 14	Create and save a form.
Unit 17, Topic A, Pg 8, 9, 13	Use a form to enter, modify, delete records.
Unit 17, Topic A, Pg 2	Go to next record, previous record, first record, last record, specific record using form display.
Unit 17, Topic A, Pg 6	Add, modify text in Headers, Footers in a form.
Unit 17, Topic B, Pg 14	Delete a form.
Unit 17, Topic B, Pg 14	Save and close a form.
Unit 17, Topic C, Pg 15	Use the search command for a specific word, number, date in a field.

Location	Knowledge item
Unit 17, Topic C, Pg 18	Apply a filter to a table, form.
Unit 17, Topic C, Pg 18	Remove a filter from a table, form.
Unit 17, Topic D, Pg 20, 22	Create and save a single table query, two-table query using specific search criteria.
Unit 17, Topic D, Pg 26, 27	Add criteria to a query using any of the following operators: < (Less than), <= (Less than or equals), > (Greater than), >= (Greater than or equals), = (Equals), <> (Not equal to), And, Or.
Unit 17, Topic D, Pg 26, 27	Edit a query by adding, removing criteria.
Unit 17, Topic D, Pg 24-25	Edit a query: add, remove, move, hide, unhide fields.
Unit 17, Topic D, Pg 20-21	Run a query.
Unit 17, Topic D, Pg 28	Delete a query.
Unit 17, Topic D, Pg 23, 28	Save and close a query.
Unit 17, Topic C, Pg 17, 23	Sort data in a table, form, query output, in ascending, descending numeric, alphabetic order.
Unit 18, Topic A, Pg 2-7	Create and save a report based on a table, query.
Unit 18, Topic B, Pg 13, 14, 18	Change arrangement of data fields and headings within a report layout.
Unit 18, Topic B, Pg 8, 9	Group data under a specific heading (field) in a report in ascending, descending order.
Unit 18, Topic B, Pg 8, 9	Present specific fields in a grouped report by sum, minimum, maximum, average, count, at appropriate break points.
Unit 18, Topic B, Pg 14	Add, modify text in Headers, Footers in a report.
Unit 18, Topic B, Pg 17	Delete a report.
Unit 18, Topic A, Pg 5, 7	Save and close a report.

Location	Knowledge item
Unit 18, Topic C, Pg 18	Preview a table, form, report.
Unit 18, Topic C, Pg 18	Change report orientation: portrait, landscape. Change paper size.
Unit 18, Topic C, Pg 20-21	Print a page, selected record(s), complete table.
Unit 18, Topic C, Pg 20-21	Print all records using form layout, specific pages using form layout.
Unit 18, Topic C, Pg 20-21	Print the result of a query.
Unit 18, Topic C, Pg 20	Print specific page(s) in a report, complete report.
Unit 19, Topic A, Pg 3	Open (and close) a presentation application.
Unit 19, Topic A, Pg 3	Open one, several presentations.
Unit 19, Topic A, Pg 3	Switch between open presentations.
Unit 19, Topic B, Pg 10	Use available Help functions.
Unit 19, Topic D, Pg 19	Close a presentation.
Unit 19, Topic A, Pg 8	Understand the uses of different presentation view modes.
Unit 19, Topic A, Pg 8	Change between presentation view modes.
Unit 19, Topic A, Pg 4	Start a slide show, start a slide show on any slide.
Unit 20, Topic A, Pg 2, 3	Create a new presentation (default template).
Unit 19, Topic C, Pg 13	Save a presentation to a location on a drive.
Unit 19, Topic C, Pg 18	Save a presentation under another name.

Location	Knowledge item
Unit 19, Topic C, Pg 15-16	Save a presentation in another file type such as: Rich Text Format, template, image file format, software specific file extension, version number.
Unit 20, Topic B, Pg 16	Use magnification/zoom tools.
Unit 20, Topic A, Pg 2, 3	Add a new slide with a specific slide layout such as: title slide, chart and text, bulleted list, table
Unit 20, Topic B, Pg 8	Change background color on specific slide(s), all slides.
Unit 20, Topic A, Pg 5	Add text into a presentation in standard, outline view.
Unit 20, Topic A, Pg 6	Edit slide content, notes pages content by inserting new characters, words.
Unit 20, Topic B, Pg 13	Change text appearance: font sizes, font types.
Unit 20, Topic B, Pg 11	Apply text formatting such as: bold, italic, underline.
Unit 20, Topic B, Pg 20	Apply case changes to text.
Unit 20, Topic B, Pg 13	Apply different colors to text.
Unit 20, Topic B, Pg 13	Apply shadow to text.
Unit 20, Topic C, Pg 24	Align text: left, centre, right in a slide.
Unit 20, Topic B, Pg 16	Adjust line spacing before and after bulleted, numbered points.
Unit 20, Topic B, Pg 11, 16	Change between the style of bullets, numbers in a list from built-in standard options.
Unit 20, Topic C, Pg 26	Use the undo, redo command.
Unit 22, Topic C, Pg 14	Duplicate, move slides within the presentation, between open presentations.
Unit 20, Topic A, Pg 6	Delete a slide, slides.

Location	Knowledge item
Unit 20, Topic C, Pg 22-23, Unit 21, Topic A, Pg 7- 9	Duplicate text, pictures, images within the presentation, between open presentations.
Unit 20, Topic C, Pg 22-23, Unit 21, Topic A, Pg 7-9	Move text, pictures, images within the presentation, between open presentations.
Unit 21, Topic D, Pg 22	Insert a picture into a slide.
Unit 21, Topic D, Pg 23	Insert an image into a slide.
Unit 21, Topic A, Pg 9	Resize pictures, images in a presentation.
Unit 21, Topic A, Pg 12	Delete text, pictures, images in a slide.
Unit 23, Topic A, Pg 2-5	Input data to create, modify different kinds of built-in charts/graphs in a slide: column, bar, line, pie.
Unit 21, Topic A, Pg 2-5	Add different types of drawn object to a slide: line, free drawn line, arrow, rectangle, square, circle, text box, other available shapes.
Unit 21, Topic A, Pg 3-6	Change drawn object background color, line color, line weight, line style.
Unit 21, Topic A, Pg 13	Change arrow start style, arrow finish style.
Unit 21, Topic B, Pg 14	Apply a shadow to a drawn object.
Unit 21, Topic B, Pg 14	Rotate, flip a drawn object.
Unit 21, Topic A, Pg 13	Align a drawn object: left, centre, right, top, bottom of a slide.
Unit 21, Topic A, Pg 9	Resize drawn object, chart within the presentation.
Unit 21, Topic A, Pg 4	Bring an object to the front, back.
Unit 21, Topic A, Pg 7, Unit 23, Topic A, Pg 3	Duplicate a chart/graph, drawn object within the presentation, between open presentations.

Location	Knowledge item
Unit 21, Topic A, Pg 9, Unit 23, Topic A, Pg 3	Move a chart/graph, drawn object within the presentation, between open presentations.
Unit 21, Topic A, Pg 12, Unit 23, Topic A, Pg 3	Delete a chart/graph, drawn object.
Unit 22, Topic C, Pg 14-20	Add preset text, image animation effects to slides. Change preset animation effects on text, images.
Unit 22, Topic C, Pg 14-20	Add transition effects between slides. Change slide transition effects between slides.
Unit 22, Topic B, Pg 12	Add text into Footer of specific slides, all slides in a presentation.
Unit 22, Topic B, Pg 12	Apply automatic slide numbering, automatically updated date, non-updating date into Footer of specific slides, all slides in a presentation.
Unit 22, Topic E, Pg 33-36	Add notes for the presenter to slides.
Unit 22, Topic C, Pg 28	Hide, show slides.
Unit 23, Topic A, Pg 6-9	Change the background colour in the chart/graph.
Unit 23, Topic A, Pg 6-9	Change the column, bar, line, pie slice colours in the chart/graph.
Unit 23, Topic A, Pg 6-9	Change the chart/graph type.
Unit 23, Topic B, Pg 10	Create an organization chart with a labelled hierarchy. (Use a built-in organisation chart feature).
Unit 23, Topic B, Pg 12	Change the hierarchical structure of an organization chart.
Unit 23, Topic B, Pg 12	Add, remove managers, co-workers, sub-ordinates in an organization chart.
Unit 24, Topic B, Pg 6, 7, 10-11	Select appropriate output format for slide presentation such as: overhead, handout, 35 mm slides, on-screen show.
Unit 24, Topic A, Pg 2	Spell-check a presentation and make changes such as: correcting spelling errors, deleting repeated words.

Location	Knowledge item
Unit 24, Topic B, Pg 6-7	Change slide setup, slide orientation to portrait, landscape. Change paper size.
Unit 24, Topic B, Pg 8-11	Print entire presentation, specific slides, handouts, notes pages, outline view of slides, number of copies of a presentation.
Unit 25, Topic A, Pg 2	Understand and distinguish between the Internet and the World Wide Web (WWW).
Unit 25, Topic A, Pg 3-6	Define and understand the terms: HTTP, URL, hyperlink, ISP, FTP.
Unit 25, Topic A, Pg 5-6	Understand the make-up and structure of a Web address.
Unit 25, Topic A, Pg 3	Know what a Web Browser is and what it is used for.
Unit 25, Topic B, Pg 8	Open (and close) a Web browsing application.
Unit 25, Topic B, Pg 13, 14	Change the Web browser Home Page/Startpage.
Unit 25, Topic C, Pg 15	Use available Help functions
Unit 25, Topic B, Pg 10	Display, hide built-in toolbars.
Unit 25, Topic B, Pg 12	Go to a URL.
Unit 25, Topic B, Pg 11	Activate a hyperlink/image link.
Unit 25, Topic B, Pg 12	Navigate backwards and forwards between previously visited Web pages.
Unit 26, Topic B, Pg 7	Know what a Search Engine is and what it is used for.
Unit 26, Topic A, Pg 5	Be aware of the danger of infecting the computer with a virus from a downloaded file.
Unit 26, Topic A, Pg 2	Display a Web page in a new window.
Unit 26, Topic A, Pg 3	Stop a Web page from downloading.

Location	Knowledge item
Unit 26, Topic A, Pg 3	Refresh a Web page.
Unit 26, Topic A, Pg 5	Display, hide images on a Web page.
Unit 26, Topic D, Pg 16	Select a specific search engine.
Unit 26, Topic B, Pg 7, 10	Carry out a search for specific information using a keyword, phrase.
Unit 26, Topic C, Pg 11	Combine selection criteria in a search
Unit 26, Topic A, Pg 5	Duplicate text, image, URL from a Web page to a document.
Unit 26, Topic A, Pg 4	Save a Web page to a location on a drive as a txt file, html file.
Unit 26, Topic A, Pg 6	Download text file, image file, sound file, video file, software, from a Web page to a location on a drive.
Unit 25, Topic B, Pg 10	Display previously visited URLs using the browser address bar.
Unit 27, Topic C, Pg 20	Delete browsing history.
Unit 27, Topic D, Pg 26	Change Web page orientation: portrait, landscape. Change paper size.
Unit 27, Topic D, Pg 26	Change Web page margins top, bottom, left, right.
Unit 27, Topic D, Pg 24-26	Preview a Web Page. Choose Web page print output options such as: entire Web page, specific page(s), specific frame, selected text, number of copies and print.
Unit 28, Topic B, Pg 6	Understand the terms cookie, cache.
Unit 28, Topic B, Pg 8	Know what a protected Web site is, (use of username and password).
Unit 28, Topic B, Pg 9	Know what a digital certificate is.
Unit 28, Topic B, Pg 8, 9, 10	Know what encryption is and why it is used.

Location	Knowledge item
Unit 28, Topic A, Pg 4	Be aware of the possibility of being subject to fraud when using a credit card on the Internet.
Unit 28, Topic B, Pg 11	Understand the term firewall.
Unit 28, Topic A, Pg 2	Complete a Web-based form and enter information in order to carry out a transaction.
Unit 29, Topic A, Pg 2	Understand the make-up and structure of an e-mail address.
Unit 29, Topic A, Pg 2, 3	Understand the advantages of e-mail systems such as: speed of delivery, low cost, flexibility of using a Web-based e-mail account in different locations.
Unit 29, Topic A, Pg 3	Understand the importance of network etiquette (netiquette) such as: using accurate descriptions in e-mail message subject fields, brevity in e-mail responses, spell checking outgoing e-mail
Unit 29, Topic A, Pg 4	Be aware of the possibility of receiving unsolicited e-mail.
Unit 29, Topic A, Pg 4	Be aware of the danger of infecting the computer with a virus by opening an unrecognized mail message, an attachment contained within an unrecognized mail message.
Unit 29, Topic A, Pg 4	Know what a digital signature is.
Unit 29, Topic B, Pg 6	Open (and close) an e-mail application.
Unit 29, Topic C, Pg 15	Use available Help functions
Unit 29, Topic B, Pg 13	Display, hide built-in toolbars.
Unit 30, Topic A, Page 4	Open a mail inbox for a specified user.
Unit 30, Topic A, Page 4	Open one, several mail messages.
Unit 30, Topic A, Page 4	Switch between open messages.
Unit 30, Topic A, Page 10	Close a mail message.

Location	Knowledge item
Unit 30, Topic A, Page 3, 4	Add, remove message inbox headings such as: sender, subject, date received.
Unit 30, Topic B, Page 23	Flag a mail message. Remove a flag mark from a mail message.
Unit 30, Topic A, Page 4	Mark a message as unread, read.
Unit 30, Topic B, Page 16	Open and save a file attachment to a location on a drive.
Unit 30, Topic A, Page 7	Use the reply, reply to all function.
Unit 30, Topic A, Page 7	Reply with, without original message insertion.
Unit 30, Topic A, Page 5	Create a new message.
Unit 30, Topic A, Page 6	Insert a mail address in the 'To' field.
Unit 30, Topic A, Page 5	Copy (Cc), blind copy (Bcc) a message to another address/addresses.
Unit 30, Topic A, Page 5	Insert a title in the 'Subject' field.
Unit 30, Topic A, Page 14	Use a spell-checking tool if available and make changes such as: correcting spelling errors, deleting repeated words.
Unit 30, Topic B, Page 16	Attach a file to a message.
Unit 30, Topic B, Page 21	Send a message with high, low priority.
Unit 31, Topic D, Page 16	Send a message using a distribution list.
Unit 30, Topic B, Page 18	Forward a message.
Unit 30, Topic A, Page 8	Duplicate, move text within a message, or between other active messages.
Unit 30, Topic A, Page 8	Duplicate text from another source into a message.

Location	Knowledge item
Unit 30, Topic B, Page 8	Delete text in a message.
Unit 30, Topic B, Page 16	Delete a file attachment from an outgoing message.
Unit 31, Topic A, Pg 2	Recognize some techniques to manage e-mail effectively such as creating and naming folders, moving messages to appropriate folders, deleting unrequired e-mail, using address lists.
Unit 31, Topic D, Pg 16	Create a new address list/distribution list
Unit 31, Topic D, Pg 19	Add a mail address to an address list.
Unit 31, Topic D, Pg 20	Delete a mail address from an address list.
Unit 31, Topic D, Pg 19	Update an address book from incoming mail.
Unit 31, Topic B, Pg 6-9	Search for a message by sender, subject, mail content.
Unit 31, Topic A, Pg 2	Create a new folder for mail.
Unit 31, Topic A, Pg 4	Move messages to a new folder for mail.
Unit 31, Topic B, Pg 10	Sort messages by name, by date.
Unit 31, Topic A, Pg 5	Delete a message.
Unit 31, Topic A, Pg 5	Restore a message from the mail bin/deleted items folder.
Unit 31, Topic A, Pg 5	Empty the mail bin/deleted items folder.
Unit 31, Topic C, Pg 12	Preview a message.
Unit 31, Topic C, Pg 14	Choose print output options such as: entire message, selected contents of a message, number of copies and print.

ICDL/ECDL: Syllabus 4 Office 2000

Course summary

This summary contains information to help you bring the course to a successful conclusion. Using this information, you will be able to:

A Use the summary text to reinforce what you've learned in class.

B Determine the next courses in this series (if any), as well as any other resources that might help you continue to learn about ICDL/ECDL skills and concepts.

Topic A: Course summary

Use the following summary text to reinforce what you've learned in class.

ICDL/ECDL: Syllabus 4, Office 2000

Unit 1

In this unit, you learned about **information technology** (IT). You learned how to identify the characteristics of **hardware** and **software**, and you learned how to distinguish between different **computer types**. Next, you learned how to identify the parts of a computer. You also learned about **factors** that **affect computer performance**. Then, you learned how to **differentiate** between **application software** and **operating system software**. You also learned how to identify the main **types** of **application software** and how to describe the **software development process**. Finally, you learned about networks. You learned about the **characteristics** of **LANs** and **WANs**. You learned about the **features** of **telephone networking**. You also learned about the **Internet** and **intranets**.

Unit 2

In this unit, you learned about the importance of computers in daily life and about the **benefits** of computers in **work, education**, and **recreation**. You learned about the **use** of computers in areas such as **stock control, payroll, financial control, administration**, and **communication**. You also identified the benefits of using **e-mail** for communication. Next, you learned about the **impact of information technology** on **society**. You also learned about the **Information Superhighway** and **e-commerce**. Then, you learned about computer-related **health hazards** and **safety measures** taken to prevent them. You also learned about **security considerations**, such as **passwords, data backups, antivirus software**, and **UPSs**. Finally, you learned about the need for **copyright** and **data protection**.

Unit 3

In this unit, you learned how to turn off your computer properly by using the **Shut Down Windows** dialog box. You learned how to view basic system information, such as the **amount of memory available** and the **operating system installed**. You also learned how to view your **computer's desktop configuration**. Next, you learned how to use **Windows Help**, and you learned about the tabs in the **Help Viewer**. Then, you learned how to identify the **main components of the desktop**. You also learned how to **create** and **delete desktop shortcuts**. Then, you learned how to **work with Windows 2000 window components**. You learned how to use the Control menu buttons to **move, resize**, and **close** windows. Finally, you learned how to **change** the **date, time, volume, display settings**, and **keyboard language**. You also learned how to use the **Print Screen feature**.

Unit 4

In this unit, you learned how to use **My Computer** and **Windows Explorer** to **browse** the **contents** of a PC. You also identified various **file** and **folder attributes**. Next, you learned how to work with files and folders. You learned how to **create, rename, move,** and **copy files** and **folders**. Then, you learned how to **manage** files in a folder. You also learned that files in a folder can be sorted by **name, date, type,** and **size**. In addition, you learned how to **save disk space** by **compressing files**. You also learned how to **encrypt** files and folders. Next, you learned how to **delete** and **restore** files and folders by using the **Recycle Bin**. Finally, you learned how to use a **text editing application**, such as **WordPad**, to **create** and **save documents**.

Unit 5

In this unit, you learned how to **install** a printer and set it as the **default** printer. You learned how to **preview** and **print** a document. You also learned how to **monitor print jobs** and **set printer options**. Then, you learned how **viruses** affect computer performance. You also learned how to protect your computers by using **antivirus software** and by **scanning files**.

Unit 6

In this unit, you learned how to **start Word**. You learned about the **components** of the Word window. You also learned how to **open a document, create** and **save** a document, **close a document,** and **close** Word. Next, you learned how to use **templates** to **create letters, memos,** and **reports**. Then, you learned how to **change the page display**, use the **page view magnification tool** to zoom in or out on a page, change the **default settings** of Word by using the **Options dialog box,** and **modify the toolbar**. Finally, you learned how to use **Help** and the **Office Assistant**.

Unit 7

In this unit, you learned how to **insert text** in a Word document and use the **Undo** and **Redo** commands. You also learned how to **insert a paragraph** and **special characters**. Next, you learned how to **select text** by using the **keyboard**, the **mouse**, and the **selection bar**. You learned how to **copy** and **move** text **within a document** and between documents. You also learned how to **delete** text. Then, you learned how to **find** and **replace** text in a document. Finally, you learned how to **format** text. You learned how to apply **fonts, font sizes,** and **styles** to text. You also learned how to use the **style list options, change case,** and **control hyphenation** in a document.

Unit 8

In this unit, you learned how to **format paragraphs** by **aligning** text, setting **indents**, and setting **line spacing** and **tab stops**. Next, you learned how to create a list by using **bullets** and **numbering**. You also learned how to add **borders**. Then, you learned how to **format** a document by changing the **page setup**, inserting **page breaks**, and setting **margins**. Next, you learned how to add **headers** and **footers** and **set page numbers**. You learned how to **create tables** and **add text** to them. You also learned how to **resize rows** and **columns** and **align tables**. Next, you learned how to **add rows** and **columns** to a table, **add borders**, and **AutoFormat** a table. Finally, you learned how to **delete rows, columns,** and **tables**.

Unit 9

In this unit, you learned how to **insert clip art**, **charts**, and **pictures** into a document. You also learned how to add an **AutoShape** and delete a **graphic**. Then, you learned how to **create** a **form letter** and a **data source**. You also learned how to **add fields** to a form letter and **merge the data source** with the **form letter**.

Unit 10

In this unit, you learned how to check spelling both automatically and manually. You also learned how to use Word's **grammar checker**. Next, you used Word's **Print Preview** feature to preview a document before printing. Then, you learned how to **print** a document. You also learned how to **change printing options** by using the Print dialog box.

Unit 11

In this unit, you learned how to **start Excel**. You learned how to **open a workbook** by using the **Open dialog box**. You learned how to **change** and **update** a workbook. You also learned how to **open multiple worksheets**, **create** a **workbook**, and **save** a workbook. Then, you learned how to use the **Help** features, **close** a **spreadsheet**, and close **Excel**. Next, you learned how to **change** the View and **General options** by using the **Options dialog box**. You learned how to use the **page magnification tool** to zoom in and zoom out on a worksheet. You also learned how to **show** and **hide** the **toolbars**. Finally, you learned how to **freeze panes** to keep selected row or column headings and groups of cells in place while scrolling through a worksheet.

Unit 12

In this unit, you learned how to add worksheet **labels** and **values**, **select cells**, and **insert** and **replace cell contents**. You used the **Undo** and **Redo** commands in Excel. You also learned how to **copy**, **move**, and **delete** data. Then, you learned how to use the **Find** tool to **search** for **specific words** in a worksheet. Next, you learned how to use the **Replace** tool to **replace multiple occurrences** of a word. You also learned how to **sort data** to organize the data in a worksheet. Finally, you learned how to **insert**, **delete**, **move**, **copy**, and **rename worksheets**.

Unit 13

In this unit, you learned how to **enter formulas** by **typing** and by using the **mouse**. You learned about **formula error messages**. Then, you learned about **relative, absolute,** and **mixed references**. You also learned how to use the **Sum, Average, Minimum, Maximum, Count,** and **IF** functions. Next, you learned how to **format numbers**. You learned how to use **special formats** and **date** and **time formats**. You also learned how to **format text** by using the toolbar and the **Format Cells dialog box**. You learned how to **set alignment** and apply **borders** to cells.

Unit 14

In this unit, you learned how to **create** a chart by using the **Chart Wizard**. You examined the **elements** of a **chart** and learned how to **identify** various **types** of **charts**. Next, you learned how to **format chart objects**. You also learned how to **move, resize, copy,** and **delete chart objects**. Then, you learned how to **preview** and **print worksheets**. You learned how to **set printing options** and how to **insert** and **modify headers** and **footers**. Finally, you learned how to **preview a document, set** and **clear print areas, display gridlines,** and **print a worksheet**.

Unit 15

In this unit, you learned about **database terminology**. You also learned how to **plan** a database. Next, you learned how to **start Access** and **open a database**. You learned how to **create** and **save** a database. You learned how to use the **database templates**. You also learned how to **add** and **remove toolbars** and how to **add commands** to a toolbar. You learned how to **close** a database and Access. Then, you learned how to **create** a table by using the **Table Wizard**. You also learned how to create a table in **Design view**. You learned how to **save**, **close**, and **delete** a table. Finally, you learned how to use the **Microsoft Access Help window**. You learned about the **Contents**, the **Answer Wizard**, and the **Index tab**. You also learned how to use the **Office Assistant**.

Unit 16

In this unit, you learned how to **work** with **tables**. You learned how to **add** and **delete fields**, **modify field names**, and **set field properties**. You also learned how to **set primary keys** and **create single-** and **multiple-field indexes**. Next, you learned how to **manipulate data** in a **table**. You learned how to **add, edit,** and **delete records** in a table. You also learned how to **undo changes** made in a table. Then, you learned how to **sort records** by a **single field** and **multiple fields**. You learned how to **filter records**. You also learned how to **navigate** in a table, **move columns**, and **change column width**. Finally, you learned how to **normalize** a table and establish **one-to-one** and **one-to-many relationships** between tables. You also learned how to use **cascading deletes** and how to **delete records** from **related tables**.

Unit 17

In this unit, you learned how to create an Access form in **Design View** and by using the **Form Wizard**. You also learned how to add a **title** to a form. Next, you learned how to **open a form** and **enter data**. You also learned how to **modify** and **align controls** in a form. You learned how to **save** and **close** a form. Then, you learned that when you're **adding** or **modifying** records by using a form, you can use the **find, sort,** and **filter** features. You used these features on a form. Finally, you learned how to create a **simple query** and **run a query**. You also learned how to **add fields** to a query and **save** it. You learned about using **criteria** in a query. You also learned how to **close** and **delete** a query.

Unit 18

In this unit, you learned how to **create** a **report** by using the **Report Wizard**. You also learned how to **create reports** based on **queries**. Then, you learned how to **group** and **sort records** in a **report** in ascending or descending order. Next, you learned how to **add summary information**. You also learned how to **change** the **layout** and **style** of a report and add **headers** and **footers**. You also learned how to **delete** a report. Next, you learned how to use the **Page Setup** dialog box to **change** the **orientation** and **paper size** of a report. Finally, you learned how to **preview** and **print** a report.

Unit 19

In this unit, you learned how to **start PowerPoint**. You learned how to **open** and **run** a **presentation**. You explored the **PowerPoint environment** and learned about the various **components** of the PowerPoint window. You also learned how to change to various **views**. Next, you learned how to get **Help** in PowerPoint and how to use the **Office Assistant**. You also learned how to **find information** and **help** on the **Web**. Then, you learned how to **save** a presentation in an **existing** folder and in a **new** folder. You also learned how to **update** presentations. Finally, you learned how to **close** a **presentation** and close **PowerPoint**.

Unit 20

In this unit, you learned how to **create a presentation** by using the **File, New** command. You also learned how to **enter text** in slides. Next, you learned how to **add slides** to a presentation and how to select different slide layouts from the **New Slide** dialog box. You also learned how to **delete** slides. Next, you learned how to use the **Formatting toolbar**. You learned how to change the **font, font size**, and **font color** and how to apply **shadow effects** to text. You learned how to **change bullet styles**, create a **numbered list**, and **adjust** the **line spacing** in a bulleted or numbered list. You also learned how to **format text** by **changing** the **case**. Then, you learned how to **change** the **background color** of a slide and use the **magnification tools** to zoom in and out on a slide. Next, you learned how to use the **Cut, Copy**, and **Paste** commands. You also learned how to **align text** on a slide. Finally, you learned how to use the **Undo** and **Redo** commands.

Unit 21

In this unit, you learned how to **create drawing objects** by using the **Drawing toolbar** in PowerPoint. You also learned how to **duplicate, move, resize, delete**, and **align** objects. Then, you learned how to add shapes by using the **AutoShapes** menu on the Drawing toolbar. You also learned how to **format AutoShapes**. Next, you learned how to **add text** to objects and then modify that text by using the **Formatting toolbar**. Finally, you learned how to **insert** an **image** into a slide. You learned how to apply **color effects** to an image. You also learned how to **insert clip art** from the Clip Gallery.

Unit 22

In this unit, you learned how to **create a presentation** based on a design template. You also learned how to **apply a design template** to an existing presentation and how to **change the template** applied to a presentation. Then, you learned about the various **elements** of a **slide master**. You learned how to **modify** the slide master. Next, you learned how to **add transition effects** and **timings** to an individual slide and to an entire presentation. You learned how to **animate objects** on a slide and how to **customize** the **animation** by setting **time intervals** and **sound effects**. Next, you learned how to **reorder** the **animation effects**. You learned how to **hide** and **unhide** slides in a slide show, **set up** a **slide show**, and **customize a slide show**. Then, you learned how to **customize** the **PowerPoint environment** by **modifying toolbars**. You also learned how to use the **Options dialog box** to modify the default settings of PowerPoint. Finally, you learned how to **add speaker notes** to slides. You also learned how to add **headers** and **footers** to the **notes pages**.

Unit 23

In this unit, you learned how to create a **chart** by using **Microsoft Graph** and enhance the chart by using the **Chart Options** dialog box. You also learned how to change the chart type by using the **Chart Type** dialog box. Then, you learned how to create an **organization chart** by using the **Microsoft Organization Chart** window. You learned how to **add** and **remove** levels in the organization chart. You also learned how to enhance the organization chart by using the **Text** and **Boxes** menus.

Unit 24

In this unit, you learned how to **proof** a **presentation**. You learned how to **check spelling** and how to use the **style checker**. Then, you **modified** the **page setup** so that you can print a presentation in a variety of formats. Finally, you used the **Print dialog box** to **print** the **entire presentation, individual slides, handouts,** and **speaker notes**.

Unit 25

In this unit, you discussed the **history of the Internet** and the **requirements for connecting** to the Internet. You learned that **TCP/IP** is the standard communications protocol, and you identified the components of an **Internet address**. Next, you **launched Internet Explorer** and became acquainted with the components of the Internet Explorer window. You learned how to browse Web pages by clicking **hyperlinks**, entering an address in the **Address bar**, and clicking buttons on the **Standard Buttons toolbar**. Finally, you discussed the basic features of Internet Explorer **Help** and learned how to use **Web Help**.

Unit 26

In this unit, you learned how to display a Web page in a new window. You learned how to **save, stop the download of,** and **refresh** a Web page. You also learned how to **download files** from **Web sites**. Next, you learned how to **search** the **Internet**. You learned how to use the **Search Assistant window** to **find people**. You also learned how to use **Autosearch** to perform a **search** based on **keywords**. Then, you learned how to use **advanced searching techniques** and how to perform a **multiple-word search**. Finally, you learned how to customize the search features. You also learned how to change the **Autosearch settings** and **customize** the **Search Assistant window**.

Unit 27

In this unit, you learned how to save frequently visited Web pages by using the **Favorites** feature. Then, you learned about navigation techniques. You also learned how to **create, delete,** and **organize items** in the Favorites folder. Next, you used the **Links bar** to browse the Web. You also customized the Links bar by **adding, deleting,** and **rearranging** Links buttons. Then, you learned how to use the **History** button to view **recently visited** Web sites. You saw how History links are **sorted**, and you added one to the Favorites list. You also learned how to use **AutoComplete**. You specified a Web site as your **home page**, deleted **temporary Internet files**, and modified **History** and **AutoComplete settings**. In addition, you examined the capabilities of the **Content Advisor**. Finally, you learned about the **print features**; you examined the Print dialog box options for **printing frames** and **linked documents**.

Unit 28

In this unit, you learned how to shop on the Internet and how to order online by filling out **Web-based forms**. Then, you learned about the importance of **Web security**. You also learned how **cookies** and **caching** can increase the speed of Web browsing. You learned about various measures for **protecting** Web sites. Next, you learned about **digital certificates** and **encryption**. Finally, you learned how **firewalls** can protect an intranet from hackers and sometimes from spam and viruses.

Unit 29

In this unit, you learned how **e-mail** works and learned about the **advantages** of e-mail over other types of communication. You also learned that you need **e-mail addresses** to send and receive e-mail messages. You learned about **e-mail etiquette**. You also learned that it's necessary to secure your e-mail messages. You learned about two methods of e-mail security: **encryption** and **digital signatures**. Next, you learned how to **start** and **close Outlook**. You examined the Outlook 2000 window elements and the Outlook **folders**. You used **Outlook Shortcuts** to access the Outlook folders. Finally, you learned how to use the **Help** window.

Unit 30

In this unit, you learned about the Outlook **Inbox** and its interface. You learned how to **read**, **create**, and **send e-mail** messages. You also learned how to **edit**, **format**, and **check spelling** in messages. Next, you learned how to **attach** a file to a message. You also learned how to **save an attachment** for later reference. Then, you learned how to **forward** and **recall** a message. Finally, you learned how to **set the priority** of a message and **flag** a message.

Unit 31

In this unit, you learned how to **create** a **personal folder** and **move messages** between **folders** in Outlook. Then you learned how to **delete** and **restore messages**. Next, you learned how to use the **Find** and **Advanced Find** features to find e-mail messages, and you learned how to **sort messages**. You also learned how to **set printing options** by using the **Page Setup** dialog box and how to **print messages** by using the Print dialog box. Next, you learned how to **create** and **use** a **distribution list**. Finally, you learned how to **update** an **address book** with an **e-mail address** from an incoming message and how to **delete addresses** from the address book.

Topic B: Continued learning after class

It's impossible to learn to use any software effectively in a single day. To get the most out of this class, you should begin working with the applications covered in this course to perform real tasks as soon as possible. Course Technology also offers resources for continued learning.

Next courses in this series

This is the only course in this series.

Other resources

You might find some of the other resources useful as you continue to learn about ICDL/ECDL skills and concepts. For more information, visit www.course.com.

ICDL/ECDL: Syllabus 4 Office 2000

Quick reference

Button	Shortcut keys	Function
Windows		
Start	CTRL + ESC	Displays the Start menu.
		Enlarges the window to the size of the desktop.
		Closes the window and exits the application.
		Reduces the window to a task button on the taskbar.
		Restores a maximized window to its previous size.
		Moves one level up in the folder hierarchy.
		Opens the New Folder dialog box.
		Moves a file to a specified folder.
	DELETE	Deletes the selected file(s) or folder(s).
		Displays a print preview of a document.
Word		
	CTRL + N	Creates a new blank document.
		Displays the document in Normal view.
		Displays the document in Web Layout view.
		Displays the document in Print Layout view.
		Displays the document in Outline view.

Button	Shortcut keys	Function
⊞	F1	Displays Microsoft Word Help.
¶	CTRL + *	Displays all nonprinting characters.
↰	CTRL + Z	Undoes the last action.
↱	CTRL + Y	Redoes the last action.
	SHIFT + ←	Selects the text to the left of the insertion point, one character at a time.
	SHIFT + →	Selects the text to the right of the insertion point, one character at a time.
	SHIFT + ↑	Selects text from the left of the insertion point to the same place in the previous line.
	SHIFT + ↓	Selects text from the right of the insertion point to the same place in the next line.
	SHIFT + HOME	Selects text from the left of the insertion point to the beginning of the current line.
	SHIFT + END	Selects text from the right of the insertion point to the end of the current line.
⧉	CTRL + C	Copies the text to the Clipboard.
⧉	CTRL + V	Pastes the copied text.
✂	CTRL + X	Moves the selected content to the Clipboard.
B	CTRL + B	Applies a bold format to the selected text.
I	CTRL + I	Applies italics to the selected text.
U	CTRL + U	Underlines the selected text.
✍		Copies the formatting of a selection to another selection.
≣	CTRL + L	Left-aligns the selected paragraphs.
≣	CTRL + E	Centers the selected paragraphs.
≣	CTRL + R	Right-aligns the selected paragraphs.

Button	Shortcut keys	Function
	CTRL + J	Justifies the selected paragraphs.
	CTRL + SHIFT + N	Applies bullets to the selected paragraphs.
		Applies numbers to the selected paragraphs.
		Inserts a page-number field in a header or footer.
		Inserts the total number of pages in the document.
		Opens the Page Number Format dialog box, where you can format the page number.
		Inserts a current-date field in a header or footer.
		Switches between the header and footer.
		Inserts a graphic in the document.
		Opens the Mail Merge Helper dialog box.
		Merges the data source with the form letter.

Excel

Button	Shortcut keys	Function
	CTRL + O	Opens a workbook.
	CTRL + N	Creates a new worksheet.
	CTRL + SHIFT + $	Applies the currency format to the selection.
		Decreases the number of decimal places shown.
	CTRL + SHIFT + %	Applies the percentage format to the selection.
		Merges and centers the selection.
		Displays the Chart Wizard.
		Formats the selected chart object.

Button	Shortcut keys	Function
A		Opens the Font dialog box (for formatting headers and footers).
[#]		Inserts a code that prints the page number.
		Inserts a code that prints the file name of the active workbook.
		Inserts a code that prints the name of the active worksheet.
		Inserts a code that prints the current time.
Access		
		Adds all of the fields from one list to another.
		Opens the indexes.
		Finds a value in a table.
	(↓)	Moves the record selector to the next record.
	(↑)	Moves the record selector to the previous record.
	(CTRL) + (END)	Moves the record selector to the last record.
	(CTRL) + (HOME)	Moves the record selector to the first record.
		Adds a field from one list to another.
		Opens the Toolbox.
Aa		Adds a title to the form.
ab		Adds a text box to the form.
		Inserts a new record.
		Modifies the properties of a form.
...		Opens the relevant build tool.
		Switches to Form view.
		Opens a table in Design view.

Button	Shortcut keys	Function
		Sorts the records in ascending order.
		Filters records.
		Shows filtered records.
		Runs a query.
		Sorts and group records.
		Adds an image control.

PowerPoint

Button	Shortcut keys	Function
		Switches to Outline view.
		Switches to Slide view.
		Switches to Slide Sorter view.
		Switches to Slide Show view.
		Switches to Normal view.
		Saves a presentation.
		Draws a rectangle.
		Draws an oval.
		Draws a line.
		Applies color effects to an image.
		Rearranges the animation effects.
		Toggles a slide.
		Toggles a datasheet.
		Checks the spelling.

Button	Shortcut keys	Function
Internet Explorer		
← Back	ALT + ←	Returns to the previously displayed Web page.
→	ALT + →	Moves to the next Web page, after you've moved back from it.
Home	ALT + HOME	Moves to your home page.
Hide		Hides the left frame in the Help window.
Show		Shows the left frame in the Help window.
Web Help		Initiates Support Online.
(stop)	ESC	Stops the current activity.
(refresh)	F5	Refreshes the Web page, updating information that has changed since the page was cached.
Favorites	CTRL + I	Displays links to your frequently visited Web sites. Clicking this button displays the Favorites list in the Explorer bar.
History	CTRL + H	Displays a list of previously viewed Web pages that are categorized by date and time. Clicking this button displays the History list in the Explorer bar.
Outlook		
(folder)		Displays the Folder list.
✕	CTRL + D	Deletes selected e-mail messages, appointments, meetings, tasks, and other items.
▾	CTRL + SHIFT + G	Opens the Flag for Follow Up dialog box.

Index